We work with leading authors to develop the strongest educational materials in accounting, bringing cutting-edge thinking and best learning practice to a global market.

Under a range of well-known imprints, including Financial Times Prentice Hall, we craft high-quality print and electronic publications which help readers to understand and apply their content, whether studying or at work.

To find out more about the complete range of our publishing, please visit us on the World Wide Web at: **www.pearsoned.co.uk**

AUDITING FUNDAMENTALS

Marlene Davies and
John Aston

**Financial Times
Prentice Hall
is an imprint of

Harlow, England • London • New York • Boston • San Francisco • Toronto • Sydney • Singapore • Hong Kong
Tokyo • Seoul • Taipei • New Delhi • Cape Town • Madrid • Mexico City • Amsterdam • Munich • Paris • Milan

Pearson Education Limited
Edinburgh Gate
Harlow
Essex CM20 2JE
England

and Associated Companies throughout the world

Visit us on the World Wide Web at:
www.pearsoned.co.uk

First published 2011

© Pearson Education Limited 2011

ISBN: 978-0-273-71173-5

British Library Cataloguing-in-Publication Data
A catalogue record for this book is available from the British Library.

Library of Congress Cataloging-in-Publication Data
Davies, Marlene.
 Auditing fundamentals / Marlene Davies and John Aston.
  p. cm.
 ISBN 978-0-273-71173-5 (pbk.)
 1. Auditing. I. Aston, John, MBA II. Title.
 HF5667.D384 2011
 657'.45—dc22

                                                                 2010026549

10 9 8 7 6 5 4 3 2 1
14 13 12 11 10

Typeset in 9.5/12.5 pt Stone Serif by 73
Printed by Ashford Colour Press Ltd, Gosport

This book is dedicated to the late Evelyn and Harry Aston, my mother and father, to whom I owe everything.

I also dedicate this book to my wife, Diane, who is a great source of encouragement and support to me. I am in her debt.

John Aston

This book is dedicated to my parents, the late Morwenna and Hugh Jenkins who were an inspiration to me.

I also dedicate this book with all my love to my husband, Frank, and daughters, Catherine and Helen.

Marlene Davies

Brief contents

Contents

This textbook will provide a fundamental introduction to the principles and practices of auditing and has been written and designed for anyone who has an interest in the science. Traditionally, many textbooks on this subject tend to specialise in external audit, often at the expense of internal audit. In fact, history often suggests that internal audit is a 'Cinderella' of all the finance functions. The development of corporate governance, social responsibility, risk evaluation, the need to review our main systems and the continuing requirement to maximise value for money all mean that internal audit has an important and growing role within the organisation. The recent problems of toxic debt management portfolios within the banking system, contemporary worries of identity theft and weaknesses within the chip and pin system all add up to the growing stature of internal audit within the profession, reporting to the highest level of management. It is only hoped that senior management listens and can evaluate and understand the advice on offer. It is also hoped that the role of external audit will continue to develop in such a way that their reporting will be of importance to shareholders, both present and future. Many contemporary problems of corporate governance within our banking system suggest that there is still work to be done to benefit the external audit function.

The primary aim of the book is to provide a straightforward and comprehensive approach to enhance an understanding of auditing. It takes both theoretical and practical approaches. Then, taking this a step further, it integrates theory into practice in a pragmatic and applied manner. Students of accounting and finance will certainly find this book useful. Professional bodies such as ICAEW, ICAS, ICA, ACCA and CIPFA will find elements of the book useful as will students of the IIA and AAT. In many universities, both traditional and new, accounting and finance are vibrant subjects providing vocational degrees leading to good jobs. Whilst aspects of this book are core to any undergraduate course, it can be used alongside other material for postgraduate students, many of whom are studying risk assessment and modelling, uncertainty and control as part of financial resource management studies. In fact this book is suitable for any aspiring professional who wants to understand the fundamentals of auditing.

One thought which became clear to both of us whilst writing this book is that anyone employed in the area of auditing 25 or 30 years ago would find contemporary techniques almost unrecognisable. Internal audit, in particular, is now a vibrant and fully developed profession. However, there is still much research to be done to develop the science further.

This book may well mean many things to many people. It has the potential to become one of the market leaders in its field. The greatest selling point of this book is that it concentrates on both external and internal audit. In the global environment where many developing countries are looking to grow their financial infrastructure, it is likely that this publication will have international appeal and we have therefore incorporated details of the revised (2009) International Standards on Auditing (ISAs) produced by the Auditing Practices Board (APB), itself part of the Financial Reporting Council (FRC), and which is fully committed to the worldwide harmonisation of auditing standards.

Finally, our thanks go to our families and colleagues who have been a great source of wisdom, support, encouragement and patience.

We hope you enjoy reading this as much as we look forward to developing it over the years.

Marlene Davies
John Aston

Marlene Davies is Divisional Head for Accounting and Finance at the University of Glamorgan Business School. Marlene's area of expertise is in audit and corporate governance, having worked in the public sector prior to becoming an academic. She has taught extensively in Europe and in Hong Kong and been an external examiner for CIPFA and IIA, UK and Ireland. More recently she has been involved in developing modules in forensic audit and accounting. She is a regular commentator on public finance and local government issues for BBC Radio Wales and S4C.

John Aston was Subject Head of Business Studies at Brunel University. He has extensive experience in both the public and private sectors. He is a former Head of Audit and External Examiner for The Chartered Institute of Public Finance and Accountancy. He is an experienced tutor who has taught overseas in 10 different countries and for major organisations such as IBM, DHL, InterContinental Hotels, Cable and Wireless and National Savings. John is a visiting associate at Henley Business School, The College of Estate Management and The London School of Commerce. He is a licensed Lay Minister for the Church of England.

Acknowledgements

We are grateful to the following for permission to reproduce copyright material:

Figures

Figure 10.2 from The Passport Office, Crown Copyright material is reproduced with permission under the terms of the Click-Use Licence; Figure 12.3 from *Understanding Organizations,* 4th ed., Penguin (Handy, C.B. 1993), Reproduced by permission of Penguin Books Ltd.

Tables

Table 5.1 adapted from a table by David Geatrell.

Text

Extracts on pages 14–16, page 17, pages 17–18 after *APB Guidelines for Internal Audit,* Auditing Practices Board, © Financial Reporting Council (FRC). Adapted and reproduced with the kind permission of the Financial Reporting Council. All rights reserved. For further information please visit www.frc.org.uk or call +44 (0)20 7492 2300.

In some instances we have been unable to trace the owners of copyright material, and we would appreciate any information that would enable us to do so.

Introduction to audit

Objectives

After reading this chapter you will be able to:

- understand the background and purpose of auditing;
- appreciate the need for audit;
- understand the auditors' objectives;
- know the difference between external and internal auditors.

Introduction

The word 'audit' is from the Latin *audire,* meaning to hear. Its roots go back to a time when financial affairs were reported by word of mouth and the auditor would give an independent account that the steward who had managed the situation was accurate in their report.

Many of the people who invested funds knew little, if anything, about the business they were investing in and therefore could not be sure how credible the account was. This was solved by appointing an independent third party to investigate and examine, where necessary, in order to give an opinion as to its reasonableness. The account was given orally, and after hearing it, respected listeners would report their opinion. Such people became known as **auditors**. As business expanded and became more sophisticated, the oral account became a written one, but the name auditor (the hearer) remained.

Demand for auditors grew, as did the skill and expertise in investigating the accounts and reporting. Financial statements may contain errors, or could be misleading or even contain a substantial fraud. Of course, many financial transactions may contain some degree of error or mistake. Minor errors can be easily covered up, particularly if the system is large. This is why the auditor only concentrates on material items. In the world of accounting and finance, materiality means size. Potential investors and lenders must be able to rely with reasonable assurance on the reasonable accuracy of the financial statements. This degree of reasonable accuracy is known as a true and fair view. It is not possible for the auditor to confirm that the accounts are 100% because the cost and time involved in examining every transaction down to the very last penny would be prohibitive and uneconomic. The terms true and fair have never been defined in law but a sensible way of defining them would be that the financial statements are intellectually honest. If the figures have been measured correctly, for example equipment was purchased on 1 March 2008, then the accounts are presented truthfully. If the value is written down by 25% over the next year to present, for example, the net book value then the decision to depreciate by that amount is a fair one.

It is worth making clear at this point three essential facts:

- The responsibility for the preparation and accuracy of the financial statements rests with the management of the business.
- The responsibility for ensuring that systems of internal control exist rests with management.
- The auditor does not seek to uncover all fraud and error.

However, the auditor is expected to carry out tests of the records supporting the financial statements in such a manner that there is a reasonable expectation of uncovering a major fraud or error, should either exist.

In the UK there are a large number of different accountancy, or accountancy-related, institutes and associations, including the following:

- Institute of Chartered Accountants in Ireland (ICI);
- Association of Chartered Certified Accountants (ACCA);

- Institute of Chartered Accountants in England and Wales (ICAEW);
- Chartered Institute of Management Accountants (CIMA);
- Association of Accounting Technicians (AAT);
- Chartered Institute of Public Finance and Accounting (CIPFA);
- Institute of Chartered Accountants of Scotland (ICAS);
- Institute of Internal Auditors (UK & Ireland) (IIA).

All these bodies vary from each other, depending on the nature of their aims and the specialism their members wish to attain. They are all, however, characterised by various attributes common across the accounting profession:

- stringent entrance requirements (examinations and practical experience);
- strict codes of ethics;
- technical updating of members and a commitment to keep up to date by continued professional development.

Membership of a professional accountancy body is essential for any auditor who has attained and maintained a professional qualification. There is one body that specialises in internal audit only, the Institute of Internal Auditors (IIA). This body is big in the USA and Canada and fairly small in the UK by comparison. Nevertheless, its members specialise as internal auditors in both commercial and public sector bodies and provide a valuable service to management.

There are two different types of audit, external audit and internal audit, and it is important to have an early appreciation of their different roles.

External audit

The majority of external audits undertaken in the private sector are statutory audits of limited companies under company law. Auditors are appointed by the shareholders, as the owners of the company, and have a duty to carry out such investigations that will enable them to form an opinion. Every company that has a turnover greater than £5.6 million is subject to a statutory audit, which is the maximum level permitted under a Companies Act 1989 requirement. Any company that has a turnover exceeding £5.6 million that is a public limited company must submit themselves for audit.

Companies entitled to an audit exemption must deliver accounts to the Registrar of Companies. Unaudited accounts must include, on the balance sheet, a director's signature and a statement that says the following:

- The company is entitled to an exemption for that financial year.
- There is no notice from members requiring an audit.
- The company keeps proper accounting records.
- The directors acknowledge their responsibility for preparing accounts that give a true and fair view.
- All relevant accounting standards have been complied with.

Most external auditors are qualified accountant members of a supervisory body. In the vast majority of cases, these tend to be the ICAEW, the ACCA and their

Scottish or Irish equivalents, ICAS or ICI. When a partnership is appointed, it is the firm and not the individual employee that is regulated. Under the Companies Act 1985 the auditor must be totally independent of the company. Auditors are ineligible for appointment if:

- they are an officer of the company;
- they are a partner or employee of such a person;
- the company is a partnership in which such a person is a partner;
- they are ineligible by virtue of the above for appointment as auditor of any parent or subsidiary undertaking;
- there exists between them or any associate (of his or hers) and the company (or company as referred to in above) a connection of any description as may be specified in regulations laid down by Secretary of State.

It should be noted that the legislation does not prohibit the appointment of an auditor who owns shares in the company or who is a creditor or debtor. It also does not disqualify a close relative of an employee of the business. The key to all of this is that the auditor or the practising firm should be totally independent of the company.

The external auditor's duties are as follows:

- to form an opinion as to whether the financial statements are true and fair;
- to ensure the company has kept proper accounting records;
- to ensure the records agree with the financial statements;
- to ensure the statements comply with statutory and stock market requirements;
- to ensure that appropriate accounting policies have been applied consistently.

Auditors report their opinion formally in an audit report. This report is presented to the members of the company (normally the shareholders) and, to aid communication, should be placed before the financial statements.

The duties of the external auditor of a limited company are onerous. To help auditors carry out these duties, the Companies Act accords them certain powers, including the following:

- a right of access at all times to the books, accounts and vouchers of the company;
- the right to obtain from officers (including directors) of the company such explanation and information that is required;
- the right to receive notice of and attend meetings and to report on any matter that concerns the auditor;
- the right to make a report to the members on their findings, including failure on the part of the officers of the company to supply all the information and explanations.

To summarise, auditors must carry out a sufficient level of work to form a reasonable basis for their opinion that the financial statements show a true and fair view. Alternatively they may have carried out a sufficient level of work to have a reasonable chance of finding any material misstatement, error or irregularity. The external auditor will normally submit an unqualified audit report when the financial statements are true and fair. There are instances when the auditor's opinion is such that it needs to be qualified.

Internal audit

Internal audit is a part of the financial structure of very large organisations. Internal auditors are employees of the organisation and work exclusively for it. Their responsibility is to the management of the organisation, to whom they report. In the past, the internal audit division reported to the finance director, or to the chief executive, but due to codes of best practice in corporate governance many internal auditors new report directly to the Audit Committee of the organisation.

Internal audit is defined in the Auditing Practices Board's auditing guideline, *Guidance for Internal Auditors,* as:

> . . . an independent appraisal function established by the management of an organisation for the review of the internal control system as a service to the organisation. It objectively examines, evaluates and reports on the adequacy of internal control as a contribution to the proper, economic, efficient and effective use of resources.

The key to this is that despite the fact that internal auditors are employees of the company, they must maintain their independence and be able to report to the highest level of management unedited in their own name. This means they have the same right of unrestricted access to records and employees as the external auditor. They determine their own priorities but that is done in consultation with the Audit Committee On occasions they are given a remit to carry out a particular study, for example into the high level of telephone or heating costs. They have the right to report to all levels within the organisations. The internal auditor is not a part of any financial system and should not be employed to keep accounting records. If internal auditors are used for non-auditing duties, it could jeopardise their independence.

A considerable proportion of the duties of an internal auditor are directed towards a systems-based approach and internal control evaluation and testing. Systems-based audit (SBA) is essential for management to ensure that the controls within an organisation's systems provide an assurance of sound quality control. According to the Auditing Practices Board, in their *Internal Audit Guidelines* (1990):

> To achieve full effectiveness the scope of the internal audit function should provide an unrestricted range of coverage of the organisation's operations, and the internal auditor should have sufficient authority to allow him access to such records, assets and personnel as are necessary for proper fulfilment of his responsibilities.

It is a management responsibility to determine the extent of internal control in the organisation's systems, and it should not depend on internal audit as a substitute for effective controls. Internal audit, as a service to the organisation, contributes to internal control by examining, evaluating and reporting to management on its adequacy and effectiveness. Internal audit activity may lead to the strengthening of internal control as a result of audit evidence and management response. One of the objectives of internal auditing is to assist management in the pursuit of value for money. This is achieved through economic, efficient and effective use of resources. Internal audit also has a role to play in risk management, where it can act in an advisory role to management.

It is a management responsibility to maintain the internal control system and to ensure that the organisation's resources are properly applied in the manner, and to the activities, intended. This includes a responsibility for the prevention and detection of fraud and other illegal acts. The internal auditor should have regard to the possibility of such malpractice and should seek to identify serious defects in internal control which might permit the occurrence of such an event. An internal auditor who discovers evidence of, or suspects, malpractice should report firm evidence, or reasonable suspicions, to the appropriate level of management. It is a management responsibility to determine what further action to take.

Summary

This chapter introduces the reader to the world of auditing. As well as considering the background and purpose of auditing, it splits the audit function into two very different approaches, namely external and internal audit. External audit is a statutory function and an integral part of the regulation process. In some organisations, such as local government, an internal audit section is a legal requirement. (NB Accounts and Audit Regulations.) However, in the commercial sector it is a discretionary service – highly recommended and very desirable yet discretionary. However, there is momentum for change because corporate governance requirements in the UK have driven management to assess risk, materiality and internal control. It is clear they need a strong internal audit section to help them achieve their objectives.

The requirements of external and internal audit and the importance of their relationship are developed further in the next chapter.

? PRACTICE QUESTION

What are the purpose and objectives of both external and internal audit, and what kind of service do they supply to management?

Chapter 2

External and internal audit

Objectives

After reading this chapter you should:

- understand the role and function of external audit;
- be aware of key case law;
- understand the role and function of internal audit;
- be able to discuss how to measure the effectiveness of internal audit.

Introduction

This chapter builds on Chapter 1 but takes the issues of external and internal audit a step further and considers the importance of a good working relationship.

External audit

Accountancy bodies have a responsibility for inspecting and monitoring their registered auditors on a regular basis. This is undertaken by the Professional Oversight Board's Audit Inspection Unit. The following features should be transparent in each accounting/audit practice:

- recruitment of suitable staff;
- proper training, both academically and on the job;
- continuing professional development;
- quality control and supervision of work;
- proper planning and approach;
- appropriate fee-charging policy, which is based either on an hourly rate or a percentage of turnover;
- a commitment to ethical guidelines;
- internal peer review at appropriate intervals.

The visit during the monitoring process is substantive or compliance-based. The inspectors will assess a certain number of audit files selected at random, and also files from categories known to be high-risk. The substantive approach will seek to verify that:

- planning, recording, supervision and review work have been carried out to a satisfactory professional standard;
- the work recorded provides a sound basis for the audit opinion.

Each inspection ends with an interview, and the findings of the inspection are fully discussed together with any recommendations. If the inspection is not satisfied then the auditor or the firm will have their practising certificate withdrawn as a last resort.

The typical structure of an audit department in an audit firm is shown in Figure 2.1.

External auditor's reports to users and to management

Audit reports are the end product of the work and must be completed to the highest standard. They are governed by the 1985 Companies Act as amended by the Companies Act 1989 and 2006 and also by the international auditing standard ISA 700, *The Auditor's Report on Financial Statements*. The 1985 Act places a duty on auditors to examine the financial statements and to express an opinion on whether they show a true and fair view at the year end. The auditor should not express an opinion on the statements until they have been approved by the directors and the auditors have considered all available evidence.

Figure 2.1 **Structure of an audit firm**

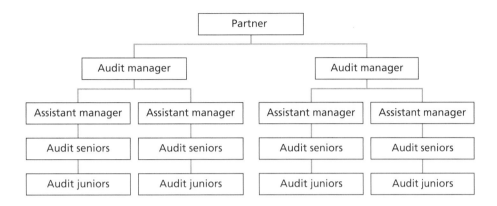

There are two types of audit report, an unqualified report and a qualified report.

Unqualified reports

This is the most common report issued with the financial statements. It is known as a clean report. The auditing standard ISA 700 states that 'An unqualified opinion on financial statements is expressed when in the auditor's judgement they give a true and fair view and have been prepared in accordance with relevant accounting or other requirements.' This judgment concludes:

■ The financial statements have been prepared using appropriate accounting policies which have been consistently applied.

■ The financial statements have been prepared in accordance with relevant legislation regulations or applicable accounting standards (and that any departures are adequately explained in the financial statements).

■ There is adequate disclosure of all information relevant to the proper understanding of the financial statements.

Qualified audit reports

There are three types of qualified report, which become appropriate depending on the circumstances. These reports will contain:

■ an 'except for' opinion
■ an 'adverse' opinion
■ a 'disclaimer of' opinion.

This type of reporting is covered in Chapter 17.

Management representation letters

As part of the completion stage of the audit, a letter is prepared by the auditor on behalf of the management of the company to remind the directors that the responsibility for the preparation of the financial statement is theirs. Because the auditor frequently has to rely on information provided by management, it is usually good practice to confirm this in writing. The content of such a letter is as follows:

- Directors acknowledge their responsibilities under the Companies Acts.
- Issues arising from the audit where management judgment and opinion are noted.
- The draft financial statements do not need to be revised because of post balance sheet events known to the directors but not reported to the auditors.
- There are no significant fixed assets held off the balance sheet which would necessitate its revision.
- There are no liabilities of a material nature not included in the balance sheet.
- There are no contingent liabilities of a material amount for which provision has not been made.

This letter of representation is signed by the chairman and company secretary and minuted by the board of directors.

The management letter

An effective written report to the board of directors preceded by an executive summary is an essential part of communication. Auditors will report on matters that have come to their attention during the course of the audit. These will include:

- changes in risk assessment which are an issue;
- weaknesses in internal controls;
- weaknesses within management information systems;
- comments on the work and reliance of internal audit;
- issues that relate to the financial statements;
- recommendations for change.

Management letters are private communications which the board may well delegate to the Audit Committee. They are considered by all parties to be important and fundamentally useful.

External audits in the public sector

External audit reports of central government departments and quangos are undertaken by the Comptroller and Auditor General (C&AG) who is not a civil servant but an officer of the House of Commons. The C&AG is responsible for the National Audit Office, with a duty not only to carry out value-for-money reviews but also to audit the government's appropriation accounts. The C&AG is required to give an opinion that sums expended have been applied for the purposes authorised by parliament and that the account properly presents the expenditure and receipts for the year.

Audits in local government and the National Health Service are carried out by the Audit Commission in England, a body that controls the audit and inspection process of these public sector bodies. The Audit Commission is an independent body made up of the District Audit Service, comprising civil servants with a financial background and the large firms of chartered accountants that apply for this type of work. One significant feature in this area is that the audit is rotated and fees are paid by the Audit Commission itself. It is a commonly stated view that this system promotes audit independence and should be used by the private sector. However, this was considered by the Smith Report in January 2003 (see Chapter 5 for a discussion of this report) and rejected as inappropriate, which some might argue was a missed opportunity. (The Smith Report is now incorporated into the Financial Reporting Council's combined code.)

An important difference between local government and the private sector is that financial statements and appropriate supporting documents are put on public view for inspection and query. Members of the public on the electoral roll may take this further by raising objections if they feel expenditure or income is unlawful and the local authority or its employees or elected members have acted with culpable neglect. The auditor has the power to issue a 'certificate of loss', which is a surcharge requesting the return of public money from an individual. The most famous case involved the surcharge issued to Dame Shirley Porter who was leader of Westminster City Council. She faced accusations of 'gerrymandering', resulting from several major housing construction projects aimed at importing affluent voters to London's Westminster constituency. Dame Shirley later faced a surcharge of £27 million after being accused of selling houses for votes by the Audit Commission. She eventually settled in 2004 with a payment of £12m. Once again the auditor must provide an opinion which if unqualified would state that the statement of accounts presents fairly the financial position of the Council for the year end.

Auditor liability

A major error or oversight by the auditor can result in an incorrect opinion. If this happens, the auditor then has a liability to parties who suffer a loss. There are cases of early law which are covered here but the most recent influential contemporary case was the House of Lords' ruling in the Caparo case in 1990. Some of the early case law is considered briefly as this is a major subject area. Figure 2.2 outlines the auditor's legal position.

Figure 2.2 **Auditor liability – legal aspects**

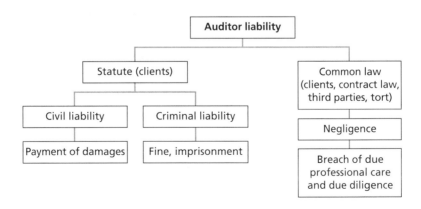

Re London and General Bank (1895)

In this case the company had taken credit for interest accrued on loans which were never likely to be repaid. Many of these loans were statute barred (i.e. uncollectable). The auditor was aware of the problem and reported only to the directors and not to the shareholders. Subsequently the financial statements did not show a true and fair view. In summing up, the judge stated that the auditor had a duty to shareholders to report any dishonest acts that had occurred. He said the auditor could not expect to find every error but had a duty to use due care and skill.

Re Kingston Cotton Mill Co. Ltd (1896)

In this case the accounts had been falsified to a very considerable extent by the managing director, by extensive overvaluations of stock. In this instance the auditors were deceived, and although they acted with due care, they had understandably missed the deception. Lord Justice Lindley stated that the auditor is not bound to be a detective; he is a watchdog and not a bloodhound. In this instance the directors are liable to the shareholders for fraud.

Both this case and *Re London and General Bank* represent a cornerstone for auditor liability.

What are the auditor's duties?

The Companies Acts do not expressly state how an auditor should discharge their duty of care. L. J. Lopes, in *Re Kingston Cotton Mill*, stated.

> It is the duty of the auditor to bring to bear on the work he has to perform that skill, care and caution which a reasonably competent, careful and cautious auditor would use. What is reasonable skill, care and caution must depend on the particular circumstances of each case.

Donoghue v. Stevenson (1932)

This case established that a duty of care is owed to parties outside a contractual relationship. This case refers to the sale of goods and relates to a situation where a customer was sold a bottle of drink with a slug at the bottom. It established the principles of duty of care.

Candler v. Crane Christmas (1951)

Although the court confirmed that no duty of care is owed to third parties outside a contractual agreement, the dissenting judgment of Lord Denning signalled the way the law would develop in the future by stating that the accountant owes a duty to any third party who sees the accounts and invests money but that this duty cannot be extended to include strangers.

Hedley Byrne & Co. Ltd. v. Heller & Partners (1963)

The court accepted the Denning reasoning that a duty of care is owed to third parties where it can be shown that a special relationship exists. The counsel's opinion was that there is a duty of care only if:

■ It is clear that the financial loss is attributable to reliance upon the negligently prepared document and no other cause.

- The party issuing the document knew the purpose for which it was being prepared and knew (or ought to have known) that it was to be relied upon in that particular context.

Therefore, there was no duty of care to individual shareholders who place reliance on the audit report for investment decisions. The financial statements and the audit report are prepared for the purpose of stewardship and not for future investors.

Hedley Byrne v. Heller and Partners (1963)

In this case it was determined that the judgment in *Candler* v. *Crane* was wrongly decided. Hedley Byrne were advertising agents who wished to extend credit to the company Easipower Ltd. They asked Heller, as the company's bankers, for a reference in relation to the company's creditworthiness. The reference was given that the company was respectable but the reference included a disclaimer on the part of the bank if the information was relied on for any investment or business decisions. The advertising agency lost money and sued the bank for negligence.

The case was dismissed because of the disclaimer; however, the judge in this instance held that there was a duty of care even though no contractual or fiduciary relationship existed.

Jeb Fasteners Ltd v. Marks, Bloom & Co. (1981)

In this instance, the auditors conducted an audit for a company facing solvency difficulties. They were also subject to a takeover. The assets in the balance sheet were seriously overvalued, hence forcing the company to be taken over at an artificial price. Lord Justice Woolf said that the auditors could reasonably foresee that a takeover company would rely on the audited accounts and therefore suffer a loss if they were inaccurate.

Caparo Industries plc v. Dickman & Others (1990)

In 1984 Caparo Industries acquired a company called Fidelity on the basis that the company profits were in excess of £1 million. After the takeover, Caparo claimed that the accounts were inaccurate and the reported profit should have been a substantial loss. Caparo claimed that the auditors Touche Ross owed a duty of care to investors and sued them. They claimed Touche Ross should have seen the vulnerability of the company and therefore foreseen the likelihood of a takeover. However, the Law Lords were unanimous that auditors do not have a duty of care to individual shareholders or future investors. They also came to the conclusion that some previous cases, including *Jeb Fasteners* v. *Marks Bloom & Co.*, had been decided wrongly. However, Caparo went on to successfully pursue their action for damages against the directors of Fidelity, namely the Dickman brothers.

In relation to the Caparo judgment, Lord Bridge laid down the following circumstances in relation to proximity: the auditor will only be liable to the third party if the following circumstances are met:

1. The auditor is aware of the nature of the transaction which the third party is contemplating.

2. The auditor knows that the report will be communicated to the third party either directly or indirectly.
3. The auditor knows that the third party is likely to rely on the report in deciding whether or not to engage in the transaction in contemplation.

The Caparo judgment is a significant one since the courts are clearly reluctant to impose an unacceptable burden on auditors. Yet given the costs involved in lengthy court cases, it is not a surprise that so many cases in recent years, such as Barlow Clowes, BCCI, Maxwell Enterprises and Polly Peck, have been settled out of court.

In recent years the collapse of Enron and WorldCom in the USA and the consequences for the auditors Arthur Andersen, who were implicated in the scandal, resulted in the USA introducing the Sarbanes Oxley Act 2002. In the UK the courts have been concerned about the burden placed on external auditors since the Caparo case. In order to limit this burden, some auditors have formed limited liability companies; in other cases limited liability partnerships were created as an alternative.

Relationship between external and internal audit

During the course of their planning, the external auditors should perform a preliminary assessment of the internal audit function, when it appears that certain internal audit work is relevant to their external audit. A favourable assessment might allow the external auditors to modify the nature, timing and extent of external audit procedures.

External auditors may make use of the work of internal audit in forming their opinion. During the course of their work they will want to measure the effectiveness of internal audit. They do this against the *Internal Audit Guidelines* approved by the Auditing Practices Board (APB) in 1990.

However, it must be stated that external auditors have sole responsibility for their statutory responsibility to provide an audit opinion.

Internal audit

The Institute of Internal Auditors define internal audit as an independent assurance and consulting activity designed to add value and improve the organisation's objectives. It also helps an organisation accomplish its objectives, and it improves the effectiveness of risk management, control and governance processes. Figure 2.3 for the typical structure of an internal audit department.

Internal audit is defined by the APB in its 1990 *Internal Audit Guidelines* as an independent appraisal function established by the management of an organisation for the review of the internal control system as a service to the organisation. It objectively examines, evaluates and reports on the adequacy of internal control as a proper, economic, efficient and effective use of resources. The essential features of an effective internal audit department are as follows:

■ independence
■ appropriate staffing and training

Figure 2.3 **Typical structure of an internal audit department**

- relationships
- due care
- planning, controlling and recording
- evaluation of the internal control system
- evidence
- reporting and follow-up.

It is a management responsibility to determine the extent of internal control and not to depend on internal audit as a substitute for those controls. Internal audit will assist management in its assessment of risk and its corporate governance responsibility of internal control.

One of internal audit's objectives is to assist management in the pursuit of value for money.

It is management's responsibility to maintain the internal control system and to ensure that resources are properly directed. This, of course, will include a responsibility for the prevention and detection of fraud. If an internal auditor discovers evidence of, or suspects, fraud or some other malpractice, they should report their suspicions to the appropriate level of management. It is a management responsibility to determine what further action to take.

Independence

This is achieved through the organisational status of internal audit. Clearly it should have freedom to function effectively. The support of management is essential and internal audit should determine its own policies, in consultation with management. The head of internal audit should have direct access to, and freedom to report to, all senior managers, including the chief executive, finance director, board of directors and, of course, the Audit Committee. The key attribute of independence is the ability to report unedited in the head of audit's own name to the highest level of management. Each internal auditor should have an objective attitude of mind and be able to exercise independent judgment, express opinions and make recommendations without any degree of pressure.

Staffing and training

The APB guidelines state that:

- The effectiveness of internal audit depends substantially on the quality, training and experience of its staff. The aim should be to appoint staff with the appropriate background, personal qualities and potential. Thereafter, steps should be taken to provide the necessary experience, training and continuing professional education.
- The internal audit unit should be managed by a head of internal audit who should be suitably qualified and should possess wide experience of internal audit and of its management. They should plan, direct, control and motivate the resources available to ensure that the responsibilities of the internal audit unit are met.
- The full range of duties may require internal audit staff to be drawn from a variety of disciplines. The effectiveness of internal audit may be enhanced by the use of specialist staff, particularly in the internal audit of activities of a technical nature.
- The internal audit unit should employ staff with varying types and levels of skills, qualifications and experience in order to satisfy the requirements of each internal audit task.

Auditors need to be trained and kept up to date with changes of procedure and legislation. All audit staff should undertake continuing professional development in order to keep themselves up to date. This should be checked by the annual staff appraisal process.

Source: After *APB Guidelines for Internal Audit*, Auditing Practices Board, © Financial Reporting Council (FRC). Adapted and reproduced with the kind permission of the Financial Reporting Council. All rights reserved. For further information please visit www.frc.org.uk or call +44 (0)20 7492 2300.

Relationships

Auditors have dealings with a wide range of employees and managers and it is important for them to have confidence in the audit process. Many senior managers feel a real need for internal audit in helping them verify that their systems work in accordance with their expectations. It is acknowledged that at the lower end of the company some first-line managers do question the need for audit as see it as a drain on their time. Audit interpersonal skills are very important in this instance.

Discussions with management are an important part of the audit, and the pre-audit interview is an essential ingredient in the planning process. When the audit is completed, the auditor will want to discuss the findings and recommendations with management prior to the report being issued. This is an essential and important feature of a good working relationship between the auditor and management.

Due care

The auditor can never give a total assurance that control weaknesses don't exist but they must be able to demonstrate that due care is exercised and their working papers are consistent. The ethical guidelines published by the professional accountancy bodies are particularly relevant to the work of auditors. The head of internal audit should exercise some degree of quality control over the work of the department's staff.

Planning, controlling and recording

The head of internal audit will want to agree a strategic audit plan with the Audit Committee, which will address the audit approach over a period of 2–5 years, the minimum level of cover required (i.e. person-days) and the balance between value-for-money reviews, systems-based and other types of approach.

The APB's internal audit guidelines state the main purposes of internal audit planning as follows:

- to determine priorities and to establish the most cost-effective means of achieving audit objectives;
- to assist in the direction and control of audit work;
- to help ensure that attention is devoted to critical aspects of audit work;
- to help ensure that work is completed in accordance with pre-determined targets.

According to the guidelines, the stages of internal audit planning are as follows:

- to identify the objectives of the organisation;
- to define internal audit objectives;
- to take account of relevant changes in legislation and other external factors;
- to obtain a comprehensive understanding of the organisation's systems, structure and operations;
- to identify, evaluate and rank risks to which the organisation is exposed;
- to take account of changes in structures or major systems in the organisation;
- to take account of known strengths and weaknesses in the internal control system;
- to take account of management concerns and expectations;
- to identify audit areas by service, functions and major systems;
- to determine the type of audit, e.g. systems, verification or value for money;
- to take account of the plans of external audit and other review agencies;
- to assess staff resources required, and match with resources available.

Source: After *APB Guidelines for Internal Audit*, Auditing Practices Board, © Financial Reporting Council (FRC). Adapted and reproduced with the kind permission of the Financial Reporting Council. All rights reserved. For further information please visit www.frc.org.uk or call +44 (0)20 7492 2300.

The audit plan is broken down into a list of weekly or monthly tasks to be undertaken by staff. Against this plan, the head of audit controls, records and approves the release of the audit report.

Evaluation of the internal control systems

A systems-based approach to internal audit is advised and recommended. This means that the internal auditor is a control expert. The APB guideline for internal auditors clearly states that controls should ensure that processes meet the systems objectives.

The main objectives of the internal control system, according to the guidelines, are as follows:

- to ensure adherence to management policies and directives in order to achieve the organisation's objectives;
- to safeguard assets;
- to secure the relevance, reliability and integrity of information, so ensuring as far as possible the completeness and accuracy of records;
- to ensure compliance with statutory requirements.

When evaluating internal control systems the internal auditor should consider the effect that all the controls have on each other and on related systems.

As part of the planning process, the internal auditor should identify the whole range of systems within the organisation. For those systems to be examined, the internal auditor should establish appropriate criteria to determine whether the controls are adequate and assist in achieving the objectives of the system. The stages of a system audit would normally be:

- to identify the system parameters;
- to determine the control objectives;
- to identify expected controls to meet control objectives;
- to review the system against expected controls;
- to appraise the controls designed into the system against control objectives;
- to test the actual controls for effectiveness against control objectives;
- to test the operation of controls in practice;
- to test an opinion based on audit objectives as to whether the system provides an adequate basis for effective control and whether it is properly operated in practice.

Source: After *APB Guidelines for Internal Audit*, Auditing Practices Board, © Financial Reporting Council (FRC). Adapted and reproduced with the kind permission of the Financial Reporting Council. All rights reserved. For further information please visit www.frc.org.uk or call +44 (0)20 7492 2300.

Evidence

Evidence is information obtained by the auditor which enables conclusions to be drawn. This will come from the output obtained by substantive testing. The head of audit must be satisfied that evidence is sufficient, reliable and relevant, because judgment will be exercised and an opinion given.

Reporting and follow-up

The APB *Internal Audit Guidelines* clearly state that the primary purposes of internal audit reports are to provide management with an opinion as to the adequacy of the internal control system, and to inform management of significant audit findings, conclusions and recommendations. The aim of every internal audit report should be:

- to prompt management action to implement recommendations for change leading to improvement in performance and control;
- to provide a formal record of points arising from the internal audit assignment and, where appropriate, of agreements reached with management.

Reporting arrangements, including the format and distribution of internal audit reports, should be agreed with management. The head of internal audit should ensure that reports are sent to managers who have a direct responsibility for the unit or function being audited and who have the authority to take action on the internal audit's recommendations. Internal audit reports are confidential documents and their distribution should be restricted to those managers who need to know, to the audit committee and to the external auditor.

Audit reports in the main can be issued quickly because the auditor is satisfied that system controls are working and meet the control objectives. These reports will therefore have no specific or detailed recommendations. Their formats are held on computer file and they can be quickly run off once the head of audit has approved them.

Auditors are expected to report on the nature of the audit and, in particular, the remit which may come from the board but is more likely to be approved by the audit committee. The report will include details of findings, the impact and effect of the findings and, specifically, recommendations for improvement. In some cases a draft report is issued, the facts are verified and discussions held with managers. In other cases, an implementation schedule is attached (see Figure 2.4).

Figure 2.4 **Implementation schedule for an internal audit report**

SUBJECT: Vehicle Purchasing   REF. NO.: TR/06/08

REPORT PARA.	RECOMMENDATION	* ACCEPT	* REJECT	DATE OF PROPOSED IMPLEMENTATION
6	Vehicles should be purchased from two competing organisations	A		30/9/XX
	Suppliers should be asked to tender on price and provide a discount for bulk buying	B		To be discussed after a schedule of local suppliers is completed

SIGNED: P. Catley   DATE: 23.5.201X

NOTE: This form should be detached from the audit report and, after completion, returned to the head of audit
not later than ....

Please attach separate memorandum to amplify recommendations replied to codes B, C or D

*CODE FOR REPLY

A. Agreed in full

B. Agreed in principle, more research necessary

C. Disagree in present form

D. Disagree – reject completely

Reports are received differently according to the varying temperaments of the person being audited. However, the audit becomes a positive tool when logical, workable and pragmatic recommendations are produced. Managers are asked to give their response in writing. Reactions to audit reports should be monitored as a performance indicator for measuring the effectiveness of the internal audit division.

Once recommendations have been agreed, a follow-up audit is advised in order to see that these have been implemented and whether the system has improved. In some cases it can be left until the next audit. This is important because, all too often, recommendations are quickly accepted and then forgotten once the audit has been completed.

The image and marketing of internal audit

Perception is a real skill for the auditor to have. It draws on instinct or gut feeling. While it is not, in itself, evidence, it can be used to direct time, attention and effort.

The image of audit has always been a matter of some concern. In our experience, some directors of finance have used internal audit as a 'dumping ground' for staff who could contribute very little, whose career path was horizontal and would remain so until they retired. Key staff in the audit section have tended to leave for pastures new. In some cases their posts were cut, frozen or filled with somebody unacceptable to the chief internal auditor.

When it comes to promotion, chief internal auditors are judged on their work record and the positive results they have obtained, so it is interesting to note how few of them become directors of finance.

Many audit sections, including some of the smaller ones, engage in a multitude of non-audit functions. They become part of the system, doing mundane work such as checking refunds, calculating pensions or issuing stationery. Cheques are examined prior to despatch and contract final accounts receive 100% of internal audit's attention. This cannot be right and it makes one wonder what the barriers to change are. If these could be addressed perhaps chief internal auditors would have a free hand to concentrate on audit issues.

The threat of competition and the changing environment mean that the incentive for review and change is great. No matter how good a service looks, it can be improved. And service delivery, presentation and reporting are among the areas that must be addressed.

Auditors must look at their own range of management skills and consider how they deal with conflict and assertiveness as well as their interpersonal skills. Contact, marketing and selling skills must also be developed as senior audit staff will become familiar visitors to the offices of the chief officers.

The promotion of the internal audit brand is a key feature of raising the department's image within the company. A business card and a brochure with contact details can help to do this and should be provided so that managers are aware of the range of services on offer (see Figure 2.5a–c for examples).

Figure 2.5 **(a) Audit card. (b) Front cover of audit brochure. (c) Inside of audit brochure.**

ABC INTERNAL AUDIT SERVICE

Matt Ferdinandos
HEAD OF AUDIT

Tel: 081-901-2090
Fax: 081-901-9898

HQ
Council Avenue
Guildford Surrey
GU1 2SA

√ Quality, Efficiency, Reliability

(a)

ABC AUDIT SERVICE

FOR: Mr J. Ashtead

YOUR AUDIT MANAGER WILL BE: Mrs V.F. Munny, FCA
Tel.: 081 901 2999
Fax: 081 901 9898

√ Quality, Efficiency, Reliability

(b)

ABC INTERNAL AUDIT SERVICE

Services offered:

- Regulatory/probity audits
- Systems audits
- Computer audits
- VFM reviews
- Monitoring studies
- Pre- and post-audit interviews with client
- Easy access to staff throughout the week to discuss any issue, however small

√ Quality, Efficiency, Reliability

(c)

Exhibit 2.1 **Performance indicators**

Audit time
Productive time – actual vs. planned (%)
Reports produced within target time (%)
Reports exceeding target time (%)
Time spent on non-audit work (%)

Audit cost
Average cost per day
Total internal audit costs – budget vs. estimate
Total costs recharged

Audit plans
Progress against annual plan
Progress against long-term plan
Number of reports issued

Staff and skill levels
Staff in post vs. those required
Staff turnover rates
Numbers of professionally qualified staff vs. part-qualified
Ratio of trainees to total staff

Findings and recommendations
Recommendations accepted vs. recommendations made (%)
Recommendations implemented within 6 months (%)

Client reaction
Customer satisfaction survey

Performance indicators for internal audit

The head of internal audit is usually expected to prepare an annual report to the Audit Committee. Some of the performance indicators that might be included in such a report, for internal management information, are shown in Exhibit 2.1.

External audit reviews of internal audit

It is a function of external audit to evaluate the effectiveness of internal audit work. External auditors must feel a degree of assurance as to its quality, and they will want to assess the performance of internal audit. The Auditing Practices Board *Internal Audit Guidelines* provide an appropriate benchmark to do this. Some external auditors measure internal audit on a scale of A to D. In this instance, full compliance with the guidelines would receive an A, while complete non-compliance would receive a D. There is a standard, ISA 610, which requires the external auditor to assess the quality of the work of internal auditor.

A checklist is provided in Figure 2.6, which can serve as a guide in measuring the effectiveness of internal audit.

Figure 2.6 **External audit's checklist for the assessment of internal audit**

Internal Audit	Assessment	
Year ending 31 March 201X	Date:	
	....	
	....	

Status	Answer	Reference
1. Are role and objectives clearly established?	....	....
2. Does IA have unrestricted access to records?	....	....
3. Is IA independent of line management?	....	....
4. Is IA well regarded in the authority?	....	....
Staffing		
5. Is staffing adequate for size and scope?	....	....
6. Is complement complete in year?	....	....
7. Are specialist skills available, e.g. computers, contracts?	....	....
8. Do any staff have non-audit duties?	....	....
Planning		
9. Does IA have a strategic plan?	....	....
10. Is a satisfactory annual plan prepared?	....	....
11. Is the plan being met in this year?	....	....
Scope and procedures		
12. Is there a manual or equivalent?	....	....
13. Are instructions/work programmes adequate?	....	....
14. Are audit procedures satisfactory?	....	....
15. Have matters of concern been discovered?	....	....
16. Is balance of coverage satisfactory – main systems, sub-systems, other regularity, projects, VFM etc.?	....	....
Management		
17. Is IA work properly supervised?	....	....
18. Does CIA manage effectively?	....	....
Reporting		
19. Is the method of reporting satisfactory?	....	....
20. Is progress on recommendations monitored?	....	....
21. Is an annual report prepared?	....	....
22. Does IA have access to top management	....	....
Overall conclusion	....	
	....	
	....	

Summary

This chapter builds on Chapter 1 and goes into more depth of the features of external audit and internal audit.

The statutory requirement of external audit is investigated and its key function, which is to provide an opinion on the financial statements, is analysed. External audit case law is examined from early times through to the Caparo case, which is currently the legal precedent for the United Kingdom. There has always been a debate about the effectiveness and usefulness of external audit and the issue of liability should things go wrong. However, its role remains a cornerstone to certify the integrity of the financial statements. Within the regulatory framework, external auditors have a duty to shareholders to perform the role of a watchdog. They are required to check and verify internal audit's work as part of the process, so that they can be reassured as to the reliability of internal control verification.

Internal auditors, whilst having a degree of independence, are salaried employees of the company and are considered to be independent by virtue of their objectivity and provide an appraisal function as a service to management. They are an integral part of the function of internal control.

? PRACTICE QUESTION

As part of their review, external auditors must comment on the reliance and effectiveness of internal audit. Discuss how they will go about doing this.

Auditing standards

Contents

Objectives

After studying this chapter you should be able to:

- discuss the current international standards in auditing and their major concepts;
- explain the impact of auditing standards on the auditing profession;
- appreciate the relevance of adhering to auditing standards as a means of ensuring quality;
- identify the auditing regulatory bodies within the UK.

Introduction

The role of auditing standards is multi-faceted, covering five key aspects:

- *Quality control.* Auditing standards provide a framework that enables delivery of a consistent and acceptable standard of audit service between practitioners. They also add to the credibility of the audit, allowing the client and those interested in the audit report to be reassured that the audit was undertaken according to recognised guidelines.
- *Practitioner education.* Auditing is a dynamic subject area and auditing standards contribute to the continuing education of professionals. Auditing standards, by their nature, must be subject to review, thus enabling a response to developments in the business environment in a positive manner to meet expectations. In this way, such changes are reflected in the audit work, which in turn ensures a process whereby auditors are continually developing their skills and knowledge.
- *The disciplinary role.* Auditing standards enable the profession to determine whether the performance of an individual auditor or that of an auditing firm is commensurate with what is expected of the auditing profession as a whole.
- *The legal role.* In instances of litigation against an auditor, professional auditing standards act as a guideline in a court of law to determine whether the auditor has been negligent in undertaking the audit work.
- *The political role.* Auditing and accounting standards can be used by the profession to demonstrate that it is capable of regulating and controlling itself rather than subjecting itself to government regulation.

Background to the adoption of international auditing standards

History and development

The groundwork for an international set of auditing standards was laid in 1969 with the publication of a number of reports focusing on international auditing by the Accountants International Study Group, comparing the situations in Canada, the UK and the USA. A few years later, in 1973, the establishment of the International Accounting Standards Committee (IASC) generated many calls for similar bodies to be set up to review the introduction of standards for auditing. In the late 1970s the Council of International Federation of Accountants (IFAC) created the International Auditing Practices Committee (IAPC), which would be a standing committee of the IFAC Council and subsequently the IFAC Board (renamed a board in May 2000).

During the period between 1980 and 1991, the IAPC issued International Auditing Guidelines (IAGs) along with addendums. The first International Standard on Auditing (ISA) was issued in 1991, and this has remained the series to the present day. The IAPC's definition of these international standards is as follows:

> National standards on auditing and related services published in many countries differ in form and content. The International Auditing Practices Committee (IAPC) takes cognizance of such documents and differences, and, in the light of such knowledge, issues ISAs, which are intended for international acceptance.

The IAPC becomes the IAASB

On 19 July 2001, the IFAC Board issued a press release entitled 'IFAC Seeks Comments on Role of International Auditing Committee', which included a discussion of a number of issues and resulted in a recommendation from the Review Task Force to specifically address the future of ISAs. It said it was looking to 'more clearly establish and communicate the authority of IAPC International Standards on Auditing and other guidance'.

As a result of the review, the IAPC was renamed the International Auditing and Assurance Standards Board (IAASB) in mid-2002. It had a remit to ensure that it encouraged changes to the processes and transparency of its work and included a widening of its membership to include non-auditors. On 1 January 2003 the IAASB made available the full text of its International Standards on Auditing for free on its website and agreed that all future final pronouncements were also to be published for free online.

The International Auditing and Assurance Standards Board

The IAASB has a remit to serve the public interest by:

- setting, independently and under its own authority, high-quality standards dealing with auditing, review, other assurance, quality control and related services;
- facilitating the convergence of national and international standards.

This contributes to enhanced quality and uniformity of practice in these areas throughout the world, and in so doing is meant to strengthen the public's confidence in financial reporting.

International Standards on Auditing

In 2004 (and revised in 2009) the UK and Ireland adopted the International Standards on Auditing (ISAs) that set out the principles and essential procedures that auditors should follow in undertaking their audit of financial statements. These ISAs replaced the existing Auditing Practices Board (APB) Statement of Auditing Standards (SAS) guidance for auditors that existed in the UK and Ireland prior to 2004.

Standard-setting

The responsibility for standard-setting rests in the hands of the IAASB, based in New York. It determines when new auditing standards are needed or when existing standards need to be amended. A subcommittee of the IAASB is tasked with producing an exposure draft (ED), which is then reviewed by the IAASB and, if acceptable, is circulated for consultation among interested parties (the APB in the UK is one of these parties). Comments on the ED are fed back to the IAASB and, if considered relevant, it is amended. Eventually the ED will become a new ISA. In the UK, the ISA is then reviewed by the APB and issued as an ISA (UK & Ireland). The ISA may be issued in the same format as the international version, or it may have small amendments to reflect UK legal and regulatory requirements. The policy is to make as few amendments as possible.

Conflict situations

There are circumstances in which conflict may arise, despite the desire to have internationally accepted standards. For example, a country may have a 'local' audit requirement for an engagement letter to be sent every 3 years for recurring audits. However, ISA 210, *Agreeing the Terms of Audit Engagements*, paragraph 13, recommends that the auditor considers annually whether a letter is needed on a recurring audit, and provides examples of situations when a new letter should be sent. The local and ISA requirements are therefore at odds in this situation. In order to resolve this conflict, a number of issues need to be considered:

- ISAs are not designed to overrule the specific requirements of an individual country. If there is a conflict, then the specific country's regulation is to be followed. However, the IAASB normally recommends that changes are eventually introduced in that country's legislation in order to bring it in line with the ISA.
- If the ISA requirement is seen to provide a stronger auditing policy, then the country can adopt the ISA and withdraw the local audit regulation. This is why the APB in the UK decided to adopt the ISAs rather than amend some of the existing SASs.
- In a situation where there is no comparable auditing standard in the country, the ISA can be used immediately.

In summary, ISAs are followed within a country whenever possible. Similarly auditors will follow the auditing procedures for their own country, which will eventually become ISAs. In the rare situation where the ISA is inappropriate for the country from an audit point of view, an auditor may depart from the ISA and follow the national/local standard. But deviation from the international standard is not encouraged and auditors must consider carefully the consequences of non-compliance, particularly as courts may view the ISA as the standard that they should follow.

Accounting and auditing regulation in the UK

The Financial Reporting Council

The Financial Reporting Council (FRC) is the UK's independent regulator, responsible for promoting confidence in corporate reporting and governance. By pursuing this aim the FRC has a strategy that ensures UK companies with a primary listing in the UK are led in a way that facilitates entrepreneurial success and the management of risk. Corporate reports must contain information that is relevant, reliable, understandable and comparable. These reports need to be useful for decision-making and stewardship decisions. The corporate reports must be of a level such that users of audit reports can place a high degree of reliance on the audit opinion as to whether the financial statements show a true and fair view. In terms of actuarial information, the users need to be able to place a high degree of reliance on the relevance, transparency of assumptions, completeness and comprehensibility of the information. Clients and employers of professionally qualified accountants and actuaries, and of accountancy and actuarial firms, can rely on these professionals to act with integrity and competence, having regard to the public interest.

The FRC has a role to be an effective, accountable and independent regulator, which actively helps to shape UK approaches, and to influence EU and global approaches, to corporate reporting and governance. The functions of the FRC are outlined in Exhibit 3.1.

The FRC incorporates five operating boards:

- The Accounting Standards Board;
- The Auditing Practices Board;
- The Financial Reporting Review Panel;
- The Accountancy Discipline and Investigation Board;
- The Professional Oversight Board.

Source: www.frc.org.uk

The Professional Oversight Board

The FRC's regulatory responsibilities in relation to audit and to the accountancy profession are exercised by the Professional Oversight Board (POB). The POB contributes to the achievement of the FRC's own fundamental aim of supporting investor, market and public confidence in the financial and governance stewardship of listed and other entities by:

- independent oversight of the regulation of the auditing profession by the recognised supervisory and qualifying bodies;
- monitoring the quality of the auditing function in relation to economically significant entities;
- independent oversight of the regulation of the accountancy profession by the professional accountancy bodies;
- independent oversight of the regulation of the actuarial profession by the professional actuarial bodies and promoting high-quality actuarial work.

Exhibit 3.1 **The functions of the FRC**

- Promoting high standards of corporate governance
- Setting, monitoring and enforcing accounting and auditing standards
- Setting actuarial standards
- Statutory oversight and regulation of auditors
- Operating an independent investigation and discipline scheme for public interest cases
- Overseeing the regulatory activities of the professional accountancy and actuarial bodies

In relation to audit, the board achieves its aims by discharging on behalf of the FRC the statutory responsibilities delegated to it by the Secretary of State for authorising professional accountancy bodies to act as supervisory bodies and/or to offer a recognised professional qualification. As part of this activity, the board will assess whether:

■ the recognised supervisory and qualifying bodies comply with all the statutory requirements for recognition set out in the Companies Act 1989;
■ the recognised supervisory bodies comply with the independent standard-setting, monitoring and disciplinary arrangements which the legislation provides for.

The POB monitors also the audit quality of economically significant entities through an independent Audit Inspection Unit (AIU). The unit monitors audit quality by reviewing audit processes including audit judgments. It will agree with audit firms amendments to their procedures where appropriate and make recommendations to the recognised supervisory bodies for appropriate regulatory action.

In relation to the regulation of the accountancy profession, the POB reviews the regulatory activities of the professional accountancy bodies in relation to their members, including education, training, continuing professional development, standards, ethical matters (except those which are the responsibility of the Auditing Practices Board), professional conduct and discipline, registration and monitoring, including making recommendations on how these activities may be improved. The professional accountancy bodies have the primary regulatory responsibility for the supervision of their members acting in their professional capacity. In relation to audit, as recognised qualifying bodies (RQBs), they are required to have effective arrangements in place in order to ensure that their audit qualifications meet the statutory requirements and, as recognised supervisory bodies (RSBs), they must have in place appropriate and effective arrangements for the registration, monitoring and disciplining of their auditor members.

The Auditing Practices Board

The Auditing Practices Board (APB) is a part of the FRC and was re-established in April 2002, and replaced a previous APB which had been in place since 1991. The APB has as its remit a commitment to lead the development of auditing practice in the UK and Ireland so as to:

■ establish high standards of auditing;
■ meet the developing needs of users of financial information;
■ ensure public confidence in the auditing process. It reviews the ISAs for their applicability to the UK and if necessary awards the ISA to meet with UK legal/ regulatory requirements.

Audit risk, fraud and quality control were issues plaguing the auditing profession during the latter part of the 20th century. As the body responsible for promoting the principles and procedures expected during an audit, the APB realised that the UK auditing standards needed to be reviewed in the context of financial reporting irregularities in the UK, US and continental Europe. This was to ensure that the standards in existence were as effective as possible in addressing fraudulent financial reporting and aggressive earnings management. Rather than working on this in isolation, the APB decided that it would be more effective to contribute to the international effort, through the IAASB, and thereby demonstrate its commitment to the worldwide harmonisation of auditing standards, the ISAs, rather than updating its own Statements of Auditing Standards (SASs).

In 2004 the APB announced its intention that new ISAs relating to audit should apply in the UK and Ireland for audits of accounting periods commencing on or after 15 December 2004. The revised standards of 2009 are effective for accounting periods ending on or after 15 December 2010.

In adopting the ISAs issued by the IAASB, the role of the APB changed to that of ensuring that the quality of the ISAs that apply to the UK and Ireland are maintained.

Maintaining the quality of the UK's and Ireland's auditing standards

As part of the incorporation of the International Standards on Auditing into the UK profession, the APB reviewed all of its existing SASs to identify instances where they contained higher standards than those in equivalent ISAs. As a result, the APB decided it was necessary to incorporate some material from the existing SASs into the ISAs to avoid any dilution of UK and Irish standards. Over time, the intention is that the APB will withdraw any supplementary material to the relevant ISAs when revised by IAASB.

Adopting the ISAs helps maintain the status of UK and Irish standards internationally. In the aftermath of corporate failures in the US and continental Europe, securities regulators and governments recognised the value of harmonised standards. The European Commission in the meantime introduced an amended directive on the statutory audit that required the adoption of ISAs by all Member States.

The adoption also enables the APB to benefit efficiently from future improvements to ISAs. APB members are involved in working parties to revise the ISAs and in so doing focus on the issues pertinent to the UK and Ireland.

International Standards on Auditing: an introduction

www.frc.org.uk

ISA 200: Overall Objectives of the Independent Auditor and the Conduct of an Audit in Accordance with International Standards on Auditing (UK and Ireland)

ISA 200 provides a definition of the audit of financial statements by stating that the 'objective of an audit of financial statements is to enable the auditor to express an opinion as to whether the financial statements are prepared, in all material aspects, in accordance with an identifiable financial reporting framework'.

ISA 210: Agreeing the Terms of Audit Engagements

ISA 210 states that the 'the auditor and client should agree the terms of the engagement'. These agreed terms need to be in the form of an engagement letter, which clearly defines the auditor's responsibilities to minimise any misunderstandings or disputes at a later date. The letter acts as confirmation of the appointment and outlines the scope of the audit, the format of the report that will be forthcoming on completion of the audit plus any non-audit services.

ISA 220: Quality Control for an Audit of Financial Statements

ISA 220 emphasises the importance of quality control policies and procedures both at audit firm level and the at individual audit level. The revised standard on quality control of audits of historical financial information outlines specific responsibilities of the personnel involved in the individual audit engagements.

ISA 230: Audit Documentation

ISA 230 states that 'the auditor should prepare, on a timely basis, audit documentation that provides a sufficient and appropriate record of the basis of the auditor's report, and evidence that the audit was performed in accordance with ISAs and applicable regulatory requirements'.

ISA 240: The Auditor's Responsibilities Relating to Fraud in an Audit of Financial Statements

ISA 240 outlines the auditor's responsibility in being aware that there may be possible misstatements within the financial statements due to fraud. The auditor must be professionally sceptical when it comes to fraud and must consider how the fraud could occur, and by whom. This ISA integrates into the audit planning and risk assessment standards in that they all fit together in terms of the assessment of the risk that fraud may be present. ISA 240 states that

> . . . when identifying and assessing the risk of material misstatement due to fraud the auditor shall evaluate which types of transaction or assertions give rise to such risks. The auditor shall treat those assessed risks of material misstatements due to fraud as significant risks and accordingly, to the extent not already done so, the auditor shall obtain an understanding of the entity's related controls relevant to such risks.

ISA 250A: Consideration of Laws and Regulations in an Audit of Financial Statements; ISA 250B: The Auditor's Right and Duty to Report to Regulators in the Financial Sector

ISA 250 states that 'when designing and performing audit procedures and in evaluating and reporting the results thereof, the auditor should recognise that non-compliance by the entity with laws and regulations may materially affect the financial statements'.

ISA 260: Communication with those charged with governance

ISA 260 states that 'the auditor should communicate audit matters of governance interest arising from the audit of financial statements with those charged with governance of an entity'. This relates to matters that have come to the attention of the auditor during the course of the audit. Communication can be to the whole board, the audit committee or the supervisory board, depending on the governance structure of the organisation.

ISA 265: Communicating Deficiencies in Internal Control to those Charged with Governance and Management

ISA 265 (a new 2009 standard) states that the auditor on identifying deficiencies in internal controls must communicate this in writing to those charged with governance. The auditor needs to identify whether these deficiencies lead to material misstatements.

ISA 300: Planning an Audit of Financial Statements

ISA 300 states that the 'auditor should plan the audit so that the engagement will be performed in an effective manner'. An effective and efficient audit relies on sound planning procedures in order to give a framework to work against and also to ensure that all issues relating to the particular audit client are covered.

ISA 315: Identifying and Assessing Risks of Material Misstatement through Understanding the Entity and its Environment

ISA 315 states that 'the auditor should obtain an understanding of the entity and its environment, including its internal control, sufficient to identify and assess the risks of material misstatement of the financial statements whether due to fraud or error, and sufficient to design and perform further audit procedures'.

ISA 320: Materiality in Planning and Performing an Audit

ISA 320 on audit materiality requires the auditor to consider materiality when, 'determining the nature, timing and extent of audit procedures, and evaluating the effect of misstatements'. Materiality should be reviewed constantly during the audit, as changes or developments may mean that a reassessment of the situation has to be undertaken.

ISA 330: The Auditor's Responses to Assessed Risks

ISA 330 refers to the response to assessed risk and states that 'in order to reduce risk to an acceptably low level, the auditor should determine overall responses to assessed risks at the financial statement level, and should design and perform further audit procedures to respond to assessed risks at the assertion level'.

ISA 402: Audit Considerations Relating to an Entity Using a Service Organisation

ISA 402 provides guidance to the auditor when its client uses a 'service organisation'. The guidance outlines the auditor reports from the service organisation that the auditor must obtain, while the 'auditor should consider how an entity's use of a service organisation affects the entity's internal control so as to assess the risk of material misstatement and to design and perform further audit procedures'.

ISA 450: Evaluation of Misstatements Identified During the Audit

ISA 450 (a new 2009 standard) requires the audit to consider whether the overall strategy and audit plan need to be revised if misstatements identified have an impact on the audit work. The auditor must also communicate all misstatements and request that they be corrected.

ISA 500: Audit Evidence

ISA 500 is core to the work of the auditor – gathering evidence is an important feature of the audit work. The standard requires the auditor to 'obtain sufficient appropriate audit evidence to be able to draw reasonable conclusions on which to base the audit opinion'. Sufficient and appropriate are key words here as they apply to both tests of control as well as substantive procedures.

ISA 501: Audit Evidence – Specific Considerations for Selected Items

ISA 501 concerns contingencies relating to litigation and legal claims, and states that the 'auditor should carry out procedures in order to become aware of any litigation and claims involving the entity which may have a material effect on the financial statements'.

ISA 505: External Confirmations

External confirmation, as the words imply, refers to third party confirmation of evidence. In relation to this, ISA 505 states that the auditor must maintain control over the external confirmation requests and send follow-up communications. Where management refuse auditor contact then the auditor must perform alternative audit procedures.

ISA 510: Initial Audit Engagements – Opening Balances

ISA 510 states that the 'auditor must consider whether opening balances reflect the application of appropriate accounting policies and that those policies are consistently applied in the current period's financial statements'.

ISA 520: Analytical Procedures

In ISA 520, analytical procedures are described as similar information for prior periods, anticipated results of the entity, from budgets or forecasts, predictions prepared by the auditors and industry information such as comparison of the client's ratio of sales to debtors with the industry average. In undertaking analytical review the auditor should 'apply analytical procedures as risk assessment procedures to obtain an understanding of the entity and its environment and in the overall review at the end of the audit'.

ISA 530: Audit Sampling

ISA 530 outlines a form of obtaining evidence that meets the objective of the audit: 'When designing audit procedures, the auditor should determine appropriate means of selecting items for testing so as to gather sufficient appropriate audit evidence to meet the objectives of audit procedures.'

ISA 540: Auditing, Accounting Estimates, Including Fair Value Accounting Estimates, and Related Disclosures

ISA 540 relates to accounting estimates which are approximations of the amount of an item when there is an absence of precise methods of measurement. In the vein of sufficient appropriate evidence, this standard stipulates that the auditor should 'obtain sufficient appropriate evidence regarding accounting estimates'.

In terms of the fair value measurements and disclosures, the auditor must ensure that there are appropriate mechanisms in place to ensure that sufficient appropriate evidence is gathered to support the fair value measurements.

ISA 550: Related Parties

ISA 550 relates to the audit role in terms of existence and disclosure of related parties, the entity's transactions with related parties, and the adequacy of related party disclosures in the financial statements. The definition of 'related party' is adopted from ISA 24 and the financial reporting standard FRS 8.

ISA 560: Subsequent Events

ISA 560 provides the standard approach that the auditor should employ, stating that the auditor 'should consider the effect of subsequent events on the financial statements and on the auditor's report'. Auditors have a responsibility to review subsequent events before they sign their audit report and must ensure that sufficient and appropriate evidence exists relating to all events up to the date of the auditor's report that may require adjusting or disclosing within the financial statements.

ISA 570: Going Concern

ISA 570 states that 'when planning and performing the audit procedures and in evaluating the results thereof, the auditor should consider the appropriateness of management's use of the going concern assumption in the preparation of the financial statements'. Management have to make an explicit assessment of the company's ability to continue as a going concern by taking into account any uncertainties, financial indications, operating indications and any other indications affecting a going concern.

ISA 580: Written Representations

ISA 580 defines management representations and details the audit responsibilities, whereby the auditor should obtain appropriate representations from management. It states: 'The auditor should obtain audit evidence that management acknowledges its responsibility for the fair presentation of the financial statements in accordance with the applicable financial reporting framework and has approved the financial statements.'

ISA 600: Special Considerations – Audits of Group Financial Statements (Including the Work of Component Auditors)

ISA 600 sets out procedures for the auditor in terms of using the work of component auditors, whereby the professional competence of the other auditors should be reviewed in respect of the context of the specific assignment. There is an expectation that the work of the other auditor is adequate for the principal auditor's purpose. This refers to the audit of group financial statements.

ISA 610: Using the Work of Internal Auditors

ISA 610, in considering the work of internal audit, states that the 'external auditor should obtain a sufficient understanding of the internal audit activities to identify and assess the risks of material misstatements of the financial statements and to design and perform further audit procedures'. The external auditor may make specific use of internal audit work, in which case the external auditor should evaluate and perform audit procedures on the work to confirm its adequacy for external auditor purposes.

ISA 620: Using the Work of an Auditor's Expert

ISA 620 has a requirement for auditors to ensure that if they use the work of an expert then they must obtain sufficient appropriate audit evidence to confirm that the work of other experts is fit for purpose in terms of the audit being undertaken. There is a need to confirm the professional competence of experts and their objectivity.

ISA 700: The Auditor's Report on Financial Statements

Note: the APB has not adopted the IAASB ISA 700 Forming an Opinion and Reporting on Financial Statements. It has issued a clarified version (revised in 2009). ISA 700 is an important standard as it outlines the form and content of the auditor's report after the completion of the audit of the financial statements. It states that 'the auditor should evaluate the conclusions drawn from the audit evidence obtained as the basis for forming the opinion on the financial statements'.

ISA 705: Modifications to Opinions in the Independent Auditor's Report; ISA 706: Emphasis of Matter Paragraphs and Other Matter Paragraphs in the Independent Auditor's Report

These two ISAs were adopted by the APB in 2009 and replace ISA 701. They identify circumstances when a modification to the auditor's opinion is required and when the auditor considers it necessary to draw the user's attention to important matters deemed fundamental to the understanding of the financial statements.

ISA 710: Comparative Information – Corresponding Figures and Comparative Financial Statements

This standard is effective for audits of financial statements for periods ending on or after December 15, 2010.

The auditor's objectives are to obtain sufficient appropriate audit evidence about whether the comparative information included in the financial statements has been presented, in all material respects, in accordance with the requirements for comparative information in the applicable financial reporting framework; and to report in accordance with the auditor's reporting responsibilities.

For purposes of clarification the following definitions have been provided:

- *Comparative information* – The amounts and disclosures included in the financial statements in respect of one or more prior periods in accordance with the applicable financial reporting framework.
- *Corresponding figures* – Comparative information where amounts and other disclosures for the prior period are included as an integral part of the current period financial statements, and are intended to be read only in relation to the amounts and other disclosures relating to the current period (referred to as 'current period figures'). The level of detail presented in the corresponding amounts and disclosures is dictated primarily by its relevance to the current period figures.
- *Comparative financial statements* – Comparative information where amounts and other disclosures for the prior period are included for comparison with the financial statements of the current period but, if audited, are referred to in the auditor's opinion. The level of information included in those comparative financial statements is comparable with that of the financial statements of the current period.

In respect of ISA 710, therefore, the auditor should determine whether the comparatives comply in all material respects with the financial reporting frameworks applicable to the financial statements being audited.

ISA 720A: The Auditor's Responsibilities Relating to Other Information in Documents Containing Audited Financial Statements; ISA 720B: The Auditor's Statutory Reporting Responsibility in Relation to Directors' Reports

The ISA 720A provides guidance to the auditor on dealing with other information found in documents containing audited financial statements. The auditor may not have any obligation to report on this information, but 'the auditor should read the other information to identify material inconsistencies with the audited financial statements'.

ISA 720B requires the auditor to assess whether the information in the director's report is consistent with the financial statements.

International Standard on Quality Control (UK and Ireland)

The International Standard on Quality Control (ISQC) (UK and Ireland) contains basic principles and essential procedures together with related guidance in the form of explanatory and other material, including appendices. Systems of quality control in compliance with the ISQC (UK and Ireland) became applicable to firms in the UK and Ireland on 15 June 2005.

Practice notes and bulletins

In addition to ISAs there exist practice notes which are intended to assist auditors in applying general auditing standards to particular circumstances and industries. The APB also issues bulletins to provide auditors with timely guidance on new and emerging issues.

Practice notes and bulletins are persuasive rather than prescriptive. They are indicative of good practice, even though they may be developed without the full process of consultation and exposure used for standards.

Summary

The introduction of standards provides a firm foundation for the auditing profession to display quality in its audit work. Standards offer benchmarks by which the profession can assess audit activity, and provide a sound basis for instruction and guidance in the training of auditors.

? PRACTICE QUESTION

What is the role of the Auditing Practices Board in the UK regulatory framework? Discuss whether it has been successful in achieving its objectives.

Chapter 4

Professional ethics and code of conduct

Objectives

After studying this chapter you should be able to:

- explain the concepts of professional ethics;
- describe the aspects contained within the professional ethics codes of conduct;
- discuss the issues relating to professional ethics within the context of confidentiality and conflicts of interest;
- distinguish between the elements of professional ethics applicable to internal auditors and those applicable to external auditors.

Introduction

When defining 'ethics' it is worth noting how the word fits with 'professional' in terms of the auditing and accounting profession. The word 'ethics' is derived from the Greek word *ethos*, meaning 'character'. Ethics, as defined by the *Cambridge dictionary* is 'a system of accepted beliefs which control behaviour, especially such a system based on morals'. This 'system of accepted beliefs' is what underpins the auditor's role and is described by Mautz & Sharaf (1961, p. 232)[1] as follows:

> Ethical behaviour in auditing or in any other activity is no more than a special application of the general notion of ethical conduct devised by philosophers. . . . Ethical Conduct in auditing draws its justification and basic nature from the general theory of ethics.

In Western cultures the tradition of ethics is sometimes called moral philosophy. While morality focuses on the 'right' and 'wrong' of human behaviour, ethics focuses on how and why people act in a certain manner. It therefore concerns itself more with a study of morality.

Ethics are standards of behaviour that describe how people react when they encounter different situations. This is reflected in their reaction to the circumstances and situations as well as the people involved, e.g. friends, parents, business people and professionals. Ethical standards provide a framework for human behaviour and human interaction and deal with the question of what is right and what is wrong. The concept of 'ethics' applies when an individual has to decide on a response when there are various alternatives regarding moral principles. All individuals and societies possess a sense of ethics, in that they come to some sort of agreement as to what is right and what is wrong. Modern business ethics holds that there is no established set of principles as such that meets with this concept of right and wrong. In the tale of Robin Hood, was Robin right or wrong in stealing from the rich to give to the poor? Was he acting ethically?

The term professional ethics can be derived from the above-mentioned definitions, and describes the behaviour and interaction within a group of professionals – a set of standards governing the conduct of members of a certain occupation. The professional ethics code is a part of ethics which answers the question: how should the profession be practised? By establishing a set of professional ethics they provide values, which can then characterise the profession. Ethics therefore act as a code of conduct that embraces a high standard of professionalism. This, in turn, provides an expectation that there will be auditor integrity, objectivity and independence. Failure to abide by a code of conduct will bring the profession as a whole into disrepute.

Why is there a code of professional ethics?

Ethics affects all processes of auditing, as the auditor is faced with decisions at all stages of an audit. The code can act as a guideline for the entire auditing process. The ethical code is not merely a guide to how an auditor must behave whilst

[1]Mautz RK, Sharaf HA (1961). *The Philosophy of Auditing*. Sarasota, FL, USA: American Accounting Association.

undertaking the auditing process, but also designs the framework for the relationship between client and auditor. For example, the importance of a standard embracing integrity, independence and objectivity can be easily explained using the following scenario:

> Auditor A owns shares in a client company that A is currently auditing. During the audit, A does not question the overly aggressive accounting approach undertaken by management to indicate higher earnings. This is because A knows that the indicative higher earnings will increase the company's share price and benefit the auditor as well as other shareholders.

This example shows the importance of the ethical code in ensuring that the actions of the auditor are not influenced by the opportunity for personal gain, in this instance a share price increase. The independence of audit provides a certain level of reliability and public confidence. By acting unethically the auditor's action would not only damage the reputation of the audit firm, but could also lead to a reduction in the level of trust in the whole audit process.

The Jefferson Institute of Ethics identified 'six pillars of character':

- truthfulness
- respect
- responsibility
- fairness
- caring
- citizenship.

From these six pillars of character there emerged 10 universal values most people expect in terms of ethical behaviour in society:

- honesty
- integrity
- promise keeping
- loyalty
- fairness
- caring for others
- respect for others
- responsible citizenship
- pursuit of excellence
- accountability.

Why is there a need for an ethics guideline for professional auditors?

Ethics for professional auditors are guidelines for ensuring a professional attitude and conduct in a way that enhances the image of the auditing profession. Auditors should strive for the highest standards of professionalism, as they act as assurance providers for the shareholders and the public. Therefore, by inference, the standards of the profession are of concern to the shareholders and public. The code of professional ethics for auditors is different from that of other professions in its emphasis on independence, especially the appearance of independence.

Background

In 1995 the ethical principles in place for external auditors, as laid down by the Auditing Practices Board's (1995) Statements of Auditing Standards (SASs), stated that 'In the conduct of any audit of financial statements auditors should comply with the ethical guidance issued by their relevant professional bodies' (SAS 100.2).

These 1995 principles, applying to external auditors, consisted of 'integrity, objectivity, independence, professional competence and due care, professional behaviour and confidentiality'. Under the guidance of the Chartered Accountants' Joint Ethics Committee (CAJEC), the UK adopted the Guide to Professional Ethics in 1996. This was regarded as a foundation stone in terms of evaluating the professional ethics and independence of auditors. This guidance introduced the 'conceptual framework' and dispensed with the strict rule of conduct. This conceptual framework offered a set of structured ideas to provide auditors with a method for adopting a consistent approach in decision-making.

Leading on from this guidance, each recognised supervisory body (RSB) then went on to introduce their own tailored ethical statements. These statements embraced the concepts included in the CAJEC's statement. The statement used by the Institute of Chartered Accountants in England and Wales (ICAEW) was, in fact, the original CAJEC statement, which identified four key areas:

- Section A – objectivity, independence and the audit;
- Section B – objectivity and independence in financial reporting and similar non-audit roles;
- Section C – objectivity and independence in professional roles other than those covered in sections A and B;
- Section D – definitions.

The Association of Chartered Certified Accountants (ACCA) wrote a similar statement, which had the title 'Statement 1: Integrity, objectivity and independence' and included a summary stating that:

- A member's objectivity must be beyond question if he (or she) is to report as an auditor. That objectivity can only be assured if the member is, and is seen to be, independent. The threat to independence may be reduced by the nature and extent of the precautions taken by the practice to guard against loss of objectivity.

Despite the existence of a guide for professional ethics there was an element of doubt surrounding the ethics of the profession in the late 20th century. Around the turn of the century a series of high-profile corporate scandals, including those of Robert Maxwell, Polly Peck, BCCI, Enron and WorldCom, along with the collapse of the audit firm Arthur Andersen, led to a decline in confidence in the auditing profession. This loss of confidence dented the value of the existing ethical guidance and indicated that there were flaws present in the ethical codes. Questions were raised as to how ethical it was for auditors to provide additional services and consultancy along with the legally required audit opinion. In an attempt to address this loss of confidence the UK Financial Reporting Council appointed the Auditing Practices Board (APB) to review the guidelines on ethics and introduce new ethical standards. The rebuilding of trust was necessary to regain the public's confidence in the profession. The perception of independence and the existence of independence required some confirmation. One route to achieve this was the introduction of a code of ethical standards, providing:

- a standard framework for the profession;
- a sense of consistency resulting from that framework;
- a distinction between the audit profession versus the audit as a business, which was necessary after the impact of the scandals.

Professional ethics and codes

The term professional ethics refers to the code of behaviour, rules and guidance that is set out for accountants and auditors to follow. Audit firms and auditors are expected to go about their daily business in a professional manner which should adhere to the guidelines set out by the APB. Professional ethics are the principles and standards that underlie the auditor's responsibilities and conduct when undertaking an audit.

Reasons for adopting ethical standards

In view of the background to the publication of the new standards in 2004 (subsequently revised in 2008) by the APB – the low level of public of confidence in the audit profession resulting from the accounting scandals – there may very well have been a need to do something to reinstate the reputation of the accounting and auditing profession as a valued and trustworthy service. The accounting scandals identified gaps and flaws in the system and therefore the review and development of new standards and codes of professional ethics were deemed necessary in order to enhance the credibility of auditors.

Ethical standards are important for the following reasons:

- They are essential in protecting an auditor's reputation – without a good reputation the whole industry will fail; confidence in the auditor's ability to undertake an audit is imperative to the client, customer, stakeholder and society in general.
- Auditors must be completely trustworthy, truthful, honest and fair, which again reflects expectations from the profession.
- Auditors must resist any pressure to misrepresent information – this is part and parcel of being objective and able to act without fear of conflict of interest or undue pressure from parties with an interest towards their own benefit.
- An audit provides the basis for reliance to the public, which ensures that confidence is relayed in terms of the work undertaken.
- Auditors must observe the law at all times, which again ensures that the audit work is within the law and is what is normally expected of the auditor.

The APB's five ethical standards became effective for audits of financial statements for periods commencing on or after 15 December 2004. From the APB's perspective there were three main reasons for the introduction of the standards:

- maintaining auditor independence;
- enhancing public confidence in the value of audit;
- reinstating confidence in the accounting profession.

The main objective, therefore, of the APB's ethical standards for auditors is to ensure that they are independent of the companies they audit by adhering to a set of principles and a number of detailed rules.

The APB's five standards address the key issues that affect auditors in terms of an ethical approach to their work. The standards look at the areas of integrity, objectivity and independence, business and personal relationships. They also consider the aspect of any long-term associations with the audit client, fees, remuneration, gifts and hospitality; and also the contentious issue of undertaking non-audit services. The standards establish basic principles and essential procedures with which auditors are required to comply during the audit of financial statements. These standards replaced the existing guidance for auditors, issued by the auditors' professional bodies.

The five ethical standards are as follows:

- APB Ethical Standard 1 – Integrity, objectivity and independence;
- APB Ethical Standard 2 – Financial, business, employment and personal relationships;
- APB Ethical Standard 3 – Long association with the audit engagement;
- APB Ethical Standard 4 – Fees, remuneration and evaluation policies, litigation, gifts and hospitality;
- APB Ethical Standard 5 – Non-audit services provided to audit clients.

The Companies Act 2004 required the RSBs to adopt these ethical standards from 6 April 2005. Non-compliance was not an option, as ultimately the RSB status would be withdrawn by the Financial Reporting Council.

At the time that these standards were published, the APB Chairman, Richard Fleck, said:

> These standards represent a comprehensive revision of the ethical guidance that currently governs the auditing profession, and are designed to enhance public confidence in the quality of the audit process. In my view, they are rigorous, clear and therefore likely to be consistently applied and effective in practice.

A brief outline of the content of the ethical standards is given in Exhibit 4.1.

Exhibit 4.1 Brief outline of the content of the APB's ethical standards

- No over-familiarity with clients
- Limitations on loans of staff to clients
- No client to constitute more than 10% of practice income
- Declarations to be made of financial interests and family members' relationships with clients
- Audit partner rotation normally after 10 years, or 5 years for a listed company
- Sufficient staff on audit to comply with auditing and ethical standards, irrespective of fees
- A partner nominated as being responsible for the firm's ethics
- Gifts from a client are banned unless insignificant
- Hospitality from a client is banned unless reasonable
- Non-audit services banned if incompatible with the role of the auditor
- Where an auditor also conducts internal audit, there is to be no overlap of personnel and it is banned in some circumstances
- Ban on auditors providing valuation, actuarial valuation, litigation support and legal services in most circumstances

APB Ethical Standard 1 – Integrity, objectivity and independence

Ethical Standard 1 (ES1) includes standards on integrity, objectivity and independence, where auditors have a responsibility to be straightforward and honest in performing their professional work. One of the key requirements of this new ethical standard is that firms are now required to appoint an ethics partner with 'responsibility for the adequacy of the firm's policies and procedures relating to integrity, objectivity and independence; its compliance with APB ethical standards; and the effectiveness of their communication to partners and staff within the firm.'

Integrity

This refers to the professional way in which auditors should be honest, reliable and truthful when carrying out their audit. The APB states that auditors should aim not only for honesty 'but a broad range of qualities such as fairness, candour, courage, intellectual honesty and confidentiality'. Confidentiality is a major factor that is mentioned several times in the standards. It is important that the auditor does not give out any information about the company that is being audited, because the auditor could provide competitors with vital information, or give other stakeholders information that should be only known by the company. If directors and management cannot depend on the auditors to be confidential, they may be tempted to withhold information from them for fear of it being leaked to third parties. Directors and management also expect auditors to be intellectually honest and fair. This implies that the standard has been set to meet these expectations of directors and management as well as those of the stakeholders.

Confidentiality

Auditors should not disclose or use to their advantage client information. Insider dealings are illegal, while giving sensitive information to competing clients does nothing for the integrity of the auditor or the confidence that others will have in the auditor and the profession.

However, confidentiality must be broken if:

- the courts order it;
- the client is suspected of terrorism;
- the client is suspected of drug-trafficking or money-laundering;
- under certain circumstances the client is not a fit and proper person;
- it is in the 'public interest' – sometimes referred to as 'whistle-blowing'.

In such circumstances there is a requirement for the auditor to report suspicious transactions. Before disclosing any information, an auditor must consider whether all the relevant facts are known. The auditor may need to obtain professional legal advice.

Objectivity and independence

Many argue that 'independence' is the key link to maintaining the integrity and objectivity of auditors. Ethical Standard 1 provides the necessary guidelines for auditor independence, summarising that:

> Independence is freedom from situations and relationships which make it probable that a reasonable and informed third party would conclude that objectivity either is impaired or could be impaired. Independence is related to and underpins objectivity. However, whereas objectivity is a personal behavioural characteristic concerning the auditors' state of mind, independence relates to the circumstances surrounding the audit, including the financial, employment, business and personal relationships between the auditor and the audited entity.

The standard details how auditors should follow professional ethics in respect of objectivity and independence. These are two of the biggest factors on auditors carrying out their work in a professional manner. The APB describes objectivity as 'a state of mind that excludes bias, prejudice, and compromise and that gives fair and impartial consideration to all matters that are relevant to the task in hand, disregarding those that are not'. Basically, objectivity is all about the auditor being able to judge that what has been written in the financial statements gives a true and fair view based on the audit evidence. This involves auditors being confident enough to disagree with the judgment of the directors, and to qualify their audit opinion on the financial statements.

Professional independence is basically an attitude of mind characterised by integrity coupled with an objective approach to professional auditing work. The auditing profession involves a lot of judgment on the part of professional auditors and it is extremely important that this judgment and objectivity are not impaired in any way by a third party as this affects independence. There are many types of threat to objectivity and independence. These are listed in the ES1 and include:

- self-interest threats
- self-review threats
- management threats
- advocacy threat
- familiarity threat
- intimidation threat.

None of these threats stands alone and a situation can often cause more than one threat to arise. ES1 suggests that an assessment by the audit partner of the potential threats to objectivity and independence is essential when considering whether to accept or retain any audit work. This implies that threats to independence should be taken very seriously when deciding to carry out an audit and also whilst undertaking an audit. These threats are just as applicable to the aspects considered within the other four ethical standards.

Auditors have to maintain two types of independence to comply with the ethical standards set by the APB:

- legal independence
- ethical independence.

Ethical independence requires that auditors behave with integrity in all professional relationships. They must strive for objectivity in all professional judgments and should not accept or undertake work that they do not feel competent to complete. Auditors must carry out their professional work with due skill, care, diligence and appropriate consideration for both technical and professional standards.

Ensuring objectivity

In order to protect their objectivity, most firms have review procedures in place to check that each new or continued engagement may be properly accepted.

Client screening is performed on three levels: legal, ethical and practical. Undertaking the audit of client knowing that there are illegal activities taking place is clearly something to avoid. Screening on ethical grounds requires the auditor to review the ethical standards in terms of any issues affecting objectivity, conflicts of interest or threats to independence. On a practical level, client screening requires the auditor to establish whether there are sufficient resources with the appropriate skills and expertise to undertake the audit.

Other safeguards include rotation of audit partners and managers, registers for declarations of interest, use of ethics committees, documentation of audit procedures to maintain objectivity, and auditors making judgments on the evidence available, not on the opinions or pressures from others.

These other safeguards take into account the length of the audit relationship with the client – long associations may need to be reviewed. Recognising that there may be potential conflicts of interest and a declaration to that effect may help to maintain independence in fact as well as independence in appearance.

Reasons to question auditor's independence

There are occasions when the auditor's independence may be brought into question. For example, independence can be compromised if the auditor is financially dependent on the client for a substantial amount of its income. If there is huge competition within the external audit market, the quality of audit may become dependent on the amount of fee charged.

There is also considerable debate about the impact of non-audit consultancy work on audit independence. Specifically, if the audit firm provides non-audit services, does it impinge on the audit opinion given where the non-audit fee is substantial? Independence can also be compromised if there is a degree of laxity in the regulatory framework.

The simple answer for an auditor to preserve independence is to withdraw from any engagement where there is the slightest threat to it. However, in some cases, withdrawing from an audit is not as easy as it sounds. Professional ethics are not hard and fast rules; they are given only as guidance. Therefore it is up to the auditor to judge whether any threats are likely to influence their objectivity.

APB Ethical Standard 2 – Financial, business, employment and personal relationships

Ethical Standard 2 (ES2) explains the importance of ethics with regard to the different types of relationship auditors may be faced with during their working life. These include financial, business, employment and personal relationships. A financial relationship includes the possibility of the auditor having some kind of financial interest in the audit client or its affiliates, either directly or indirectly. The ethical standard states that where a financial interest is held, the 'entire financial interest is disposed of, and a sufficient amount of indirect financial interest is disposed of so that the remaining interest is no longer material, or that person does not retain a position in which they exert such influence on the audit engagement'.

Business relationships are very similar to financial relationships in that they involve any direct or indirect interest in the company, but in this case the interest is commercial. ES2 states that this 'may create self-interest, advocacy or intimidation threats to the auditor's objectivity and a perceived loss of independence'. ES2 also states that basically the only business relationship that should occur between an audit firm and an audited entity or its affiliates is where it involves the purchase of goods and services from the audit firm or the audited entity in the ordinary course of business and on an arm's length basis and the value involved is not material to either party.

The important phrase to note is the 'ordinary course of business'. Where a business relationship exists outside of the ordinary course of business, this relationship should be terminated in order for the audit to be undertaken. There is a very important need for both these standards to be in place, as any financial or commercial interest that an auditor or audit firm may hold in the audit client will affect objectivity and independence. This is because the audit firm or auditor would have an interest in the company's financial statements and/or the running of the business, and the result of the work they carry out could affect the interest that they have in the company.

Employment relationships have to do with what the ES2 refers to as 'dual employment'. This is where a person might be employed by both the audit firm and the potential audit client. Dual employment results in an employment interest and the audit cannot be carried out. As well as permanent dual employment, there are also issues concerning an audit firm 'loaning' a partner or employee to work for the audit client. This would still be considered to be dual employment unless the company and the audit firm follow the ethical standard where there is an 'agreement that the individual concerned will not hold a management position, and [the audit firm] acknowledges its responsibilities for directing and supervising the work to be performed'. The problem with an audit firm loaning an employee to an audit client is that this can result in threats to objectivity and independence, which is the case with any employment relationship.

Ethical Standard 2 also points out that there is a self-interest threat associated with a partner in the audit firm or member of the engagement team for a particular audit client leaving the firm and taking up employment with that audit client. Where this is the case, a number of different factors need to be considered to evaluate the significance of the self-interest, familiarity and intimidation threats. These include the position held in each company and the length of time between working in each company. The inclusion of these factors in the standard is to give an audit firm a sound basis to decide on whether to engage in an audit based on employment relationships.

The last relationship in ES2 concerns family and personal connections. This can be linked to the other types of relationship in that a close family member may affect the audit firm's or affiliate's interest financially or commercially, or may be employed by the audit client thus creating employment relationship issues, all of which are threats to independence.

All relationships that exist must be reported to the engagement partner. The relationship issues can then be evaluated to come to a conclusion as to whether the audit should be carried out by the audit firm or whether they will have to decline or terminate the contract.

APB Ethical Standard 3 – Long association with the audit engagement

This standard is concerned with long associations with the audit engagement, and states that 'the audit firm should establish policies and procedures to monitor the length of time that audit engagement partners, key audit partners and staff in senior positions serve as members of the audit engagement team for each audit'. The need for ES3 is that if the key audit staff, senior audit staff and engagement partners have had a long association with the audit firm then this can create a threat to the auditor's objectivity and independence. Again, factors such as self-interest and familiarity need to be considered. These factors focus on the role of the person and the amount of time that they have been associated with the audit engagement.

Ethical Standard 3 suggests the introduction of safeguards to limit such threats, including the rotation of senior members of the team after a predetermined number of years; a review by an additional partner; and the application of independent internal quality reviews to the audit assignment. The standard recommends that a continuous 10-year period in a role should be considered as a long association, particularly for an audit engagement partner, and that the suggestions above should be considered before the end of this period is reached. This is because independence and objectivity could be impaired and it is suggested that the audit client should be made aware of the long association. ES3 also sets out clear guidelines on the rotation of audit partners for the audit of listed companies, which may be summarised as: engagement or independent partners should only have continuous service of 5 years; key audit partners should serve no more than 7 years continuously; and senior audit team members should be involved no more than 7 years continuously. This different guideline for listed companies is because of increased self-interest and familiarity threats to the auditors' objectivity.

APB Ethical Standard 4 – Fees, remuneration and evaluation policies, litigation, gifts and hospitality

This standard explains the importance of ethics concerning fees, remuneration and evaluation policies, litigation, gifts and hospitality. Again, many of these factors can affect independence and the guidelines are in place to avoid jeopardising it. The primary issue considered is that of the audit fee. In a business market where there is competition between audit firms, there is a danger that if thresholds and restrictions are placed on fees, they may be driven down to below the level at which a proper audit can be done. The standard suggests that the audit engagement partner should assign partners and staff with sufficient time and skill to perform the audit in accordance with all applicable standards, irrespective of the fee. It thus underlines the need for a quality audit to be performed whether the fee is large or small; the quality of the audit should not be linked to the fee charged. ES4 also states that 'an audit should not be taken on a contingent fee basis'; in other words, the fee of the audit should not be dependent on its outcome.

In addition to looking at the fees agreed in an audit about to be undertaken, it is also important to look at fees that may still be outstanding from previous audits. An audit firm will have to consider whether it is a viable option to undertake the audit of a client for the next period if that client has not yet paid the bill for the previous one. The standard states there is a need for the engagement partner and ethics partner to discuss this matter and decide 'whether the audit firm can continue or whether it is necessary to resign'. There is a need for them to consider whether a self-interest threat to their independence and objectivity would arise if they were to continue to act as auditors for a client who is also one of their creditors. This is because they may feel an unqualified audit report will enhance their chances of receiving payment.

A guideline for the percentage of total value of fees from one client is suggested by the standard. The standard recommends not accepting an appointment where fees are regularly in excess of 15%, or 10% for listed clients. For listed company fees regularly in excess of 5%, a disclosure of this expectation to the ethics partner is required. Again there is a need for the standard, as it implements appropriate safeguards. A standard that provides both auditing firms and audit clients with clear guidelines about fees ensures that there can be little argument about what is expected from both parties.

The second part of ES4 looks at remuneration and evaluation policies, litigation, gifts and hospitality issues. In relation to remuneration and evaluation policies, the standard states that it is important that cross-selling of non-audit services is not part of the audit team's objectives, performance evaluation or remuneration. The standard also points out that the audit engagement partner should look at threatened or actual litigation that could arise, or has arisen, between the audit firm and the client. If this is the case, the partner should strongly consider not continuing or not accepting the audit as there would be self-interest, advocacy and intimidation threats associated with such an engagement. Finally, a quite obvious ethical standard that needs to be complied with for reasons of independence is that auditors and their immediate families should not accept gifts or hospitality from audit clients unless insignificant or reasonable in terms of frequency, nature and cost. Unfortunately, there are no safeguards which can reduce the threat to objectivity and independence in this case. It can also be difficult to determine what counts as too big a gift or too much hospitality and this is often up to the auditor and the audit firm to judge.

APB Ethical Standard 5 – Non-audit services provided to audit clients

This standard addresses 10 specific areas of non-audit services, including internal audit, legal, valuation, recruitment and remuneration, and general accounting services. These apply to audits of financial statements in both the private and public sectors. There is a need to identify the threats and safeguards in relation to non-audit services. Ethical matters relating to non-audit services that are to be provided should be understood by the audit engagement partner and the audit should only be undertaken if a reasonable and informed third party considered it to be consistent with audit objectives.

A further threat has to do with a perceived loss of independence where the fees for non-audit services are greater than the fees for normal audit services. The standard provides auditing professionals with guidance on identifying the different kinds of threats that could arise if non-audit work is carried out and offers advice on what action needs to be taken.

Audit firms as advisory companies

An ethical issue arises when an audit firm acts as a consultant, providing business services based on its wide knowledge and experience gained from working with companies. Consulting services can generate a considerable amount of an auditing firm's turnover. The big four firms are the ones most likely to benefit from and be affected by this kind of advisory role. The wide experience they possess puts them in a favourable position to offer non-audit services. Where non-audit service fees can outweigh the income generated from audit opinion fees, many believe this can create a situation that compromises auditor independence.

Differences between *independence in fact* and *independence in appearance*

There are instances where actions or involvement by the auditor may not affect independence in fact but are likely to affect independence in appearance. Auditors must not only maintain an independent attitude in fulfilling their responsibilities, but the users of financial statements must have confidence in that independence. These two objectives are frequently identified as 'independence in fact' and 'independence in appearance'. Independence in fact exists when the auditor is able to maintain an unbiased attitude throughout the audit, thereby being objective and impartial, whereas independence in appearance is the result of others' interpretation of this independence. For example, ownership of a small number or very low percentage of the total shares of an audit client does not, in fact, jeopardise an auditor's independence, but any ownership of shares will give the impression that the auditor is not independent.

Any financial involvement with a client can have an impact on independence and may cause interested parties to believe that independence has been impaired. Financial involvement with a client comes in different guises and can take the following forms:

- direct financial interest in a client where there is a direct payment in return for an investment received or given;
- indirect material financial interest as a consequence of being an administrator of an estate or trust that has a financial interest in the client company;
- loans to or from the client or any director or major stockholder in the client company;
- financial interest due to a joint venture with a client or employee(s) of a client.
- financial interest in a non-client that has an investor or investee relationship with the client.

Proper conduct

There is no doubt that auditors must consistently uphold the reputation of the profession, and in so doing must refrain from participating in any activity that could diminish public confidence or discredit themselves or the profession. When an auditor encounters an issue that might have an impact on their objectivity, integrity and independence, there is a duty to inform the appropriate authority or person who has the ability to prevent the misdeed or misconduct.

There is an expectation that the auditor will act in a manner that maintains the reputation of the profession. Arthur Andersen's actions in the Enron case not only affected that firm but had an impact on the profession as a whole, by creating the danger that all audit firms would be tarred with the same brush. Auditors must act responsibly towards their clients, shareholders, third parties, other members of the auditing profession and stakeholders, including the general public.

Ethical Standard: Provisions Available for Small Entities 2005, revised 2008

This standard was re-issued in April 2005 and again in 2008 following intense criticism of the standards released in December 2004 and their effects on small businesses. Critics argued that requiring an owner-managed business to appoint one firm to prepare its accounts and deal with the tax and a second firm to audit the accounts would simply lead to duplication of costs and a poorer service for the client. Although the standard has been widely criticised, it tries to provide small businesses with provisions to help them follow the professional ethical guidelines set out in the standards.

The revised standards recognise that some of the requirements in Ethical Standards 1 to 5 are difficult for small entities to apply. This means that while the standards are appropriate in establishing the integrity, objectivity and independence of auditors, there is an acceptance that certain dispensations are appropriate to ensure the cost-effectiveness of an audit of small entities' financial statements.

This has resulted in alternative provisions that apply in terms of threats arising from economic dependence and where tax or accounting services are provided. This allows the option of taking advantage of exemptions from certain of the requirements of Ethical Standards 1 to 5 for a small entity audit engagement. When the audit takes advantage of the exemptions, it must: take the steps described in the standard; and disclose in the audit report the fact that the firm has applied small entity audit exemptions.

Revised Ethical Standards 2008

Following a review, the APB published revised ethical standards for auditors in 2008. The board did not make any major changes, only amendments which were required to comply with UK and Irish legislation that implemented the EU statutory Audit Directive. This directive, 2006/43/EEC, also referred to as the Eighth Company Law Directive, created an auditing standard framework for the European Economic Area (EEA) for regulation and supervision of all aspects of the activities of auditors and audit firms, aimed at ensuring that the wider aspects of the international capital markets are taken into account. Two key aspects under this directive that are highly topical are the treatment of non-EEA audit firms and the possible introduction of the audit firm's liability for statutory audits.

Other revisons include the fact that ethical standards continue to adhere to the principles of international ethical standards and that the amendments add clarity to the existing standards and assist their implementation in practice.

Internal audit ethics

It is not easy for auditors to remain independent vis-à-vis their company, especially when that company pays their wages. Internal auditors who are members of the Institute of Internal Auditors UK and Ireland are governed by a separate code of ethics from those of external auditors.

The Code of Ethics is an authoritative guidance for the internal audit profession that comes from the Global Institute of Internal Auditors. The code is developed and updated by the global Ethics Committee and is part of the International Professional Practices Framework. The Code of Ethics is a statement of principles and expectations governing behaviour of individuals and organisations in the conduct of internal auditing. It provides a description of minimum requirements for conduct and describes behavioural expectations rather than specific activities. These rules of conduct describe norms of behaviour that are expected of internal auditors. These rules act as a guide to the interpretation and application of the principles to practice and are intended to guide the ethical conduct of internal auditors.

The IIA (UK and Ireland) defines internal audit as an:

> . . . independent, objective assurance and consulting activity designed to add value and improve an organisation's operations. It helps an organisation accomplish its

objectives by bringing a systematic, disciplined approach to evaluate and improve the effectiveness of risk management, control, and governance processes.

The practical guidelines are designed for those who provide the internal audit service irrespective of whether they are members of the IIA (UK & Ireland).

The IIA's Code of Ethics outlines four key principles:

- *Integrity.* The integrity of internal auditors establishes trust and provides the basis for reliance on their judgment. Internal auditors should perform their work honestly, observing the law, while contributing to the legitimate and ethical objectives of the organisation.
- *Objectivity.* Internal auditors should exhibit the highest level of professional objectivity in gathering, evaluating and communicating information. Internal auditors make a balanced assessment of all relevant circumstances and are not unduly influenced by their own interests or by others. Internal auditors avoid activities and relationships that might be seen to undermine their objectivity .
- *Confidentiality.* Internal auditors respect the value and ownership of information they receive and do not disclose information without appropriate authority, unless there is a legal or professional obligation to do so. Internal auditors should use information prudently and not for their personal benefit.
- *Competency.* Internal auditors apply the knowledge, skills and experience needed for their role. They perform their work in accordance with the International Standards and engage in continuing professional development.

Although these principles are also applicable to the external auditor, the external auditor must be seen to be adhering to the key external principle, which is independence. This is of paramount importance to the public and all users of financial statements, as their opinion must be seen to be unbiased.

Standards and quality of audit

The quality of an audit could be defined as the probability that a given auditor will both discover a breach in the client's accounting system, and then report the breach. There are numerous characteristics that companies use to evaluate the quality of the audits they receive:

- integrity of the audit firm
- technical competence of the firm
- the quality of the working relationship with the audit partner
- good reputation
- technical competence of the audit partner.

Large audit firms are more likely to lower their audit quality opportunistically in order to keep existing clients than are smaller firms. This is because the larger audit firm is likely to have many clients, and if they lose one, it will not have a significant effect on their overall fee income for the year. The opposite is true for smaller audit firms. However, if a 'breach' is found in the accounts of the larger audit firm's client then the larger firm stands to lose more than the smaller audit firm in terms of reputation and technical competence.

International Federation of Accountants (IFAC) ethics guidelines

The IFAC requires an accountant to comply with fundamental principles, that include the role of the auditor.

- *Integrity.* 'Integrity' means that a professional accountant should be straightforward and honest when undertaking professional services. A 'professional service' is any service that necessitates accountancy or related skills performed by a professional accountant. This includes accounting, auditing, taxation, management consulting and financial management services.
- *Objectivity.* 'Objectivity' is a combination of impartiality, intellectual honesty and a freedom from conflicts of interest. A professional accountant is required to be fair and should not allow prejudice or bias, or the undue influence of others to override objectivity.
- *Professional competence and due care.* When a professional accountant agrees to provide professional services, the ethics guideline requires that he or she is competent to undertake the services. In addition, knowledge, skill and experience will be applied with reasonable care and diligence. The professional accountant is required to perform all services with due care, competence and diligence. He or she has a continuing duty to maintain professional knowledge and skill at a level required to ensure that a client or employer receives service based on up-to-date developments in practice, legislation and techniques. This is known as a requirement to maintain 'continued professional development' as a member of the accountancy and auditing profession.
- *Confidentiality.* Professional accountants should respect the confidentiality of information obtained when performing professional services. The professional accountant should not use or disclose any of this information without proper and specific authority of the parties concerned.
- *Professional behaviour.* The guidelines require the professional accountant to act in a manner consistent with the good reputation of the profession. The accountant is required to refrain from any conduct which might bring discredit to the profession when considering responsibilities to clients, third parties, other members of the accountancy profession, staff, employers and the general public.
- *Technical standards.* It is expected that professional services be carried out in accordance with the relevant technical and professional standards. These services should conform to the technical and professional standards as outlined by the IFAC through International Standards on Auditing; the International Accounting Standards Committee; a members' professional body or other regulatory body; and relevant legislation.

European Union

To provide each EU member state with a common understanding of this independence requirement, the European Union Committee on Auditing issued a Recommendation entitled Statutory Auditors' Independence in the EU: A Set of Fundamental Principles. The principles-based approach was considered 'preferable to one based on detailed rules because it creates a robust structure within which statutory auditors have to justify their actions.'

The EU framework, which parallels the threat and safeguard approach of IFAC, is based on the requirement that auditors must be independent of their audit clients both in mind and appearance. An auditor should not audit a client if there are any financial, business, employment or other relationships between them that a reasonable and informed third party would conclude compromised independence.

United States

American-based firms and firms that audit US publicly traded firms must adhere to the regulations of the Sarbanes-Oxley Act, Title II, Auditor Independence, as interpreted by the Public Company Accounting Oversight Board (PCAOB).

Under PCAOB rules, all non-audit services to clients, which are not specifically prohibited, must be pre-approved by the Audit Committee and disclosed to the shareholders. Audit partners must be rotated every 5 years. Clients cannot hire as an officer any member of the audit team within 1 year after their last audit. Determination of the independence of the auditors who audit non-publicly traded firms is left up to the regulatory authorities of the 50 states of the US.

Summary

Professional ethics are reflected in the professional code, which contains principles of ethics. There is a need for an ethical code because of the demand for auditors, and also because auditors need the guidelines to protect their reputation with respect to integrity, independence and objectivity.

Because of the growing proportion or revenues from non-audit services offered by audit companies, the need to adhere to the code of professional ethics has acquired a new dimension in order to stay competitive, on the one hand, and keep the public's trust in the independence of the audit firms, on the other. The standards are important in the auditing profession as they provide clear guidelines and, in many places, safeguards to assist audit engagement partners, audit firms and auditors to make the correct decisions in a professional and ethical manner.

? PRACTICE QUESTION

Cox and Sherlock are an established firm of accountants who carry out audit duties. They have a portfolio of over 100 clients and the largest client provides 8% of their fee income. It is company policy when issuing the audit management letter to recommend that any system weaknesses be improved by either their consultancy or IT division carrying out the work. They say that, as the auditors know the problems, a degree of liaison can lead to a cost-effective solution.

Discuss the ethical issues involved in this situation.

Corporate governance

Objectives

After studying this chapter you should be able to:

- appreciate the development of the corporate governance codes of best practice;

- discuss the factors that influence the role of auditors in corporate governance;

- describe the role and responsibilities of the Audit Committee in corporate governance;

- explain the differences between mandatory and voluntary codes of corporate governance;

- critically assess the role of executive and non-executive directors within corporate governance;

- identify the benefits of a working relationship between the audit function and the Audit Committee as a cornerstone of corporate governance;

- compare and contrast several theoretical frameworks that are applied to the corporate governance discipline.

Introduction

Corporate governance is about the separation of ownership and control. The directors may run the company but the shareholders own it. The separation of ownership and management creates a situation where the shareholders have to trust the judgment of those running the company; corporate governance therefore has to function within a framework of accountability, openness and integrity due to the expectations of those releasing funds into the organisation. The management have been trusted to run the company in the interest of the shareholders and other stakeholders. If information was freely available to all the shareholders, and even the stakeholders, in the same format at the same time, corporate governance would not be an issue. This separation between those who direct and manage the organisation and the people who own it is referred to as the agency theory. There is a need for corporate governance codes of practice to indicate whether directors are maximising shareholder returns, and keeping business risk at a reasonable level, to ensure that they are not becoming too dominant, and also that they are receiving reasonable remuneration for the work they undertake in directing the organisations they govern.

Corporate governance is also about best practice and how a company is controlled and administered. This includes the relationship between various stakeholders, namely the board of directors, the shareholders, management, employees, customers, suppliers and regulators. An important theme of corporate governance deals with issues of accountability and fiduciary duties, essentially advocating the implementation of guidelines and mechanisms to ensure good behaviour that protects shareholders and, in line with today's corporate social responsibility requirement, protects society and the environment as well.

A best-practice approach encompasses other stakeholders not merely the shareholders and the directors. According to the FRC Combined Code (2008):

> Good corporate governance should contribute to better company performance by helping a board discharge its duties in the best interests of shareholders; if it is ignored, the consequence may well be vulnerability or poor performance. Good governance should facilitate efficient, effective and entrepreneurial management that can deliver shareholder value over the longer term.

The high number and high value of corporate scandals during the first years of the 21st century have had a dramatic affect on corporate governance. Not only have there been serious frauds, such as at Enron and WorldCom, but the credit crunch in the US mortgage market of 2007 and the resulting fallout in the banking sector have also highlighted some serious governance failings. These events have had a profound worldwide impact on confidence in governance and repercussions on governance requirements. The main result has been an increase in compliance requirements, leading to higher costs in completing the relevant documentation and in the increased level of audit necessary to give the assurance expected.

Corporate governance codes

These deal with such matters as:

- the proper constitution of the board – including the presence of non-executive directors, and proper appointment mechanisms via an appointments committee;
- the proper arrangements for the remuneration of directors – including the existence of a remuneration committee;
- the proper mechanisms for shareholder relations – both for institutional investors and for private investors;
- the role of accountability and audit – covering financial reporting, internal control, risk management and the existence of an Audit Committee.

Source: www.accaglobal.com

Corporate governance developments

Corporate governance has undergone an evolutionary process in the UK, which came about as a response to various external events and increased demands for accountability from different sectors of society. As a consequence, various reports with their own recommendations for codes of best practice have been issued in the UK since 1992, resulting in the current Financial Reporting Council's (FRC) *Combined Code on Corporate Governance* 2003, amended in 2006 and 2008 and subject to review in 2009.

The emphasis in the UK is on a principles-based or voluntary approach to a corporate governance code as opposed to a mandetory one, such that 'the UK's system of business regulation, which is principles based rather than rules based, reduces the cost to global businesses of introducing procedures to comply with detailed regulations, many of which unnecessarily constrain business practice and innovation' (FRC 2006).

In the late 1980s a number of high-profile collapses of prominent UK companies occurred in rapid succession, causing ripples of discontent throughout the auditing and accounting profession, not to mention the business environment. Among the companies to fail were Maxwell Communications Corporation, the Bank of Credit and Commerce International (BCCI), Ferranti International plc, PollyPeck International plc and Barings Bank. These failures were mainly attributed to the presence of weak governance systems, a poor system of oversight of the directors of the board, and the concentration of too much control in the hands of a small number of top executives.

A summary of the governance issues that led to these failures is as follows:

- looseness in accounting standards that led to misinterpretation either on purpose or unintentionally and rendered a lack of consistency in accounting information;
- the absence of a clear framework for ensuring that directors kept under review the internal control mechanisms and risk management within their business;
- competitive pressures on companies which made it difficult for auditors to stand up to boards of directors when there were issues of concern;

- problems within the business environment and with certain private sector companies, with mismanagement, failures and scandals hitting the headlines on a regular basis, leading to a fall in confidence in the auditing profession;
- denationalisation of the utilities in the UK, which led to controversy over levels of pay and bonuses paid to directors.

To summarise, there were four key issues:

- creative accounting
- business failures and scandals
- directors' pay
- short-termism.

Source: www.acca.org.uk

The financial scandals that occurred during the latter part of the 20th century led to the publication of a number of reports as outcomes of various reviews. These reviews and subsequent reports became the recognised names of corporate governance reform in the UK at this time, namely Cadbury, Greenbury, Hampel and Turnbull. These reports attempted to improve the accountability of powerful directors, impacted on the role of the auditor, and were seen as a response from regulators to the public's perception of the problems with corporate governance.

During the late 1980s and early 1990s, therefore, a number of initiatives began to emerge, the objective of which was to provide support, guidance and protection for those within the business environment. The first of these initiatives was the review instigated in May 1991 by the Financial Reporting Council, the London Stock Exchange and the accountancy profession, when a committee was set up to investigate and report on the financial aspects of corporate governance. The Committee on the Financial Aspects of Corporate Governance was chaired by Sir Adrian Cadbury and the resulting Cadbury Report became the forerunner of a series of reports designed to improve corporate governance within UK companies.

Corporate governance in the UK focuses on the relationship between the company and the shareholders, not between the company and the regulator. There is a strong push towards encouraging good communication and dialogue between the board and shareholders on corporate governance issues. Shareholders have voting rights which bring with them rights to information (as set out in company law and also in the London Stock Exchange Listing Rules), which in turn require the board to be accountable to the shareholders.

A timeline showing the developments in corporate governance between 1992 and 2006 can be seen in Table 5.1.

London Stock Exchange Listing Rules

Compliance with UK corporate governance requirements is a requirement of Listing Rules on the London Stock Exchange (LSE). If anything should happen to the ownership of the LSE then there is the possibility that it could lead to a change in governance requirements imposed by the LSE. Assurances may be given on takeover, but if the owners of the LSE operate in a different environment it may prove to be problematic to retain the existing UK governance frameworks.

Table 5.1 **Corporate governance timeline**

When	What	Who	Why	Key requirements
1992	*The Financial Aspects of Corporate Governance* (Cadbury Report)	Sir Adrian Cadbury, Cadbury Schweppes	Response to UK corporate failures (BCCI, Maxwell)	▪ Implementation of effective internal financial controls and reporting for FTSE listed companies ▪ Establishment of an Audit Committee of non-executive directors
1995	Study Group on Directors' Remuneration (Greenbury Report)	Richard Greenbury, Marks & Spencer	Concern over high salaries in previously nationalised industries, e.g. utilities	▪ Requirements for improved reporting of directors' remuneration in published accounts ▪ Establishment of Remuneration Committee
1998	The Committee on Corporate Governance (Hampel Report)	Sir Ronald Hampel, ICI plc	Review the impact of the Cadbury Code	▪ Separation of the role of chairman and chief executive ▪ Requirement for a senior non-executive director ▪ Requirement for directors to review the effectiveness of all internal controls, not just financial ▪ Review the need for internal audit
	Combined Code	Financial Reporting Council (FRC)	Code to combine requirements of Cadbury, Greenbury and Hampel	▪ All companies incorporated in the UK and listed on the LSE are required under the Listing Rules to report on how they have applied the Combined Code in their annual report and accounts
1999	*Internal Controls: Guidance for Directors on the Combined Code* (Turnbull Guidance)	Nigel Turnbull, Rank plc	ICAEW provision of advice on implementing the Combined Code	▪ Adoption of a risk-based approach to establishing a system of internal control and reviewing its effectiveness ▪ Annual review of the effectiveness of system of internal control ▪ Use of internal audit functions
2003	*Review of the Role and Effectiveness of Non-executive Directors* (Higgs Report)	Derek Higgs, Partnerships UK plc	UK response to US corporate failures. Independent review of the role and effectiveness of non-executive directors	▪ Guidance on the composition, performance evaluation and role of the board, specifically the chairman and non-executive directors ▪ Guidance on the operation of Remuneration and Nomination committees

	Audit Committees – Combined Code Guidance (Smith Report)	Sir Robert Smith, The Weir Group PLC	UK response to US corporate failures. Independent review to clarify the role and responsibilities of Audit Committees and to develop the existing Combined Code guidance	▪ Audit Committee to include at least three members, all independent non-executive directors, with at least one member to have significant, recent and relevant financial experience
				▪ Committee to monitor and review:
				  ▪ the integrity of the financial statements of the company
				  ▪ the company's internal financial control system and, unless expressly addressed by a separate risk committee or by the board itself, risk management systems
				  ▪ the effectiveness of the company's internal audit function and to make recommendations to the board in relation to the external auditor's appointment

(continues)

61

Table 5.1 *Continued*

When	What	Who	Why	Key requirements
				◼ the external auditor's independence, objectivity and effectiveness and to develop and implement policy on the engagement of the external auditor to supply non-audit services
	Revised Combined Code	FRC	Incorporation of principles from Higgs and Smith reviews	◼ See above – company disclosures now must cover all main and supporting principles
2005	Flint Review	Douglas Flint, HSBC	Review of Turnbull guidance	◼ Re-emphasis that establishing an effective system of internal control is not a one-off exercise ◼ Endorsed flexible principles-based approach of earlier reviews, rather than changes along the mandatory Sarbanes-Oxley report
2006	Update of 2003 Combined Code	FRC	Modifications to original 2003 Combined Code	◼ Company chairs allowed to sit on Remuneration Committee if deemed independent ◼ Shareholders voting by proxy have option to withhold vote on resolutions ◼ Companies to publish details of proxies lodged on resolutions where votes are based on a show of hands

Source: Adapted from a table by David Geatrell.

Cadbury Report (1992)

Sir Adrian Cadbury's report, *The Financial Aspects of Corporate Governance* (1992), focused on the potential abuse of power and the need for openness, integrity and accountability in the decision-making process of an organisation. The Cadbury Report was published in December 1992 and 'aimed to improve information to shareholders, reinforce self-regulation and strengthen auditor independence'. It advocated that

> . . . boards of listed companies should publish a report on the effectiveness of their systems of internal control and that auditors should contribute to the reporting process; the directors' service contracts should not exceed three years without approval by the shareholders; and each listed company should establish an audit committee of at least three non-executive directors.

The key aspects of the Cadbury Code of Best Practice are outlined in Exhibit 5.1.

Audit interest in the Cadbury Report

The audit interest in the Cadbury Report was mainly due to the focus placed on controls and reporting. Directors were now expected to report on the effectiveness

Exhibit 5.1 **Key recommendations of the Cadbury Code of Best Practice**

- Clear division of responsibilities and procedures to be adopted by the board in the way it controlled and directed the company
- There should be independent non-executives and appropriate remuneration of directors
- Terms of executives' contracts to be no more than 3 years
- Audit Committee should be formally constituted as a subcommittee of the main board to whom it should report on a regular basis. It should meet at least twice a year and include within its membership at least three non-executive board members, independent of the senior management
- Compliance with code to be stated in the annual report of all listed companies in the UK. (In June 1993, compliance with the code was made an obligation for all public listed companies by the London Stock Exchange – failure to do so required an explanation)
- Auditors were to review the director's statement of compliance with the code prior to its publication in the annual report

of internal control systems which are key to any audit activity. The key issues were as follows:

- The board has to ensure an objective and professional relationship with auditor.
- By requiring the directors to give a balanced and understandable assessment of the company's position, it clearly distinguishes between the role of the director and that of the auditor.
- Directors are required to explain their responsibilities.
- The directors are expected to report on the company's position as a going concern which clearly identifies the specific role of the director.
- Directors should establish an Audit Committee of at least three non-executive directors with clear terms of reference providing a mechanism for auditor appointment and liaison with the board.
- There should be transparent procedures for the appointment of new directors to the board.
- Re-election at least every 3 years with a formal transparent policy on the remuneration packages for directors were important in terms of the audit appointment and audit activity. Remuneration packages and executive bonuses were an issue in 1992 and still remain an issue today.

A major implication for auditors was the recommendation for the establishment of Audit Committees.

Greenbury Report (1995)

In 1995 a committee was set up to review the remuneration of directors. Headed by Sir Richard Greenbury, its remit was to examine directors' pay in response to public concern over perceived salary excesses. The committee and its resulting report stated that it 'aimed to provide an answer to the general concerns about the accountability and level of directors' pay; argued against statutory control and for strengthening accountability by the proper allocation of responsibility for determining directors' remuneration, the proper reporting to shareholders, and greater transparency in the process'. The Greenbury Report produced the Greenbury Code of Best Practice, which was divided into four sections:

- remuneration committee
- disclosure
- remuneration policy
- service contracts and compensation.

The report recommended that UK plcs should 'implement the code as set out to the fullest extent practicable; that they should make annual compliance statements; and that investor institutions should use their power to ensure that best practice is followed'.

The Greenbury Report, sometimes referred to as the Greenbury Code, set out to establish a framework for director remuneration, recommending:

- the creation of a remuneration committee to be composed of non-executive directors to review the remuneration of executive directors;
- the full disclosure of directors' pay packages, including pensions, by the remuneration committee via the annual report to the shareholders;
- shareholder approval to be sought for any long-term bonus schemes;
- compliance with the code to be stated in annual reports;
- privatised utilities to review directors' pay packages;
- avoidance of service contracts longer than 2 years, and for compensation cases to shorten the period of notice to less than 1 year;

These recommendations were included in the Stock Exchange Listing Rules from October 1995.

Hampel Report (1997)

Included within the Cadbury Report was a recommendation that a review of corporate governance codes should be undertaken by a successor body. This successor body in 1997 was the Committee on Corporate Governance, chaired by Sir Ronald Hampel and hence known as the Hampel Committee. The outcome of the committee's review, the Hampel Report, contained the findings of Cadbury and Greenbury, combined with its own recommendations which, with the co-operation of the London Stock Exchange, resulted in the production of The Combined Code: Principles of Good Governance and Code of Best Practice (1998).

The Hampel Report recommended that the auditors should report on internal control privately to the directors; the directors should maintain and review all (and not just financial) controls; and companies that do not already have an internal audit function should from time to time review their need for one. The report also introduced the Combined Code, which consolidated the recommendations of previous corporate governance reports.

This Combined Code consolidated all previous reviews into one report and it reaffirmed that internal control was a major issue for both the financial and operational health of an organisation. It also illustrated that corporate governance was an important issue for regulatory bodies. Indeed, the code became mandatory for all organisations coming under the London Stock Exchange Listing Rules and from December 1998, a statement of compliance was to be included in the annual report to shareholders.

The Combined Code contained principles and detailed provisions in two parts:

- principles of good governance
- code of best practice.

The report concluded that directors should assume responsibility for monitoring both financial and non-financial risks and controls. Briefly, the recommendations were as follows:

- board to supervise the work of senior executives;
- role of non-executive directors to be extended to encourage companies to think long-term, these directors to be paid in shares;
- institutional shareholders to be encouraged to vote, and small investors to be offered better opportunities to put forward proposals at company meetings;
- small companies given exemption from Cadbury;
- directors to state that they have conducted a review of the internal controls – a change of focus from effectiveness.

The Combined Code sets principles on the subjects of directors' roles and appointment, directors' remuneration, shareholders, and accountability and audit. In this final category, one of the principles deals with internal control, which is an area focused upon in the following report, the Turnbull Report.

Turnbull Report (1999) (Turnbull 1)

During 1999, the Institute of Chartered Accountants in England and Wales (ICAEW) set up a working party under the chairmanship of Nigel Turnbull, whose objective was to assess how company directors could meet the new requirements placed upon them when monitoring and reporting on internal controls as outlined in the Combined Code in the Hampel Report.

The Turnbull Report provided guidance to assist companies in implementing the requirements of the Combined Code relating to internal control. It recommended that where companies do not have an internal audit function, the board should consider the need for carrying out an internal audit annually and also recommended that boards of directors confirm the existence of procedures for evaluating and managing key risks.

This Turnbull review expanded on the internal control provisions of the Combined Code and focused on the importance of internal control and risk management review by the directors. The review was expected to cover all controls, including financial, operational and compliance controls and risk management. The Combined Code also required companies that did not have an internal audit function to consider the need for one from time to time.

The Turnbull Report stressed the requirement and expectation for directors to maintain and review the effectiveness of internal control. Corporate boards were required to ensure they had appropriate and sufficient procedures in place to

Exhibit 5.2 **Summary of the recommendations of the Turnbull Report**

- Evolutionary shift in focus to managing organisational risk, i.e. expanding the focus beyond the financial aspects of business
- Channels opened up to allow internal audit to report on weaknesses
- Creation of a flexible system that can respond to change
- Periodic review of all aspects of internal control systems
- Companies to disclose details of internal control reviews in their annual reports
- Boards to maintain sound systems of internal control in order to safeguard shareholder investments and company assets

obtain the assurance necessary for internal control confirmation, including its need for an internal audit function. A statement from boards on the presence and operation of internal control in the statutory annual report was made a requirement of compliance. If boards could not give the full disclosure, they were required to explain their reasons – this is where the term 'comply or explain' originated. The guidance recommended that internal control should be embedded within processes and that an organisation should be able to apply the guidance in a manner best suited to its circumstances and using a risk-based approach.

Turnbull, in recognising that the board had responsibility for the system of internal control, insisted it should be regularly assuring itself that appropriate processes were functioning effectively in order to monitor risks. This assurance was invariably being provided by the internal auditors, which in turn meant a change in their role as internal auditors. Hence, directors had to disclose in the annual report as a minimum that appropriate processes had been put in place and explain how they had reviewed the effectiveness of the processes. Conversely, a failure to report required an explanation as to why they as directors were not complying with the code. The review produced its findings under the report title *Internal Control: Guidance for Directors on the Combined Code* (1999), which also acknowledged that directors could delegate aspects of review work to committees, including the Audit Committee, and thus audit committees previously experienced in dealing with financial risk and controls were called upon to broaden their remit and adopt a more challenging stance, becoming the cornerstone of corporate governance in the process. The Turnbull Report (a brief summary of its recommendations is given in Exhibit 5.2) was taken on board by the London Stock Exchange, who in turn followed what had been a requirement after Hampel that listed companies should comply with the recommendations of the Turnbull Report from 2000 onwards.

Smith and Higgs reports (2003)

In the period between 1999 and 2003, various external events made a review of the existing corporate governance codes essential. In the UK, directors' pay was increasingly a focus of national anger, while corporate scandals around the world forced all regulatory regimes to consider the robustness and effectiveness of existing corporate governance requirements.

In January 2003 an FRC-appointed group, chaired by Sir Robert Smith, published a report called *Audit Committees – Combined Code Guidance*, which was aimed at defining and strengthening the role of Audit Committees following the recent US scandals such as Enron and WorldCom. Audit Committees now play a key role in effective corporate governance, and are considered a cornerstone of corporate governance. An Audit Committee has to have non-executive directors, and is responsible for liaising between the full board, internal audit and external audit.

The main recommendations of the Smith Report were as follows:

- The company chairman must not be an Audit Committee member.
- At least three members of the committee should be independent non-executive directors.
- At least one member of the committee should have significant, recent and relevant financial experience.
- Appointments to the committee should be for up to 3 years, extendable for up to two additional 3-year periods.
- The Audit Committee chairman and members must be given induction and continuing training which should cover, among other things, the role of internal and external auditing and risk management.

In addition the Smith Report recommended that Audit Committees should play a role in:

- monitoring the integrity of the financial statements of the company;
- reviewing any financial reporting judgments that appear significant;
- reviewing the company's internal financial control system;
- reviewing the risk management policies of the company unless there is a separate risk committee;
- monitoring and reviewing the effectiveness of the company's internal audit function;
- recommending to the board their opinion on the external auditor's appointment (in the event of the board rejecting the recommendation, the committee and the board should explain their respective positions in the annual report);
- monitoring and reviewing the external auditor's independence, objectivity and effectiveness;
- developing and implementing a policy on the agreement in respect of the external auditor undertaking any non-audit services, (taking into account relevant ethical guidance in respect of non-audit services).

These recommendations stemmed from major public concern about the independence of auditors. At the time of publication Sir Robert Smith said: 'The report I am publishing develops and codifies the role of Audit Committees, building on current best practice. I believe its implementation will raise British corporate governance standards and help to maintain our position among leaders in the field. The guidance we propose will strengthen the hand of Audit Committees without breaking the unitary board structure.'

The new roles and responsibilities given to Audit Committees by Sir Robert Smith have, in relation to the audit function, provided new opportunities for auditors to enhance their standing and display their worth within companies and organisations.

At the same time, Derek Higgs, under the aegis of the FRC, published a report called *Review of the Role and Effectiveness of Non-executive Directors*, which was aimed at improving corporate governance in the UK. It also endorsed Sir Robert Smith's recommendations that non-executive directors should assist Audit Committees in increasing their effectiveness. The Higgs Report included a suggested revised Combined Code to supersede the 1998 Hampel Combined Code. The FRC incorporated proposals from both the Higgs and Smith reports.

The Higgs Report proposed that:

■ at least half the members of a company's board, excluding the chairman, should be independent non-executive directors;
■ no individual should chair more than one FTSE 100 company;
■ the roles of chairman and chief executive should be separated.

The report ensured that the board had leeway to request and ensure that there was:

■ an increased level and type of material to review;
■ established independence criteria for non-executive directors;
■ a detailed outline of the role and responsibilities of non-executive directors.

FRC Combined Code (2003)

The recommendations of the Smith and Higgs reports resulted in the publication in July 2003 by the FRC of the revised UK Combined Code on Corporate Governance; it superseded and replaced the Combined Code issued by the Hampel Committee on Corporate Governance in June 1998. The code applied to reporting years beginning on or after 1 November 2003.

The 2003 Combined Code required listed companies to report to shareholders on their compliance with key provisions. Companies failing to meet these provisions must give reasons for any areas of non-compliance.

The main features of the FRC Combined Code (2003) were to provide:

■ new definitions for the role of the board members, the chairman and the non-executive directors;
■ more open and rigorous procedures for the appointment of directors and from a wider pool of candidates;
■ a formal evaluation of the performance of boards, committees and individual directors, and an enhanced induction with an opportunity for professional development of non-executive directors;
■ at least 50 per cent of the board in larger listed companies to be independent non-executive directors (including a definition of 'independence' of non-executive directors);
■ a reinforcement of the separation of the roles of the chairman and the chief executive;
■ the chief executive should not go on to become chairman of the same company;

- a closer relationship between the chairman, the senior independent director, non-executive directors and major shareholders;
- a strengthened role for the Audit Committee in monitoring the integrity of the company's financial reporting, reinforcing the independence of the external auditor and reviewing the management of financial and other risks facing the company.

The overall aim of the Combined Code was to enhance board effectiveness and to improve investor confidence by raising standards of corporate governance. A major change in the Combined Code was the modification of the code's structure to include not only main 'principles' and 'provisions' but also 'supporting principles', thereby allowing companies to have more flexibility in how they implement it. This was especially important for the smaller to medium-sized company which could not fulfil the requirements of the code as it stood.

These modifications enabled greater flexibility in terms of allowing the board chairman to act as the chairperson for the nomination committee. The modifications provided a clarification on the roles of the chairman and the senior independent director (SID), thereby emphasising the chairman's role in providing leadership to the non-executive directors and in the communication of shareholders' views to the board. In addition, the modifications provided smaller listed companies below the FTSE 350 an opportunity for a relaxation of the rule on the number of independent non-executives to 'at least two' instead of 'at least 50%'. Finally the modifications allowed the board to undertake a rigorous review instead of a special explanation when non-executive directors are re-elected beyond 6 years.

Recommended committees in the Combined Code (2003)

The Audit Committee

The Audit Committee is a key element in good corporate governance. It has responsibility for a range of audit-related matters and, in particular, the company's relationship with its auditors. The Audit Committee is regarded as a cornerstone of corporate governance and its remit includes overseeing the work of internal and external audits and reviewing the scope and results of audits. It is also required to play a part in the appointment and dismissal of both internal and external auditors.

Some of the rules governing Audit Committees are as follows:

- All committee members must be independent directors.
- At least one member must have recent and relevant financial expertise.
- Members' period of service should not exceed 9 years.
- Audit Committees must have annual procedures to ensure the independence and objectivity of the external auditor, which should involve a consideration of all relationships between the company and the audit firm (including the provision of non-audit services).
- A separate section of the annual report should describe the Audit Committee's work.
- The Audit Committee chair should be present at the AGM to answer questions.

The key working practices of the Audit Committee, as outlined in the Combined Code (2003) are shown in Exhibit 5.3.

Exhibit 5.3 **Audit Committee – key working practices and features**

- The Audit Committee should be independent of the executive management of the company and, unless there are good reasons of impracticality, should be independent of the Finance Committee.
- The Audit Committee should report its advice directly to the board of directors or in the case of not-for-profit organisations the governing body.
- The Audit Committee must be given sufficient resources and authority in its relationships with the board, management and other appropriate parties, including external and internal auditors, to fulfil its responsibilities.
- The Audit Committee must be given written terms of reference, which deal adequately with its membership, authority, goals and duties. The terms of reference and membership of the committee should be disclosed in the annual report and accounts. The terms of reference should be periodically reviewed to ensure that they remain relevant and appropriate.
- The board must ensure that an appropriate officer is assigned responsibility to establish and maintain effective mechanisms to inform the Audit Committee members of relevant reports and other publications which impact on the committee's work. The officer responsible could, for example, be the secretary to the Audit Committee.
- The Audit Committee must comprise at least three members. Non-executive members should be in the majority. At least one member should have a background in finance, accounting or auditing, but membership should not be drawn exclusively from people with such a background.
- In order not to jeopardise, or to be perceived to jeopardise, the Audit Committee's objectivity or independence, a number of restrictions on membership may be necessary or advisable, such as the chair of the board and the chief executive must not be a member.
- The precise duties of the Audit Committee should be determined by the board in the light of the company's needs. These duties should normally include reviewing and advising the board in relation to the systems of internal control, internal audit, external audit (including consideration of annual financial statements), and such advice to the board as the committee considers appropriate.

The Audit Committee is required to review the company's internal control procedures, to review its financial statements, assess the risk management procedures and be aware of the whistle-blowing procedures established by the company. However, in doing this, it is recognised that any such system of controls can only provide reasonable and not absolute assurances against material misstatement or loss. The Audit Committee will be concerned not only with internal financial controls but also with the wider aspects of internal control, including the identification of key business risks, non-financial controls, compliance with laws and regulations as well as evaluating their financial implications and establishing policies for managing those risks.

The independence of the Audit Committee is essential, hence the role played by non-executive directors.

The Nominations Committee

This committee is responsible for overseeing the appointment, and re-appointment, of board members. Again, independence is key to this committee. The committee should consist of a majority of independent non-executive directors and is to make recommendations only – it is for the whole board to make appointments. Its role usually includes identifying the skills and experience required on the board; overseeing the recruitment process, including appointing 'head hunters'; and vetting candidates and making a recommendation to the board. Some Nominations Committees may also have a more proactive role in succession planning.

The Remuneration Committee

The Remuneration Committee oversees the remuneration policy in respect of the executive directors and the implementation of that policy. The duties of the remuneration committee include:

- recommending the overall remuneration policy;
- determining targets for any performance-related pay or bonus schemes;
- setting individual remuneration packages within the policy;
- setting policy regarding pensions and service contracts;
- reporting to shareholders.

The membership of the remuneration committee must consist exclusively of independent non-executive directors.

Tyson Report (2003)

In 2003 the Higgs Report was followed by the Tyson Report on the current role and effectiveness of non-executive directors (NEDs) and how to improve these in the future. Commissioned by the Department of Trade and Industry, the Tyson Report considered the recruitment and development of NEDs within a company. The report identified that factors such as size and age of the company, the customer and employee base, the extent of its participation in global markets, future strategies and current board membership were all important in determining the skills required by NEDs. The report recognised that there was a certain amount of training already in existence for NEDs but questioned whether that training was appropriate for the role.

Flint Report (2005) (Turnbull 2)

The review of the Turnbull Report's recommendations, known as the Flint Report, was driven by the introduction of Sarbanes-Oxley Act in the US in 2002, itself a direct result of the Enron and WorldCom scandals. Prior to the publication of the review it was anticipated that it would offer some sort of equivalence between the UK and the US and that compliance with Turnbull/Flint would be accepted as Sarbanes-Oxley compliance. What was feared to be 'Turnbull 2' with some extreme changes turned out to be merely 'Turnbull 1.1'. The Turnbull Review Group led by Douglas Flint resisted calls to follow the Sarbanes-Oxley Act 2002 (a mandatory requirement for US listed companies) and apply strict rules for providing assurance of the accuracy of financial statements and concluded that the principles-based (a voluntary code) approach was appropriate for governance in the UK. Flint concluded that some improvements were necessary but that the principles of the original Turnbull Report had led to improvements in internal control and did not require any change. The review group re-emphasised that establishing an effective system of internal control was not a one-off exercise. Flint's review did highlight the need to facilitate increased communication between the board and the shareholders on risk and its internal control mechanisms. The Flint Report therefore reiterated the two main aspects of corporate governance, namely internal control and risk management.

The FRC's updated version of the Turnbull guidance, *Internal Control: Guidance for Directors on the Combined Code*, took effect for financial years beginning on or after 1 January 2006. The updated version strongly endorsed the retention of the flexible, principles-based approach of the original guidance and made only a small number of amendments to the existing practices as outlined by the Turnbull Report of 1999.

The key conclusions of the Flint Report included the following:

- The Turnbull guidance has contributed to improvements in internal control in UK listed companies, and significant changes are not required.
- The guidance should continue to cover all internal controls, and not be limited to internal controls over financial reporting.
- No changes should be made to the guidance that would have the effect of restricting a company's ability to apply the guidance in a manner suitable to its own particular circumstances.
- The guidance should be updated to reflect changes in the Combined Code and Listing Rules since 1999 and the proposed statement of directors' duties in the draft Company Law Reform Bill.
- Boards should review their application of the guidance on a continuing basis.
- It would not be appropriate to require boards to make a statement in the annual report and accounts on the effectiveness of the company's internal control system because the requirement would be 'onerous' and of little value to shareholders, but boards should confirm that necessary action has been or is being taken to remedy any significant failings or weaknesses identified from the reviews of the effectiveness of the internal control system.
- Boards should look on the internal control statement in the annual report and accounts as an opportunity to communicate to their shareholders how they manage risk effectively, and include such information as is considered necessary to assist shareholders' understanding of the main features of the company's risk management processes and system of internal control.
- There should be no expansion of the external auditors' responsibilities in relation to the company's internal control statement.

Source: www.apb.org.uk

A clarification was also introduced that directors are expected to apply the same standard of care when reviewing the effectiveness of internal control as when exercising their general duties. In other words, companies will now have to ensure that the private review of control effectiveness that they should already be doing to comply with Turnbull is carried out with 'reasonable care, skill and diligence.'

FRC Combined Code (2006) amendments

The FRC made some changes to the original guidance, writing in the preface that it hoped to encourage companies to continually review how they are implementing the Combined Code, and that companies continued to provide shareholders with meaningful information in their annual reports about internal controls.

Among the changes in the updated version of the 2003 Combined Code was the requirement for boards to confirm in the annual report that 'necessary action has been or is being taken to remedy any significant failings or weaknesses identified from their review of the effectiveness of the internal control system, and to include in the annual report such information as considered necessary to assist shareholders' understanding of the main features of the company's risk management processes and system of internal control'.

There was also a clarification that directors are expected to apply the same standard of care when reviewing the effectiveness of internal control as when exercising their general duties.

A re-ordering of the introduction to emphasise that the guidance is intended to reflect sound business practice as well as help companies comply with the internal control requirements of the Combined Code.

Key aspects of corporate governance in the UK (FRC 2006 and 2008)

In 2006 the FRC made a small number of changes to the previous version of the Combined Code (2003). These enabled the company chairman to sit on the remuneration committee if the individual was considered independent on appointment; provided shareholders voting by proxy with the option of withholding their vote on a resolution; and encouraged companies to publish the details of proxies lodged on resolutions where votes are taken on a show of hands.

This meant that a single board became collectively responsible for the success of the company. Checks and balances appeared in the form of a separation of the roles of the Chief Executive and Chairman. A balance of executive and independent non-executive directors on the board, with a strong independent audit and remuneration committee, was established. There became a requirement for an annual evaluation by the board of its performance, including an emphasis on the objectivity of the directors in the interests of the company. Transparency on appointments and remuneration, and effective rights for shareholders, were recognised as relevant and important to company survival and success.

The FRC Corporate Governance code of 2008 removed the restriction on company chairpersons sitting on more than one FTSE 100 company. The chairperson can also sit on the audit committee if deemed independent. The Walker Report 2009 reviewed the effectiveness of risk management in the banking sector which led to further code amendments in 2010.

The essential features after the amendment are summarised in Exhibit 5.4.

The Combined Code identifies good governance practices relating to the role and composition of the board and its committees and the development of a sound system of internal control. In order to meet their obligations under the LSE

Exhibit 5.4 **Essential features of UK corporate governance**

The role and composition of the board

- A single board with members collectively responsible for leading the company and setting its values and standards.
- A clear division of responsibilities for running the board and running the company with a separate chairman and chief executive.
- A balance of executive and independent non-executive directors – for large companies at least 50% of the board members should be independent non-executive directors; smaller companies should have at least two independent directors.
- Formal and transparent procedures for appointing directors, with all appointments and reappointments to be ratified by shareholders.
- Regular evaluation of the effectiveness of the board and its committees.

Remuneration

- Formal and transparent procedures for setting executive remuneration, including a remuneration committee made up of independent directors and an advisory vote for shareholders.
- A significant proportion of remuneration to be linked to performance.

Accountability and audit

- The board is responsible for presenting a balanced assessment of the company's position (including through the accounts) and maintaining a sound system of internal control.
- Formal and transparent procedures for carrying out these responsibilities, including an Audit Committee made up of independent directors and with the necessary experience.

Relations with shareholders

- The board must maintain contact with shareholders to understand their opinions and concerns.
- Separate resolutions on all substantial issues at general meetings.

Source: www.frc.org.uk

The FRC Combined Code is available on the FRC website (www.frc.org.uk).

Listing Rules, listed companies will have to describe how they apply the Code's main and supporting principles and either confirm that they comply with the Code's provisions or provide an explanation to shareholders. Where companies consider a different approach to be more appropriate to their particular circumstances, they have to provide an explanation to their shareholders who must decide whether they are happy with this approach. The Combined Code emphasises that companies and institutional investors should enter into dialogue based on trust and mutual understanding. Companies should give helpful and informative explanations, and institutional investors should take a considered approach when evaluating them.

The 'comply or explain' approach enables a case-by-case approach to be utilised where judgments have to be made about particular governance aspects such as the independence of non-executive directors. According to research by Grant Thornton in 2005 many companies were still not up to speed with the requirements of the Combined Code that had been in place for years. The research indicated that the proportion of FTSE 350 companies fully compliant with the code dropped by half in 2005 to 28%, compared with 58% in 2004.

Among them, 59 companies in the FTSE 100 did not comply. This indicates that the vast majority of FTSE 350 companies were truly embracing the principles of 'comply or explain'.

The minor amendments to the 2003 code as a result of the 2005 Flint review gave the message to organisations that they must continue to ensure that their internal control systems develop to take account of new and emerging risks, and that boards must communicate with their shareholders in their annual reports to explain how they as boards are managing risk.

Audit and corporate governance

The Companies Act 1985 requires the external auditor to undertake an audit of the financial statements of the company to form an opinion that they show a true and fair view of the activities undertaken. If the company is a listed company on the London Stock Exchange, in line with its Listing Rules the directors have to provide a report stating that it complies with the Corporate Governance Code of Best Practice issued by the FRC in 2003. The auditor has to provide a report supporting the directors' corporate governance report published within the annual statement.

The spectacular corporate scandals and the subsequent lack of confidence in the way companies were directed and controlled during the latter part of the 20th century and the early 21st century led to an increased demand for sound assurance that resulted in a change in the roles of both the external and internal auditors.

There are three key areas for auditor involvement in corporate governance: the supervision and monitoring of the executive; ensuring that there are mechanisms for displaying accountability; and provision of assurances on the presence of risk management processes. Increasing corporate governance requirements are placing greater pressures on boards in terms of their responsibility and accountability. To enable boards to comply with and fulfil these responsibilities, they have to reconsider the source and level of assurance that they require. One of the most obvious ways of obtaining this assurance is from within their own organisation. An effective internal audit function is very often the best source to provide boards with the relevant assurance. This has led to a new role for internal audit, which in turn has led to an increased profile for this function. As the corporate governance framework keeps on moving its goalposts, organisations are seeking assurances from their internal audit function to provide the necessary independent and objective assurances on internal controls and risk management.

Audit and risk management

The Turnbull Report of 1999 helped companies that had already established a framework of risk management processes to formalise these into procedures and processes, while companies that had yet to embark on a risk management approach were pushed into thinking about one. Internal audit played a significant role in introducing and implementing risk management in many companies, which meant that compliance checking and enforcement, previously a major role, became less so. Implementing the recommendations of Turnbull led to a different role for internal audit that helped to increase its profile and added value status.

Whilst the recommendations claimed to highlight the worthwhile role of having internal audit as an integrated part of operational management, the reality was that only a few internal audit departments were completely independent of operational management. Most internal audit departments were already carrying out additional functions, especially in risk management. Against this background, internal audit acts as a means of spreading best practice, encouraging control risk self-assessment policies, and helping to develop a culture that embraces embedded risk management.

The audit of risk management in an organisation would include confirming that the organisation's objectives are clear and have been communicated appropriately to all concerned. This endorses the fact that audit has a role in establishing the identification of significant risks process and adopting a co-operative working relationship with the Audit Committee. Audit will review the adequacy of the methods for measuring the significance of risks, as well as the establishment of risk registers. The likelihood of risks occurring and their impact will need to be assessed, and audit will have a role to play in ensuring that

- these processes are present within the organisation. An overall review of risks will entail: referring to published information on risks in similar organisations and then comparing these with risks identified within the organisation;
- meeting with senior managers and discussing their concepts of risk within their areas of responsibility;
- assessing the risk appetite of the organisation and confirming whether this is being consistently applied;
- confirming that identified risks have been considered and various management approaches have been considered using the 4 Ts method of treat, tolerate, terminate and transfer.

Audit will be involved with ensuring that monitoring and management processes have been put in place for the identified risks. Finally the audit function will be involved in confirming whether risk management responsibility has been embedded within the organisation with a reporting process to allow the tracking and reporting of relevant risk management issues on a regular basis.

A summary of the key aspects of audit review of risk management is given in Exhibit 5.5.

Exhibit 5.5 **Audit review of risk management**

- The identification of key areas of risk
- Assessing risks in terms of probability, measuring impact and prioritising risk
- Evaluating the financial implications of the risks
- Monitoring and assessing progress in terms of responses and remedial action
- Reviewing the policies for managing those risks
- Taking into account non-financial controls as well as financial controls
- Compliance with laws and regulations that have an indirect impact on both internal controls and risk

Relationship between external and internal audit

A feature in achieving this 'key component of corporate governance' is the reliance placed on internal audit within an organisation. This has placed the internal audit function and head of internal audit under the spotlight in terms of the changing role and responsibilities in meeting Audit Committee requirements and expectations within organisations.

Definitions for internal audit imply that the role of the internal auditor has developed and changed from that of an appraisal, monitoring and evaluating function to that of an assurance provider and audit consultant. Does the internal audit function provide a worthwhile service in terms of being a valued member of the organisation? Is internal audit contributing to the effective management of resources, or is the audit role still at the old traditional stage of evaluating control structures?

The role of internal audit has developed considerably since the first corporate governance report was published in 1992. The Turnbull Report on internal control identified the important role that internal audit has to play in confirming the presence of an appropriate system of internal controls.

The benefits of a strong working relationship between internal and external audit are as follows:

- An awareness by both parties of individual activities can lead to a reduction in audit testing and therefore savings for the client.
- Common audit areas are not duplicated.
- Reliance can be placed on internal audit work by the external auditor.
- Internal audit can undertake certain work on behalf of external audit.
- Internal audit is part of internal control, and therefore if external audit place reliance on internal control, they in fact place reliance on internal audit.
- Some objectives of internal audit are the same as those for external audit, e.g. evaluation of accounting systems, compliance and substantive tests undertaken in the same format.
- Co-operation can release external audit resources to undertake more audit work in high-risk areas.
- Development of mutual respect can make the audit less disruptive to the client.
- In many large organisations, due to the size and nature of their activities, the external auditor has no choice but to rely on the work of the internal auditor.

The Audit Committee can be of assistance in the relationship between internal and external audit by:

- helping to avoid the duplication of work where the Audit Committee is aware of both plans of action;
- reviewing audit findings and areas of audit concern;
- clarifying any problems regarding the most suitable accounting treatment of contentious accounting items;
- clarifying the manner and degree of disclosure of any item that may affect both auditors;
- acting as a mediator when there are issues that need resolving between both auditors and the board;

Exhibit 5.6 **Key areas requiring internal and external audit input**

■ Monitoring of the executive in its decision-making process in terms of sound governance for the benefit of wealth creation for the shareholder and the general well-being of stakeholders in terms of corporate social responsibility
■ Mechanisms for ensuring that management is accountable to shareholders and stakeholders
■ Ensuring that companies are run properly and taking into account internal control and risk management
■ Audit to show a true and fair view of the financial statements in order to comply with legislation
■ Recognition of the important role that both internal and external auditors play in corporate governance
■ Advisory role to the board and Audit Committee

■ becoming involved in matters relating to auditor appointment and remuneration;
■ providing auditors with access to the Audit Committee to discuss issues that may be sensitive to certain members of management.
■ acting as a channel of communication between the corporate board for both the auditors;
■ acting as a communication link between both sets of auditors where there may be a failure to interact or communicate with certain members of the executive.

The main areas requiring input for both internal and external audit, and therefore requiring a good working relationship, are given in Exhibit 5.6.

US legislation on corporate governance – the Sarbanes-Oxley Act (2002)

The Sarbanes-Oxley Act became US law in July 2002 and was largely a response to a number of major corporate and accounting scandals, such as those of Enron and WorldCom. The US Congress passed the legislation in an attempt to curb the likelihood of similar corporate collapses as a consequence of poor corporate governance. At the time of its inception, Sarbanes-Oxley was regarded as the most important legislative document in relation to corporate governance, financial disclosure and the practice of public accounting in the USA since the securities laws of the early 1930s. The Act requires company executives, directors and auditors to comply with greater corporate accountability and transparency. It affects the way companies operate, manage and report on their organisation.

In terms of its jurisdiction, the Act only applies to companies listed on the New York Stock Exchange, non-listed companies with 300 or more shareholders, and non-US corporations who are part of any company or group in the US required to comply with the Act. The Act focuses on issues such as the presence of controls within an organisation, the processes by which the Act is applied and the way that the data used is subject to audit verification. A major impact on companies during the first year of implementation was the cost of compliance.

An important aspect of the Sarbanes-Oxley Act is that companies recognise that adherence to the legislation means that they are now monitored more closely and that company information is more public than it was before. This has forced companies to review and improve their corporate governance, thereby enhancing the potential efficiency of the organisation by focusing attention on areas of risk and weaknesses and allowing the opportunity for corrective action.

The main provisions of the Sarbanes-Oxley Act are as follows:

- The establishment of a new Public Companies Accounting Oversight Board (PCAOB) with authority over registered public accounting firms (both inside and outside the US). This PCAOB examines auditing and audit standards, audit quality control and auditor independence. Effectively this removes self-regulation from the auditing profession.
- Section 2 establishes and regulates the relationship between the auditor and its clients, including the prohibition of the provision of a wide range of non-audit services to clients and introduction of mandatory audit partner rotation.
- Section 302 requires officers to certify that the financial statements and the information given to the external auditors are complete and fair.
- Section 404 requires companies to review the effectiveness of internal control over their financial reporting and to express an opinion. Many companies have established a project comprising the following stages:
  - documentation of processes and internal controls over financial reporting;
  - evaluation of internal controls over financial reporting;
  - redesigning the control framework and internal controls over financial reporting to address any gaps or deficiencies identified;
  - ongoing monitoring and testing of internal controls over financial reporting.
- Section 406 requires that companies disclose whether they have a code of ethics for senior financial officers, and Section 407 requires the company to disclose the name of the financial expert on the Audit Committee.
- The Act also dramatically increases criminal and civil penalties and sanctions for acts of financial fraud.

Sarbanes-Oxley, internal auditing and corporate governance

The legal requirement to comply with the Sarbanes-Oxley Act 2002 can indirectly point to the need for internal audit of processes and budgets in order to meet the requirements of the Act and the International Financial Reporting Standards (IFRS). This is because of the existence of strict penalties for non-compliance, which means that many companies have set up 'heads of compliance' jobs in order to ensure that compliance issues do not adversely affect business activity. These 'heads of compliance' can be viewed as internal auditors in disguise, where establishing an internal monitoring process can make regulatory compliance a simpler task.

There are four steps to ensuring an appropriate level of compliance:

1. Evaluating which levels within the organisation have an insight into status and the budgetary issues as and when they arise.
2. Being prepared to lead the change – there will inevitably be cultural impacts on the workforce (e.g. meeting the requirements of new IFRSs) and making employees aware of the impact of their role in these changes is important.

3. Ensuring an appropriate level of efficiency by educating personnel as to the importance of security of information, having an awareness of the sensitivity of information, as well as the levels of responsibility attached to the information. The need to meet these SOX compliance requirements will require a unification of processes, technology and people.

4. Automation and consolidation, transparency and accessibility to management information are key factors in compliance achievement. In addition there is a need to ensure that the risk of inaccuracy in management information is kept to a minimum.

An internationally accepted format for corporate governance

Internationally, codes, reports and frameworks have been issued by organisations such as the Canadian Institute of Chartered Accountants, Criteria of Control Board (CoCo), the Treadway Commission, Committee of Sponsoring Organisations (COSO), and the Organisation for Economic Co-operation and Development (OECD).

In terms of auditor role in corporate governance the OECD believes that the auditor should assess corporate governance regimes under five key areas:

- the rights of shareholders
- the equitable treatment of shareholders
- the role of stakeholders
- disclosure and transparency
- the responsibility of the board.

These issues do not necessarily mean that there should be a 'one size fits all' approach to corporate governance. Whilst establishing a standardised approach may in theory seem feasible when there are numerous multinational companies operating on a global scale, in reality a one-size-fits-all approach is not practical. Emerging economies wishing to play catch-up in the global market may find themselves in a situation where they have to introduce new corporate governance frameworks. These will inevitably test the robustness of any existing governance requirements. Companies dealing with different environments may find that embedded governance that is acceptable in one county may not be acceptable in another.

The world-leading corporate governance codes and rules of the UK and the US have distinct features, but they both represent fundamental frameworks that guide the way towards sound corporate governance. The main difference between the two is that the UK code is voluntary while the US is a mandatory code. There are arguments, however, in terms of developing an international code along the lines that the international accounting and auditing standards were developed.

In dealing with acceptability and robustness of a standardised code on governance, there are two distinct cultural aspects that can influence the development of an international corporate governance code. They are commonly referred to as the ideological structure and the socioeconomic structure. The *ideological structure'* refers to societal norms and values such as collectivism, attitude towards time, professionalism, innovation, flexibility as well as the dominance of religion, sentiments, ethical principles, world views and ethos in society's everyday life. The 'socioeconomic structure' includes factors such as the political and legal systems, the power of the profession, the tax system, the education system and professional audit and accountancy training. Similarly, the extent of shared values and the degree of co-operation are determined by organisational co-ordinating activities and formality in the various socioeconomic systems. It is important, therefore, to recognise that norms and values can differ between groups even within a nation.

Limitations to the international acceptance of global corporate governance

There are a number of limitations to introducing a one-size-fits-all code for corporate governance. Specific measures can be introduced through legislation but there is no guarantee that they will work because very often there is a lack of funding available to allow the monitoring and enforcement of the codes that have been introduced. Appropriately skilled and qualified staff may be in short supply, as may resources to purchase equipment such as computers. The timeliness of audit review of financial statement audit reports cannot be assured to comply with specified time-frames which mean that any findings and possible remedial action may not be possible. The existence of legislation or a code of practice does not mean that citizens will behave morally. In circumstances where there are very few reinforcement agencies or a lack of penalties for non-compliance, the reality is that it may not operate as expected.

A network or circle of 'powerful' people can be very small and they are inevitably intricately knitted across political, business and social life. These factors will impact on the operation of sound governance in terms of expected independence, ethical behaviour and objectivity because friendships are important to 'get ahead'. Auditors will back-pedal on issues or decide to remain silent when controversial issues come to light. Even when changes in attitudes do occur, there will still be some key players in regulatory agencies that will have remained in place, making the implementation of expected codes of conduct impractical or unworkable.

A lack of transparency or a low rating on transparency in operations may exist because of traditional attitudes that exist. The accountability of public officers, including politicians and ministers of government, can be questionable due to personal greed and egotism. An attitude accepting insider trading and own stock trading by company executives as acceptable practice will not boost investor confidence or give a sense of fair play to stakeholders.

Cultural and economic factors will play a key influencing factor in how corporate governance frameworks are actually applied in practice. In countries with high unemployment, low savings and investment, and low salaries, the driving force may be survival and the exploitation of workers and stakeholders may become an acceptable practice. A few inter-linked families may own most of the businesses, and they may use their own version of a code of governance which they consider is a workable practice.

Boards of directors are charged with the role of ensuring the practice of good governance, but this may not be as straightforward as it seems because directors may be ignorant of their role and responsibility. Directors may never have received any training in governance or business. Their appointment may be dubious as they were appointed because of a 'favour' or friendship connections, and loyalties will undermine their objectivity. Often the 'uncomfortable' questions are not asked during board meetings which can undermine boardroom diligence. Very often there isn't a pool of competent directors (both executive and non-executive) available to choose from when vacancies arise on the board. The same individuals often sit on numerous boards, making it difficult for them to serve effectively as board members. It is difficult to ensure that there is a visionary chairperson on the board who can energetically promote their recommendations. It can often be difficult to have a board that reflects the main concerns and expectations of the stakeholders.

On the political horizon, governments are always looking for businesses to increase the economic prosperity of their countries, which will lead to a situation where governments will require businesses to comply with regulations and standards that can benefit both the company and the country as a whole. Very often governments will respond to the public demand for better control features, as happened with the initial corporate governance review in 1991 in the UK. Inevitably this will require better information and communication along with appropriate monitoring and review. This is key to corporate governance development which all takes time and often requires a change in attitudes and culture.

Summary   Corporate governance relates to the way a company is directed and controlled. Audit has a role to play in corporate governance by working effectively with the board, the Audit Committee and the executive. The provision of audit assurance in terms of reviewing the existence of internal control and the mechanisms for risk management contributes to the overall process of corporate governance.

? PRACTICE QUESTION

Is the UK system of corporate governance more effective than the Sarbanes-Oxley Act in preventing company fraud?

Chapter 6

Different approaches to investigation

Objectives

After studying this chapter you should be able to:

- understand and undertake a value-for-money review;
- discuss the auditor's possible role in undertaking a fraud investigation;
- discuss the role and importance of a statutory audit;
- describe voluntary audits;
- discuss the importance of social audits.

Introduction

Whilst systems and probity audits are probably the most common an auditor will undertake, there are a number of other types of, and approaches to, investigation. Sometimes they are done as part of the internal audit remit from the Audit Committee but on other occasions they are carried out by external audit because there is a special request for this type of work agreed during the pre-audit interview. Senior management at boardroom level are very much aware of their corporate governance responsibilities, particularly with regard to financial risk. They will be concerned that there may be issues relating to systems, procedures and controls which are not highlighted for their attention.

This chapter examines some of these different types of investigation, as well as covering in more detail value-for-money (VFM) reviews and financial investigations, often called fraud or forensic accounting. It is acknowledged that both VFM reviews and fraud investigations are not pure audits but they represent work done by auditors who are seen to be independent in their judgment.

Statutory audits

This is known as the audit of the final accounts and must be completed by the external auditor in order to fulfil a statutory obligation. In the case of companies, the audit must be in accordance with the Companies Acts of 1985 and 1989, and the grouping and order of items must be in accordance with that legislation. The auditor must provide an opinion that the accounts give a true and fair view of the financial position for the financial year in question. The auditor's opinion is critical because many people, including future investors, rely on it to make major financial decisions.

There are other bodies that require a statutory audit under different legislation. Local authorities, for example, require an external audit under the Local Government Acts. The 1982 Act, which set up the Audit Commission, stated that the external auditor should give an unqualified opinion that the accounts have been presented fairly, or a qualified report if that is necessary. Similarly the audit of government departments, appropriation accounts, is completed under the National Audit Act of 1983 by the Comptroller & Auditor General.

The audit of financial statements is a legal requirement and is dealt with in more detail in Chapter 13.

Voluntary audits

Small companies with a turnover of less than £5.6 million are not required to have a statutory audit. Other exceptions include charitable companies, clubs and associations whose articles state that an audit, though not a legal necessity, is required. This, then, is a voluntary arrangement whereby members of the organisation feel it is prudent to carry out an audit. Some partners in a partnership also feel that a voluntary audit is necessary because they want to keep everything 'above board'.

Companies who are entitled to the audit exemption must still file accounts with the Registrar of Companies for each financial year. Unaudited accounts must include a director's signature on the balance sheet and a statement that the directors acknowledge their responsibilities for preparing accounts that show a true and fair view.

Social audits

There is an increasing need for organisations to be seen to be behaving ethically. Organisations often hold high ethical beliefs in their aims and objectives and promote these through their annual report. Once established, however, there is sometimes a tendency to forget these high ethical beliefs. The auditor, via a social audit approach, has a duty to check that the organisation is doing what it says. For example, it would be highly embarrassing if a health company that was against smoking was found to be investing in British American Tobacco. It is far better for the auditor to pick up on these inconsistencies than for the national newspapers to expose them.

Value-for-money (VFM) reviews

This section is properly called value-for-money (VFM) reviews, rather than audits, because technically they can be done by anybody who has a strong financial and administrative background. Although it is not strictly an audit, a VFM review tends to be carried out by auditors, often as part of a longer-term project. It fits in with their other duties very well.

A VFM review is synonymous with a performance review. Obtaining good performance is all about doing the right things well. However, it is probably better to do the right things badly than to do the wrong things well. A performance review should involve assessing the extent to which services have been delivered in an economic, efficient and effective manner – the 'three Es' (see Figure 6.1).

Economy, by definition, means ensuring that the resources purchased for delivering the service are procured at the lowest possible cost while still meeting the appropriate quality standards. Economy is therefore linked with cost and subsequently cost reduction.

Efficiency is defined as the relationship between goods or services produced, known as the outputs, and the resources used to produce them, known as inputs.

Figure 6.1 **The relationship between the three Es – economy, efficiency and effectiveness**

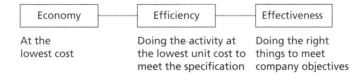

Economy	Efficiency	Effectiveness
At the lowest cost	Doing the activity at the lowest unit cost to meet the specification	Doing the right things to meet company objectives

Figure 6.2 **The value-for-money equation**

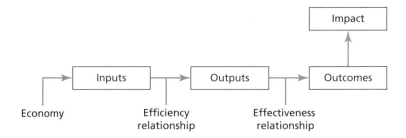

Expressed another way, efficiency means providing the required level and quality of service with the minimum of resources needed to meet the specification.

Effectiveness is a measure of how well the activity is achieving its policy objectives. In other words, is the right service level being provided to the right people at the right time and is it in accordance with strategy? If value for money is to be achieved then all the three Es need to be achieved (see the 'VFM equation' in Figure 6.2). This is a minimum because some organisations will look at an activity from a 'six E' viewpoint, the three Es already mentioned plus environmental impact, ethical considerations and the European dimension.

Considering Figures 6.1 and 6.2, it is clear that the measurement of economy is based purely on costs. The measurement of efficiency is the input divided by the output, i.e. the cost per unit of service achieved. Effectiveness is managed by determining the benefits and savings and aligning them with organisational policy. There is often a tendency to concentrate on economy and efficiency rather than effectiveness because they are easier to measure and the information is more readily available.

The management team has an objective to achieve value for money and the auditor has a role to identify where changes might be made and how they can be expedited. This means that management at board level or through its Audit Committee may issue the auditor with a remit to undertake the study. For example, they may well be unhappy about the high level of heating costs when they approved the budget and may ask audit to carry out a study. This is probably better than just cutting the budget by 10% without any clear direction on how it could be saved. The auditor will have the chance to study whether government insulation grants can be obtained, whether insulation work would save costs and whether thermostatic controls are in place and work effectively, and also to look at the costs of different forms of heating. Of course, the reverse may happen and audit may suggest an area of study to the company's Audit Committee. Ideas often come from professional journals, from friends in the profession or from stories in the newspapers.

A suggested VFM approach is as follows:

1. Obtain the remit from the Audit Committee.
2. Understand the policy objectives and how the unit audited interfaces with them.

Figure 6.3   **An overview of the value-for-money approach**

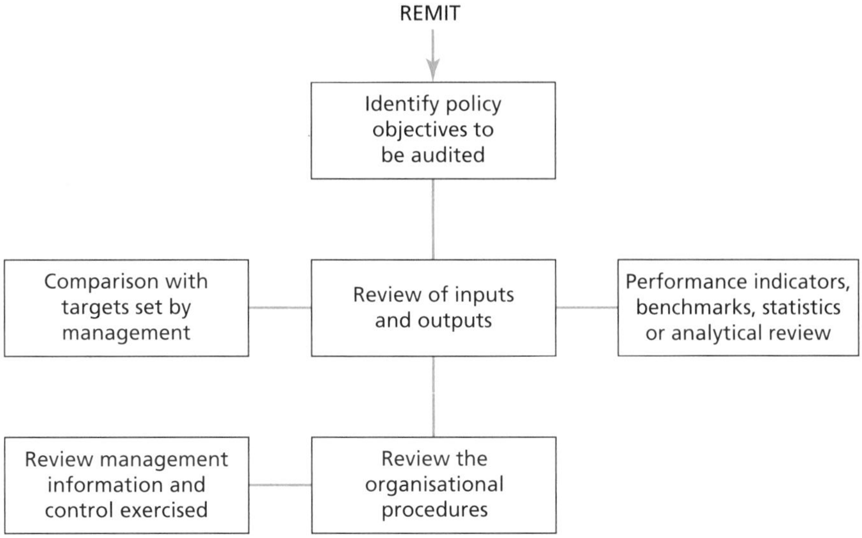

REMIT

Identify policy
objectives to
be audited

| Comparison with targets set by management | Review of inputs and outputs | Performance indicators, benchmarks, statistics or analytical review |

| Review management information and control exercised | Review the organisational procedures |

3. Review the organisation's procedures.
4. Document the systems and identify and evaluate key controls within the system.
5. Test systems to see if anything is going wrong.
6. Consider the VFM approach.
7. Review and measure inputs and outputs.
8. Determine any useful performance indicators or benchmarks.
9. Question what information is provided to management and what control is cxcrciscd.
10. Discuss with management.
11. Issue the report.

An overview of the VFM approach is shown in Figure 6.3. There are numerous tools for a VFM study which are worth examination.

Performance indicators

Performance indicators are on offshoot of VFM studies and are used to reinforce VFM study findings. However, there is no such thing as a typical or standard indicator which can be applied in all situations. Indicators must be designed to reflect the nature and culture and the dominant driving factors. Some examples of indicators are as follows:

- Time – this year vs. last year
- Service standard – actual performance vs. standard set
- Inter-firm – company's performance vs. the market leader or nearest competitor
- Utilisation rates – % used

Table 6.1 **Inter-company profit indicators**

Company – BMQ Ltd

Location	Profit margin
Putney	6.5%
Guildford	7.0%
Ealing	4.2%
Ruislip	5.5%
Oxford	6.1%
Reading	6.7%
Kingston	5.3%
Woking	2.2%
Basingstoke	6.0%

- Task times – average time to complete a particular task
- Productivity – amount of work produced per day
- Volumes of service – amount of work in volume completed
- Activity level – fee generation time compared with non-fee level work
- Service provision – measure service provision against an assessment of need, e.g. Library books issued per head of population

An example of using performance indicators within the same company is shown in Table 6.1.

From the above table the auditor will look very carefully at the performance of the Woking branch, which has a far lower profit margin than the mean and is considerably above 2 standard deviations below the mean.

Different approaches to VFM

Business process re-engineering

Many years ago business process re-engineering (BPR) was known as value analysis, but BPR is the currently favoured term. Re-engineering means a redesign of the business process to achieve a fundamental improvement in the business performance while at the same time reducing costs – in other words, providing a better service or product for less money. One key aspect of BPR is that it defines completely new and radical ways for an organisation to undertake its activities. Often these new ways cut right across an organisation, and even outside it, affecting all parts, and BPR is therefore seen as revolutionary. BPR takes place at a high level within an organisation and is driven by external and strategic demands. It should be differentiated from process improvements, which are defined as incremental changes to existing processes.

There are many definitions of BPR, often meaning different things to different people. One common application in management circles is to change the hierarchies, structures and staff roles within the organisation. From the auditor's perspective, BPR means changing the process using an opportunity cost approach (i.e. the costs or savings of the alternative). The use of IT has revolutionised change within office systems and the auditor will want to latch on to this. Of course, changes can be revolutionary, such as when Reebok attempted to remove paper from the office, but they can also be incremental, and the auditor may recommend, for example, better use of bar coding, optical character reading or electronic mail.

Income generation and cash flow

An alternative to BPR is to look at different ways of maximising income, for example through alternative revenue streams such as charging for car parking spaces, advertising or sponsorship. There is nothing wrong in auditor creativity here. A similar approach is to look at cash flow management – e.g. deferring salary dates or moving customers on to direct debits will improve cash flow and minimise borrowing costs.

Market testing

There is nothing wrong with the recommendation to test the market to ensure that VFM is maximised. This is a legitimate approach to making savings, but all too often the end product is one of cost reduction because the standard of service falls significantly. It is rare for customers to be asked how they feel about the standard of service they receive. There are occasions when outsourcing can reveal that service departments have become inefficient and expensive. However, there are other occasions when the organisation under market testing is shown to deliver a 'Rolls-Royce service'. If that is the case the auditor must be prepared to recommend hiring out the service on an agency basis to bring in an additional revenue stream. Many organisations have a successful payroll service, for example, which all too often managers and employees take for granted. However, there is a sound business case to invest in it and hire it out on agency or consultancy basis.

Technology investment

Investment in plant, machinery or other types of equipment can result in long-term savings. Examples of this are hospitals investing in large laundry tunnel washing machines or in cook-freeze catering facilities; water companies investing in water meters with a view to relating revenue generation to usage; and large companies investing in new telephone switchboard systems to reduce the number of telephone operating staff. The auditor will use the traditional tools of investment appraisal to calculate whether the investment will bring savings to the organisation. Care should be taken to separate savings from benefits received. A benefit will not result in a budgetary cutback while, of course, a saving would.

Excessive controls

When reviewing a system, it is useful for the auditor to note the controls that exist and to form a judgment on their usefulness. Controls must be justified on the basis that they achieve at least one of the following: they must be preventative, detective or corrective by prescription. If they are ineffective or excessive then they should be replaced. Controls which are excessive are often expensive and their replacement will result in savings.

Financial investigations

In many organisations the investigation of financial irregularities or fraud detection is not the responsibility of the auditor but that of a separate department. In government departments administering social security and housing benefits and in the Post Office, the sheer volume of transactions means fraud is an ongoing issue, because whatever controls, checks and balances are in place, human nature often gets the better of some individuals. In such cases the organisation finds it better to set up a separate investigation agency whose remit is to deal with these problems. In other organisations, fraud is more of an isolated issue. While any senior manager can investigate these problems, the remit often falls to internal auditors because of their independence of judgment and their financial training.

Whatever system of investigation is used, senior management has an overall responsibility for the level of fraud and its subsequent detection within the organisation. The auditor will uphold the line that prevention comes before detection and a good level of systems-based auditing will detect any problems before they arise. Nevertheless, human nature is such that whatever controls are in place somebody will try to circumvent them.

Figure 6.4 illustrates the psychology of fraud. Financial pressures and sometimes greed may drive an employee to look for a loophole or opportunity to exploit the system.

Fraud

Fraud is a major risk facing any organisation. ISA 240 outlines the auditor's responsibility to consider fraud in an audit of financial statements. The Fraud Act of 2006 states that a person can be guilty of fraud in three ways:

■ by false representation
■ by failing to disclose information
■ by abuse of position.

Figure 6.4 **The fraud triangle**

Three surveys relating to company fraud were undertaken during 2006/7. Published by accountancy firms, these surveys highlighted the losses incurred by companies as a direct result of fraud and also the fact that the greatest perpetrators were management.

Ernst & Young's 2006 survey of 19 countries concluded that one of the key tools an organisation should have in its fight against fraud is an anti-fraud policy that is communicated to its employees. In the Ernst & Young survey 72% of companies did not train their staff on the implementation and understanding of their anti-fraud policy.

A survey by KPMG in 2007 found that in the first 6 months of 2006 fraud losses amounted to £650 million, the highest recorded since 1995. The most likely perpetrators of fraud according to the survey were management.

In 2005, a survey by PricewaterhouseCoopers found that 55% of UK businesses they looked at had been subject to economic crime during 2003/4. During the previous 2 years, 35% of the businesses had experienced fraud in the form of financial misrepresentation undertaken by senior management.

Responsibility for fraud detection remains with management and those charged with governance. ISA 240 states that 'in planning and performing the audit to reduce audit risk to an acceptable level, the auditor should consider the risks of material misstatements in the financial statements due to fraud'. The standard stresses the need to consider fraud when planning the audit and that the auditor must maintain an attitude of professional scepticism. Basically the auditor needs to bear in mind that fraud is always a possibility that must not be ignored. Some examples of what fraud may involve are as follows:

- falsification or alteration of accounting records;
- misappropriation of assets or theft;
- suppression or omission of the effects of transactions from records or documents;
- recording of transactions without substance;
- intentional misapplication of accounting policies;
- wilful misrepresentation of transactions or of the entity's state of affairs.

Frauds are mainly discovered by chance. The main problem is that of financial liability where it is impossible to offer a guarantee that fraud has not taken place. When fraud is suspected, the following procedures should be adopted:

- recheck facts
- restrict questioning to verify suspicion
- retain all records
- establish all suspect areas for size of fraud
- ensure confidential communication lines
- if cash is involved, ensure both the suspect and a witness are present.

There are certain warning signs that may indicate the opportunity for, or possibility of, fraud:

- understaffing in the accounts department
- high turnover of important staff
- excessive payments for services

- incomplete files or altered accounting records
- evasive replies to auditor questions
- failure to take leave.

The management team have the overall responsibility for ensuring procedures are in place to prevent and detect fraud, but they may need assistance from various quarters. These include expert advisors who can help to set up anti-fraud systems, in which case auditors may be able to provide guidance on the need to include specific controls. Procedures can also be put in to place to check on the existence, effective operation and adherence to the controls. In this case, audit, more specifically internal audit, can provide assurances as to whether these controls are working as required. A legal system and internal organisational policy whereby any offenders/perpetrators will be brought to account will also support management in carrying out their responsibilities in relation to fraud. The existence of an anti-fraud policy within the organisation, properly communicated to all staff, is essential here and there is a role for audit to ensure that this policy is reviewed and communicated.

To investigate financial irregularities, auditors must have some knowledge of the law and the process for collecting and dealing with evidence. They must also be clear as to what constitutes a crime and theft. The Fraud Act 2006 states that 'a person is guilty of fraud if they are in breach of false representation, failing to disclose information or abuse of position'. This is slightly different to some senior judge's definition of crime, which claims that it is an act of disobedience or an omission for which some legal punishment may be inflicted. Legally a crime must have two elements, namely 'the *actus reus*' (the physical act) and 'the *mens rea*' (blameworthy state of mind). Both these elements must be proved beyond all reasonable doubt in a court of law in order to secure a criminal conviction. The Fraud Act 2006 updated the Theft Act 1968 and says specifically that if a person abuses their position to make a gain for themselves or to cause loss to another this is considered as fraud. To prove that a gain or loss has taken place, it is important to show that:

- the property belonged to somebody else
- there was an intention to permanently deprive
- the act was an act of dishonesty
- an appropriation took place.

Evidence

In legal terms, evidence is used to indicate the means by which any fact in question or in issue may be proved beyond all reasonable doubt or, for that matter, disproved. To establish this, the auditor should be aware that direct evidence is required, i.e. evidence of facts to be proved given by a witness who is prepared to make a statement of what they have seen, felt, heard or done. This is different from circumstantial evidence, which is a series of other facts, or suspected facts, from which the real fact may be proved or disproved. Hearsay evidence or gossip, which is derived from what one witness has heard another say, is unreliable and not permitted. For criminal prosecutions, courts are only concerned with the

Figure 6.5 **The fraud investigation process**

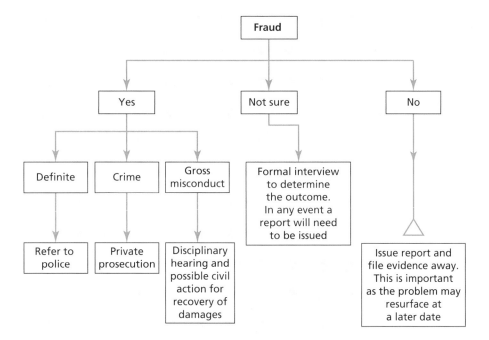

facts, which come from direct evidence alone. Opinions are not relevant unless the witness is a professional expert who is called to express a view.

Once an auditor is in possession of all the facts and evidence, which may be complete or incomplete, they now have to decide what to do. Figure 6.5 provides a systems approach to the procedure to be followed. It illustrates clearly that if a crime against the organisation has been committed then the police are the best people to investigate it and bring the perpetrator to court. However, this does not stop a civil action or a disciplinary hearing at a later date even if the criminal prosecution is lost. This is simply because the weight of evidence is less in civil or disciplinary hearings.

There will be occasions where the auditor is uncertain that the burden of proof is sufficient for either a criminal prosecution or a disciplinary hearing. There may be uncertainties that need to be cleared up before auditors can issue their report. The process for doing this is known as the 'formal interview' and it is carried out under the Police and Criminal Evidence Act 1984 (PACE) and the Criminal Justice Act 1994. PACE, Section 66, provides a code of practice for guidance to police officers and others investigating offences. There are four parts to the code but the most important one deals with the detention, treatment and questioning of suspects. It is basically a test of fairness to uphold the human rights of individuals. Therefore auditors, as investigating officers, must comply with the following:

- introduce themselves by name and position to the suspect;
- tell the suspect why they are being questioned;

- caution the suspect;
- remind the suspect of their rights to seek legal or trade union advice;
- tell the suspect that during the interview notes will be taken;
- if, during the interview, the auditor believes that there is sufficient evidence to succeed with a prosecution, questioning should cease;
- breaks are permissible but should be recorded;
- after the break remind the suspect that they are still under caution.

The words of the caution from the Criminal Justice Act (1994) are as follows: 'You do not have to say anything. But it may harm your defence if you do not mention when questioned something which you later rely on in court. Anything you do say may be given in evidence.' In effect the amendment in 1994 removed the right to silence which the Home Secretary said had been manipulated by professional criminals.

Interviews are usually recorded by handwritten notes and signed. The notes themselves are the direct evidence and not a fully word-processed transcript. This is, in contrast to the police, who prefer to use tape-recorded interviews.

Preparation for the interview is important. Try to use a quiet place where you will not be disturbed. Given the auditee notice of the interview and their right to bring a representative. Prepare a numbered list of questions and highlight which ones are core questions and which are there to just to get the suspect to talk. Very direct questions, if used, should be left to the end. Always use a desk, as this creates a degree of formality. Ensure when you question the suspect that you record their duties and responsibilities. There are frequently discrepancies here and on many occasions poor administration may be the end result of the investigation. The auditor's role is to investigate and at the end to produce a report. Suspects may offer their resignation during the formal interview but this should be rejected. It is a matter between the suspect and the HR department. Very often the suspect will offer to repay the missing sum of money during the interview. This is known as an act of restitution and should be rejected as it may harm the evidence of 'permanently seeking to deprive'. The auditor needs only to make mention of this offer in the report and to make it clear to the suspect that this is being done. An aide-memoire is useful because this can often be a stressful situation and it is very easy to make technical errors. Suspects should feel that they have been treated fairly.

The interview may often end with the suspect making a formal statement, which can be done by themselves or on their behalf by the auditor (see Figure 6.6). Statements must be written in black. Only one side of the statement must be written on. When the statement does not occupy a whole page, the witness or suspect should be asked to sign their name below the last line. The blank space should be closed by a diagonal line initialled by the auditee. The suspect or witness must finally sign their name at the lower left-hand side of the remaining pages of the statement and each page must be properly witnessed. Financial investigations can have major implications for people's careers. They must be carried out properly and in consultation with the company solicitor if necessary.

Figure 6.6 **A specimen witness statement**

WITNESS STATEMENT

Statement of: ....

Age (if over 21 enter over 21): ....

Occupation: ....

Address: ....

....

....

Telephone number: ....

This statement consisting of xx pages, each signed by me, is true to the best of my knowledge and belief and I make it knowing that if it is tendered in evidence, I shall be liable to prosecution if I have wilfully stated in it anything which I know to be false or do not believe to be true.

Signed: ....

Signature witnessed by: ....

Signed: ....

Signature: ....
witnessed by

Summary

The role and importance of statutory audits are highlighted as these are legal requirements. This is differentiated from voluntary audits, which are carried out for different reasons.

The importance of social auditing in its contemporary setting can save management much embarrassment as well as allowing for a refocusing of direction.

Value-for-money (VFM) reviews may be undertaken by anybody with a financial background. It is important to measure economy, efficiency and effectiveness in order to prove that VFM has been achieved. VFM is not just cost reduction; it is the creation of the same level of service, or a better level, at a lower cost. It is important to be able to separate out costs from savings and benefits and to be aware that there are several different approaches to VFM.

Investigating fraud requires a different approach. The auditor will have an understanding of what constitutes a crime and what evidence is required to prove it. Given the quality of the evidence, the auditor should be able to determine the best way to proceed.

? PRACTICE QUESTION

Paul Taylor has recently purchased a brand new, top-of-the-range Mercedes car. He works as a junior cashier receiving cash, cheque and credit payments for a retail furniture store. Recently a large sum of money awaiting collection by the cash-handling agents went missing. This is believed to be in excess of £30,000. You as the store manager receive an anonymous letter suggesting that Paul has stolen the money.

You are required to plan your investigation.

Planning the audit

Objectives

After studying this chapter you should be able to:

- understand the importance of planning an audit;
- describe the resources necessary to complete an audit;
- describe the information required prior to commencing audit work;
- understand the concept of materiality;
- discuss the importance of risk assessment.

Introduction

ISA 300 (UK & Ireland), Planning an Audit of Financial Statements, provides the guiding framework that the auditor should follow when planning the audit engagement. The auditor should develop a plan for the engagement in order to reduce the audit risk to an acceptably low level. Basically ISA 300 states that planning is undertaken to make the audit effective. Planning the audit is not a one-off exercise but an ongoing process that begins shortly after the end of the previous audit and continues until the completion of the current audit activity. In other words, planning is an ongoing activity.

Whilst planning an audit, the auditor should keep in mind that the audit risk is to be kept at an acceptably low level. Audit risk means the risk that the auditor may give an inappropriate audit opinion when the financial statements are materially misstated. The assessment of materiality is made by auditors based on their professional experience or opinion. There is an inverse relationship between materiality and the degree of audit risk. When conducting an audit, auditors should consider materiality and its relationship with audit risk.

Planning of audit time is important in several respects. Knowing the requirements and timescale of the audit ensures that the use of resources can be controlled so as to ensure adequate coverage of areas of risk. Control can be assessed within the agreed letter of engagement and in line with the fees for the audit work. Reporting of progress against planned activities allows management and the Audit Committee to receive assurance of continued audit coverage. Planning of required coverage also provides confirmation of the adequacy of audit resources at the relevant times during the audit. If insufficient time is available to review all the required systems, processes or risks within a cycle, additional resources may be required, and these may need to be sourced in advance. Conversely, there may be additional resources available to increase audit activity and areas identified as high risk during the initial audit planning. Resource availability will not be the only consideration; the skills and abilities of the audit staff to carry out the work will need to be factored into the equation.

The planning cycle

The planning cycle for an audit firm can be placed into three categories:

- strategic planning – where the audit firm considers its own strategic plan in terms of its objectives for the next 3–5 years;
- tactical planning – this refers to the annual plan of the firm where it considers all its clients and how they fit into its plan of activity for the year;
- operational planning – this is specific to the individual client and is often referred to as the audit plan that has been agreed at the outset in the audit engagement letter.

Basically in terms of planning, this is a case of long-term planning, short-term (1 year) planning and the audit task plan.

The auditor needs to carry out the following tasks at the start of an audit engagement:

1. perform procedures regarding the continuance of the client relationship and the specific audit engagement;
2. evaluate compliance with ethical requirements, including independence (ISA (UK & Ireland) 220, Quality Control for an Audit of Financial Statements, provides the guidance for two of these activities);
3. establish an understanding of the terms of the engagement (ISA (UK & Ireland) 210, Agreeing the Terms of Audit Engagements provides the guidance for this activity.)

The reason for carrying out these activities is to ensure that auditors have considered any event which may affect their ability to undertake the audit. Completing the preliminary activities directs the audit planning of the engagement in a manner that ensures:

- auditor independence;
- integrity of management does not hinder the auditor undertaking the audit;
- the terms of the engagement are free from any auditor and client misunderstandings.

The overall planning strategy

The audit strategy sets the scope, timing and direction of the audit and thus provides a framework for the detailed audit plan. ISA (UK & Ireland) 300 uses the following terminology: **audit strategy** → **audit plan** → **audit procedures**.

The purpose of an audit planning strategy is to determine the characteristics and priorities of the engagement that define the financial reporting framework used, industry-specific reporting requirements and the locations of components of the entity to establish the most cost-effective means of achieving the objectives of the audit. A planning strategy will help in ascertaining the reporting objectives and the nature of the communication required and deadlines for interim and final reporting, including the identification of key dates for reporting to those charged with governance.

A plan will assist the auditor in the direction and control of audit work, to ensure attention is devoted to the critical aspects of the work. The plan will also enable a preliminary identification of areas where there may be a high risk of material misstatements. It will also assist in ensuring that the resources are deployed appropriately in terms of numbers and times in the correct areas of the audit. The plan will help to ensure the audit work is completed in accordance with predetermined targets (interim audit stage, or at cut-off dates) and that review is possible of other auditors' work.

Planning will make sure the audit work generates evidence to support the required audit report, and provide a time-frame for briefing meetings pre- and post-audit. It will also assist in identifying how resources are managed, directed and supervised, and identify where and when reviews by the audit partners and managers are to take place.

Once the strategy is established, the auditor is then able to start on the more detailed audit plan. Although the plan does not have to wait until the audit planning strategy is complete, the two planning activities are closely interrelated since changes in one may affect the other. In small entities, the entire audit may be conducted by a very small team, which means communication and co-ordination between all the team members are far easier.

The audit plan

The audit plan is more detailed than the audit strategy and includes the nature, timing and extent of audit procedures. Audit planning is important because it sets the scene for the whole project, provides guidelines as to who does what and when, facilitates the reviewing process, and acts as a performance measure for audit activity. The typical audit planning schedule is as follows:

- to consider the company's background;
- to draw on the audit firm's knowledge of the client's business;
- to develop an outline plan and review last year's file;
- to meet senior management (and other staff);
- to construct an audit team/timetable;
- to undertake an audit briefing for the staff undertaking the audit.

Developing the best audit approach and making the audit fit the client's profile will help reduce the audit risk to an acceptably low level. Making the most of the audit firm's knowledge of the client enables the auditor to get the best out of applying analytical techniques, ensuring that there is a common-sense approach to assessing the audit risk whereby the constituent elements of audit risk, inherent, control and detection risk are all considered. By undertaking an organised approach to audit planning, the auditor can get to grips with the client's procedures and controls, which can facilitate a structured approach to the audit work. Finally by making the audit fit the client's profile, the auditor can ensure that the audit plan focuses the audit so as to make the best use of resources and achieve an audit appropriate to the overall objectives.

ISA (UK & Ireland) 315, Identifying and Assessing Risks of Material Misstatement through Understanding the Entity and its Environment, provides further details on this aspect of planning.

The first stage of audit planning always involves understanding the client's business. The starting point for planning is the needs assessment, which involves identifying all areas of work analysed by systems, cost centres, departments and locations. The nature, timing and extent of audit procedures required to be performed by the audit team and an assessment of the level of risk and vulnerability of each area of work will help to identify where the resources need to be concentrated. Deciding in conjunction with the client the period over which all systems and establishments will be audited and the allocation of frequencies to individual audits will facilitate the planning. Estimating the resources required to meet audit needs will require an experienced audit partner or senior audit manager to identify the risk area, the areas subject to cyclical review and any new areas requiring an audit. If the audit is not one that is for the year end or interim on the financial systems then the type of audit will need to be identified. External auditors spend their audit time forming an opinion on the financial statements. Internal auditors, on the other hand, may find that they undertake a variety of audits, including:

- risk-based audit
- systems-based audit
- transactions-based audit
- substantive audit
- value-for-money audit review
- special investigation audit
- contract audit
- compliance audit
- assurance audit
- forensic audit.

It must be emphasised that this list is not wholly exclusive to internal audit, as in undertaking the financial statement audit the external audit will focus on a risk-based, systems-based audit or forensic audit approach, while internal audit will look more at the other areas.

ISA (UK & Ireland) 330, The Auditor's Responses to Assessed Risks, provides guidance on the plan for further audit procedures.

The value of the audit plan to the audit manager/senior partner

An audit plan motivates those involved in completing the audit by providing pre-determined targets for both senior and junior staff. It assists in the production and control environment of recruitment, promotion, the training programme and continuing professional development (CPD). The plan assists the audit manager to exercise control by providing a yardstick against which the actual performance can be measured in terms of time allocation, output of audit reports and input from specific personnel involved in the audit. It also helps with the budgeting process when matching resource charge-out rates to the work programme.

The plan provides the audit manager with a means of conveying the objectives of the audit office, and ultimately the achievements, to all interested parties. The key aims of the audit plan are to:

- determine the audit approach and identify the type of audit;
- set sample sizes to establish audit evidence;
- assess and respond to audit risk;
- ensure effective control over individual assignments in terms of resources;
- avoid common errors and oversights based on previous audit experience.

Post-audit review

In terms of planning for future audits, post-audit review meetings will help to identify:

- where the audit has gone wrong or could have gone wrong;
- areas where work could have been substantially reduced;

- how the audit work could have been done more quickly;
- how the audit work could have been more cost-effective and devoid of major risks:
- where the opportunity lay for further work in terms of audit investigations and consultancy or systems and procedures.

Additional work

From time to time, circumstances dictate that additional audit work is required, extra to what was originally planned. This can result from poor estimation of time required to complete the planned audit activities or from findings during the audit that mean additional work is necessary in order to satisfy the objectives. Often requests from management for additional work arise due to their own assessment of risks, which may require the auditor to provide feedback as well as levels of assurance. New areas of activity and systems within the organisation not covered in the audit plan may require additional audit review and testing. Finally the discovery of major weaknesses, errors or fraud may dictate that additional resources are required to investigate further, in order to provide guidance or assurances to management.

The alternatives are that planned activity is not achieved if additional time is required, or that an estimate of the impact of such additional work is taken into account at the planning stage. This way an allowance in terms of a percentage of time is included in the plan. The advantage of including such an allowance for unplanned activities is that the plan is more likely to be achieved (although this still may not be the case if more unplanned work than has been allowed for arises). The disadvantage is that if less unplanned activity than anticipated is required, fewer planned activities may be completed than if all the time was accounted for in conducting the planned work.

One solution is to take a flexible approach. This would mean allowing a percentage of time (based on experience, perhaps 10 or 15%) for unexpected work, but to have a list of additional activities to spend audit time on if fewer requirements for additional work arise. These activities might be audits brought forward from the next period in the plan, or they could be additional projects that are desirable but not essential.

In conclusion, experience will allow a judgment to be reached about the likelihood and quantity of unplanned activity. While this cannot, by its nature, be predicted accurately, the planning process can take it into account and avoid the situation where planned work is unduly affected by justifiable additional activity.

Considerations for initial audit engagements

The purpose and objective of planning an audit are the same for both initial and recurring audit engagements. However, when the client is new, auditors may need to undertake additional planning activities because they will not have access to any previous audit information relating to that client.

Where the audit engagement is new, additional matters that may be considered by the auditor include:

- contacting the previous auditor to review their working papers (unless there are any issues prohibited by law);
- any major issues discussed with management in connection with the audit selection and how these might affect the overall audit strategy;
- obtaining sufficient audit evidence by reading opening balances as outlined in ISA (UK & Ireland) 510, Initial Audit Engagements – Opening Balances;
- allocating appropriate auditors with the right level of skills and experience to meet any possible risks in the new audit engagement;
- reviewing the audit firm's own quality control procedures in relation to new appointments, such as the involvement of another partner or senior auditor to review the overall audit strategy.

Direction, supervision and review

ISA (UK & Ireland) 300 states that the auditor should plan the nature, timing and extent of direction and supervision of engagement team members and review of their work.

Direction

An important function in planning the audit is the generation of material necessary for the direction of staff assigned to the audit. Staff need to receive adequate training and guidance as to the nature of the client's business and, in particular, as to any specific matters affecting the audit identified during the planning stage. These may include proposed changes or developments in the nature of the client's business, the governance and management structure or its financial structure.

ISA (UK & Ireland) 220, Quality Control for an Audit of Financial Statements, requires that auditors assigned to an audit receive direction as to such matters to enable them to carry out the audit work assigned to them. A principal aim of planning is to determine the mix of tests of controls and substantive procedures and the nature, timing and extent of those procedures. Audit staff members need to be directed accordingly to ensure that the results of the plan are documented in an audit programme which specifies the individual procedures to be performed in sufficient detail relative to the experience of the staff assigned to the engagement.

Supervision

When junior auditors are assigned to an audit, it is important that they are appropriately supervised. Naturally the more junior or inexperienced the staff, the more supervision will be required. The type of audit and length of audit engagement will dictate the amount of supervision required. On smaller audit engagements, the level of supervision will invariably be in the form of daily contact with the senior, more experienced auditor in charge of the audit. On larger audits there will be a hierarchy of staff at different levels, each with responsibility for supervising and allocating the work of the junior auditors. As part of the supervision, supervisory staff should, during the course of the audit, regularly monitor the work of junior auditors to ensure that:

■ they understand the requirements of each procedure in the audit programme to which they are assigned;
■ they have the necessary skills and competence to perform their assigned tasks;
■ the work performed is in accordance with the requirements of the audit programme.

As part of this supervision process, supervisors should make it clear to all staff involved with the audit that any important matters discovered during the audit are promptly and appropriately dealt with, while any aspects that may affect future audit work should be noted and the audit programme modified as necessary. This will ensure that audit planning is an interactive process throughout the audit engagement and one that involves all members of the audit team. The supervisor should also monitor the time spent on each aspect or stage of the audit against the budgeted time allowances established at the planning phase. If there are significant variances identified during the course of the audit, it may indicate problems in the performance of the auditors or highlight areas of the audit that require additional resources. This, in turn, may reflect on the initial audit plan, which may not be appropriate for the task in hand.

Review

Supervision also involves review of the audit work performed. There is a need to ensure that all work is reviewed to confirm that:

■ the work has been performed in accordance with the objectives identified within the audit plan and audit programme;
■ the evidence gathered and analysed has been properly documented in the appropriate audit working papers;
■ all outstanding matters identified during the audit and any from the previous audit (if applicable) have been resolved to a satisfactory level;
■ the findings and conclusions drawn from the evidence collected are in line with information obtained from other sources and are consistent with the results derived from analytical review so that they support the audit opinion or audit conclusion.

In addition to the review of audit work undertaken to gather evidence obtained as per the audit programme for the client, there needs to be a review at a higher level on the more significant audit decisions made. These include:

■ review of the audit plan and audit programme to confirm it meets with expectations;
■ assessment of inherent and control risk and the proposed audit strategy;
■ reviews of the audit working papers undertaken by staff at an appropriate level of responsibility;
■ review of the proposed audit opinion or audit conclusion based on the overall results of the audit process and audit activity.

Where the audit is a relatively small engagement, the above may not be deemed practical, in which case the overall review may be undertaken by the manager, with oversight by the audit partner that the review has been properly undertaken. For the larger audit engagements, the final review will be undertaken by the audit partner. There may, on occasion, be the need for a second partner to review the audit undertaken, someone who was not involved in the actual audit. This will entail an extra overview prior to the audit report being signed off and is sometimes called a 'hot review'.

Documentation

ISA (UK & Ireland) 300, Planning an Audit of Financial Statements, states that the auditor should document the overall strategy and the audit plan, including any significant changes made during the audit engagement. The audit documentation should record the overall audit strategy identifying the key decisions that influenced the audit plan in terms of scope, timing and conduct of the audit. Any significant changes made to the original audit strategy or audit plan (along with the reasons for theses changes) will also be documented as part of the overall audit documentation for the engagement.

The audit documentation relating to the audit plan should demonstrate the nature, timing and extent of risk assessment procedures. Further information will relate to the audit procedures at the assertion level for each material class of transaction, account balance and disclosure in response to the assessed risks. Invariably the auditor designs standardised audit programmes or checklists that are tailored to meet the different circumstances of the audit engagement. The form and extent of the documentation will depend on the size and complexity of the client, materiality and the nature of any other documentation and the circumstances of the specific audit engagement.

The auditor can communicate the nature of the audit plan to those charged with governance; it is one of the roles of the Audit Committee to consider the overall audit plan for both external and internal audit. The detailed audit plan will, however, remain the auditor's responsibility.

Working papers

ISA (UK & Ireland) 230, Audit Documentation, states that audit documentation (also referred to as audit working papers) is the record of the audit procedures performed during the audit engagement. These will include audit activities performed, tests undertaken, evidence obtained, evaluations, recommendations and conclusions leading to the audit report. If working papers are kept in a proper manner, complete and accurate on a timely basis, then an auditor with no previous connection with the audit engagement will be able to understand the nature, timing and extent of the audit procedures performed. Audit working papers are the property of the auditor and are not a substitute for the proper records that the client should keep in respect of the transactions undertaken. A typical set of working papers can be seen in Exhibit 7.1.

Exhibit 7.1 **A typical set of working papers**

- Information of continuing importance
- Audit planning information
- Auditor's assessment of the accounting system
- Detail of audit work undertaken
- Evidence that the work of audit staff has been reviewed
- Record of relevant balances/financial information
- Summary of significant points and how they were dealt with

Client files

Work relating to the client is filed in a permanent file or a current audit file. Increasingly this is in electronic format. The permanent audit file contains information that relates to the client in terms of standing data applicable on an ongoing nature. Permanent files include the memorandum or articles of association, plus information relating to legal documentation, management structures and, organisational charts.

The current audit file contains information and data relating to the audits undertaken, including standardised control questionnaires and checklists.

Other audit documents

Other documentation associated with the audit includes:

- audit planning budgets;
- audit programmes that are either specific to the audit client or standardised – the plan or audit programme should outline the tests to be performed, including the walk-through test, compliance, substantive and analytical procedures;
- internal control questionnaires (ICQs);
- risk and internal control evaluation questionnaires (ICEQs);
- supporting schedules of accounting records;
- copies of correspondence with management, letters of representation;
- audit summaries, recommendations and queries directed to management on queries identified during the audit;
- audit communication with the Audit Committee in terms of recommendations and interim reports.

Recording the audit work

Audit working papers should always be sufficiently complete, detailed and clear in order that another auditor not involved with the audit can see exactly what the audit work entailed and will reach the same conclusions as the original auditor.

One of the reasons for recording the audit work is to ensure that work allocated to staff has been properly performed; the records can be used later in the annual appraisal of staff within the audit firm. Audit working papers provide evidence of the work performed, detail the problems encountered and conclusions drawn, and can act as a detailed reference for those responsible for drawing together the audit findings/evidence which help to form the audit opinion. The need to prepare working papers encourages the auditor to adopt a methodical approach, which means that others undertaking future audits can extract the relevant information with ease and confidence.

Structured documentation

There are good reasons for having structured and standardised documentation, as it can foster a methodical approach to the audit which helps in the training of auditors.

Structured documents set out the scope of the audit, e.g. the audit programme, which, if adhered to, means that the relevant areas will have been covered within the time-frame established for the audit activity. Structured documents also help to prove what was done, e.g. ICQ/ICEQ (see Chapter 10), providing a set route for the auditor to follow in terms of tasks and questions to ask.

They help to highlight salient points, such as a failure to meet expected levels of activity in certain areas, as well as acting as a facility to check on audit work vis-à-vis the original audit plan – e.g. has the work been undertaken within the budgeted time-frame?

Structured documents are necessary for those charged with supervision and monitoring when reviewing whether the audit has gathered all the evidence and completed all the required tests. Documents and files act as a back-up, supporting the audit's findings in particular when there are controversial issues or questions of fraud and error.

Structured 'paperwork' or electronic files are especially important when detailing the systems in a client's business. The details of various accounting systems and their controls will provide a base for the auditor from which to evaluate the effectiveness of risks therein.

Having a structure to the documents and files is also of value should the Audit Committee request any further details or explanation concerning the recommendations in the audit report. Finally a structured record acts as a basis for follow-up of the current audit and as a starting point for the next audit in evaluating any areas of risk. The ability to produce an electronic record has greatly enhanced the value of standardised documents and files as an audit tool.

Other reasons for structured documentation and standardised electronic files include the following:

- They help with compliance with professional standards.
- The information helps trainee auditors in the completion of their training log.
- They are of benefit to others within the audit firm, especially the audit manager and the partners.
- They are useful to outside agencies, government departments, the Serious Fraud Office and money-laundering task forces.
- The internal audit papers will be subject to external audit review.
- They provide information to audit managers, the Audit Committee and board members.

Performance assessment

Auditors must be able to show that their work has reached an acceptable standard. Audit performance should consist of a mix of quantifiable measures, technical judgments and customer responses. This enables those assessing to review the performance from more than one source and requires:

- audits to be properly planned;
- audits to be supervised and performed by auditors of appropriate experience;
- relevant tests to be devised and properly applied in sufficient depth;
- conclusions to be soundly based on relevant and properly documented facts.

The audit documents and electronic files provide the source of material to support these requirements.

Aspects of audit activity which should be monitored on a regular basis are categorised as follows:

- inputs – the adequacy of the resources available to audit;
- processes – the way in which audit carries out its work;
- outputs – the results of audit work, both the written product and the impact.

Controlling the audit

Controlling the audit is important as it acts as a means to ensure that the work is being performed effectively. The most important elements of control are the direction and the supervision undertaken of the audit staff and the review of their audit work, in terms of the findings, assessments, evaluations and reconciliations. This will be assisted by an established audit approach and standardised documentation, including appropriate audit working papers.

Quality of audit

The quality of an audit depends to a large extent on the exercise of proper judgment by the auditor in planning audit work and choosing audit tests.

In addition to normal day-to-day supervision of internal audit work, formal reviews of performance, carried out by senior staff, will promote a high level of achievement.

In order for audit managers to ensure a good level of achievement, they must be assisted by adequate staff in terms of both quality and numbers. This means having different levels of staff qualifications and experience in the team.

Arrangements for ensuring a quality audit

To ensure a quality audit, the audit team must allocate assignments according to the ability of the auditor. The responsibilities and objectives must be understood by all audit staff, which means holding appropriate briefing meetings to communicate the scope of work to the audit team. The agreed programme of work must be approved by the partner, the audit senior and the audit staff. There must be a process that provides and documents evidence of supervision, which is especially helpful for training purposes, and for review and guidance. Adequate working papers need to be prepared in line with recommended practices and work must be carried out in accordance with the audit plan. Audit partners or managers need to investigate any significant variations form the planned work.

A research report published in 2004 by The Institute of Chartered Accountants of Scotland (ICAS), *AUDITQUAL: Dimensions of Audit Quality* by Angus Duff,[1] recommended the following to improve audit quality:

- Participants in the audit market should recognise that audit quality is multi-dimensional.
- Auditors, financial directors and fund managers rated the technical quality dimensions of reputation and capability the highest. Audit firms and accounting educators should therefore bear in mind the importance of the firm's reputation and the capability of its staff and partners.
- Audit firms can improve audit quality by monitoring clients' perceptions of it and identifying the causes of any shortfalls.
- Firms need to attract high-quality individuals with the necessary technical and interpersonal skills.
- Although it may be desirable for auditors to see themselves as relationship managers selling a complex mix of professional services, over-emphasis of client-centredness could lead to accommodating behaviours. Auditors therefore need to remember that their real client is the end-user of financial statements.

Source: www.icas.org.uk

Audit risk

Also referred to as 'ultimate risk', audit risk is the risk that the auditor will issue an incorrect audit opinion on the financial statements, i.e. that the auditor will give an opinion that the financial statements are fairly presented when they are mis-stated. Irrespective of the amount or quality of audit work undertaken, **no audit is risk-free**.

Can it be eliminated?

Audit risk cannot be completely eliminated, as this would involve the auditor examining every transaction in the financial statements. There has to be a balance between the amount of acceptable risk and the amount of additional audit work necessary to reduce the risk. Most transactions are invariably correctly stated; however, there will be varying degrees of misstatements between different types of organisations. This variation will depend on the complexity, nature and risk management found within the organisation. This will be related to the type of systems in place and the internal controls present to combat any errors, fraud and misstatements.

Figure 7.1 illustrates how audit risk can occur during normal audit activities and that audit risk cannot be completely eliminated.

---

[1]*AUDITQUAL: Dimensions of Audit Quality* by Angus Duff can be obtained from the ICAS Research Centre (contact research@icas.org.uk).

Figure 7.1 **Components of audit risk**

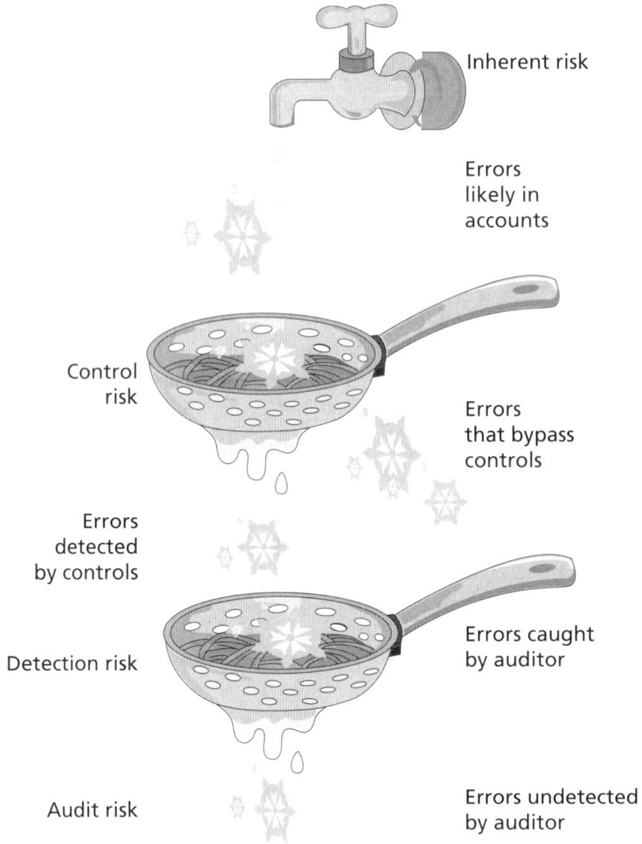

Materiality

Materiality is one of the fundamental concepts of auditing. Materiality recognises the importance of a true and fair view of the financial statements in accordance with established accounting standards. Information is deemed to be material if its misstatement (i.e. omission or incorrect/erroneous statement) can influence the economic decision of users who are basing their decisions on the financial information submitted. Materiality depends very much on the size and nature of the item. Materiality can be subjective in nature as it is often judged according to the particular circumstances of the misstatement.

ISA 320, Materiality in Planning and Performing an Audit, states that 'materiality should be considered by the auditor when determining the nature, timing, extent of risk assessment procedures; and evaluating the risk of material misstatements'.

Financial statements are materially misstated when they contain errors or irregularities whose effect (whether individually or in total) is important enough to affect the true and fair view. These misstatements may occur due to the misapplication of appropriate international accounting standards, whether it is a departure from fact or a failure to include the necessary information. The audit risk that the financial statements are misstated as well as the risk that the auditors failed to detect the misstatements while undertaking the audit comprise only one aspect of misstatements. Some misstatements will be more serious than others; this is where 'material' is used to distinguish between the more serious levels of misstatement. 'Material' in relation to financial statements refers to the amount by which the non-disclosure is likely to distort the view given by the financial statements. There are different levels relating to materiality: for the profit and loss statement, materiality could refer to turnover or to profit, while for the balance sheet it could be based on shareholders' equity, assets or liability class totals.

The level of materiality and the nature of account balances will direct the auditor in terms of identifying which account balances to audit and what audit procedures to undertake – for example, whether to use sampling or analytical procedures. The auditors will consider materiality when determining the nature, the timing and the extent of the audit procedures. Setting materiality parameters can provide guidance as to the work to be undertaken during the audit. Materiality, by its nature, is therefore an important issue to consider during the planning stage of the audit activity. Materiality depends on the size and nature of an item in the surrounding circumstances.

ISA (UK & Ireland) 320 recommends that auditors make preliminary judgments about materiality in planning the audit.

Materiality determined when planning the audit does not mean that items falling below this amount will always be regarded as immaterial. The circumstances surrounding the misstatements may render them material.

The importance of materiality

Materiality gives a level by which accounts can be in error without distorting the overall true and fair view. It influences decisions on the scope and the extent of audit work along with identifying action where errors are found. The audit work should produce evidence that material error is unlikely to exist. Any decisions on the materiality level should be noted in the audit working papers. When several materiality areas are formulated they need to be recorded on the planning section of the audit papers.

Assessing materiality

Different users of the financial statements will have different criteria on materiality. This entails comparing the magnitude of the item with the overall view presented by the accounts, comparing the magnitude of the item with its magnitude in previous years, and comparing the magnitude of the item with the total of which it forms part. Auditors must also consider the presentation and context of an item – they need to think whether it affects the true and fair view. Any statutory issues must be considered as well as bearing in mind that some items are always material, e.g. directors' emoluments.

The auditor's determination of materiality is a matter of personal judgment, and is affected by the auditor's perception of the financial information needs of the users of financial statements. The auditor will assume that:

- users will have reasonable knowledge of business activities;
- understand that financial statements are audited to levels of materiality;
- realise that judgment, estimates and future events can affect the measurement of amounts;
- users can make reasonable economic decisions based on the information within the financial statements.

Qualitative considerations

Qualitative considerations need to be taken into account when materiality is considered during the planning stage. Since the misstatements are an unknown quantity at the outset of an audit, they will only become known during the testing stage of the audit, as evidence becomes available. Qualitative considerations relate to the causes of misstatements or to misstatements that do not have a quantifiable effect. A misstatement that is quantitatively immaterial may be qualitatively material. An example is when the misstatement is attributable to an irregularity or an illegal act by the entity. The discovery of either occurrence might lead to the audit conclusion that there is a significant risk of additional similar misstatements.

In taking into consideration the relevance of risk and materiality, the audit planning process therefore covers:

- identifying all areas of work
- assessment of the level of risk
- establishing materiality levels
- deciding the time period for the audit
- allocating frequencies to the audits
- estimating the resources required
- identifying the type of audit required
- minimum level of cover.

Summary Audit planning encompasses a number of issues from the initial engagement of identifying the nature of the client's business to the assessment of risk, materiality and fraud that will fashion the approach to how the audit is planned and performed. In addition the audit objective linked to the type of audit to be undertaken will provide a framework within which the auditor will have to operate in order to fulfil the required audit.

? PRACTICE QUESTION

You are required to lead a small audit team carrying out a full audit of a medium-sized construction company that specialises in housebuilding projects. The audit will last for 6 weeks and you have five people in your team including yourself.

You are required to prepare an operational plan that highlights the risks involved and how you would carry out the work.

Chapter 8

Co-operative working between auditors and other professionals

Objectives

After studying this chapter you should be able to:

- appreciate the relevance of the client work plan, linking it to the engagement letter through to the working papers and finally the audit report;

- discuss the importance of information technology in the audit work plan;

- appreciate the contribution of others in formulating the overall audit findings and report;

- discuss the requirement that the external auditor has to assess the work of the internal auditor;

- describe how both auditors work together under the oversight of the Audit Committee.

Introduction

There is a set route, or chronology, that an auditor has to follow in order to complete the whole audit activity, as follows:

- determine scope of the audit
- plan and perform the audit
- ascertain, document and confirm the system
- assess, evaluate and test systems and controls
- test and review the financial statements
- express an opinion
- report to management/shareholders
- review and follow up.

Making the audit fit the client is important in terms of completing the audit work. If auditors are to get the best use of resources and comply effectively with the remit, their approach to audit must include:

- making the most of knowledge of the client;
- getting the best out of analytical review;
- adopting a common-sense approach to audit risk;
- getting to grips with client procedures and controls;
- focusing the audit to gain best value.

Audit activity plans will include the total number of clients and their specific requirements based on past audit activities as well as taking on board new ones. This information will need to be incorporated into the workload planning for the audit firm that looks beyond the next audit contract.

The chronology outlined above identifies the workload that the auditor will encounter once the audit has commenced. Prior to the start of the work, the auditor and client will have gone through the process of tendering for the work, an appointment process, discussions with the management and Audit Committee and communicating the outline of the work via an engagement letter.

The letter of engagement

The letter of engagement sets out the arrangements for the audit work. Its purpose is:

- to define responsibilities
- to document and confirm
- to provide written acceptance of the appointment
- to outline the objective and scope of the audit
- to describe the format of the audit report
- to minimise misunderstandings
- to state any non-audit work.

A reply from the client is expected, and this forms the formal 'contract' for the work. The engagement letter is intended to clearly establish not only what the auditor is going to do but also what the auditor is not going to do.

Exhibit 8.1 **An example of the scope of an external audit engagement**

(This outlines what the auditor is expected to do.)

- Undertake a financial review based on a risk assessment
- Ascertain the systems and risks
- Evaluate controls and risks
- Obtain adequate evidence
- Report to members via the audit opinion report
- Report to management (via the Audit Committee) with a detailed management report

The scope may also include reference to any special arrangements that may have been discussed with management and also the legal responsibilities of management in terms of providing information to the auditors.

Content of the engagement letter

The letter will start with an introduction to confirm the appointment with the client. There will also be a definition of the audit (this is a requirement of the Companies Act) and the scope of the audit (this will depend on the client needs and the type of audit to be undertaken – see Exhibit 8.1). The letter will refer to the audit responsibility for the detection and prevention of fraud. It will also include a reference to the management representations that the auditor will expect and the agreed fee, normally based on hourly rate with the anticipated number of person-days to complete the work.

The scope of the external audit engagement is ultimately to comply with legislation in terms of forming an opinion on the financial statements. This means that the audit will provide an opinion as to whether the financial statements give a true and fair view.

The objective of an audit opinion activity, as seen in Exhibit 8.1, is to draw upon the evidence gathered in order to form an opinion. In order to do this, the auditor will have to take on board ISA (UK & Ireland) 500, Audit Evidence, which states that the auditors should obtain sufficient appropriate audit evidence to be able to draw reasonable conclusions on which to base the audit opinion. Audit evidence will need to be sufficient and appropriate, where sufficiency is the measure of the quantity of audit evidence, and appropriateness is the measure of the quality and reliability of the audit evidence.

The quality of evidence will depend on how, where and when the audit evidence is sourced, namely whether it is externally sourced with third party confirmation as to its authenticity or directly by the auditor and is made up of original documents.

The procedures that the auditor employs to gather evidence will vary according to the nature of the transaction and activity, here are some examples:

- inspection of assets, which means a physical inspection;
- inspection of documents, review of electronic ledgers, original third party documents, final statements;
- observation of systems in place, methods employed by staff to complete their tasks, sitting in on processing activities;
- inquiry, from all levels of staff;

- confirmation from staff in terms of issues not clear on testing;
- recalculations/re-performance, reconciliations, matching of data;
- analytical reviews where trends and ratios can be used to confirm test results or expected outcomes.

The procedures chosen will depend on the level of risks associated with the system and sample sizes selected, whether statistical or judgmental. Written evidence is regarded as more reliable than verbal evidence as it cannot be subject to misunderstanding.

In terms of financial statements the auditor will need to confirm the following assertions:

- *Completeness* of the information;
- *Occurrence* in terms of the time at which the event or activity took place;
- *Measurement* in terms of quantity of stock or age of assets;
- *Presentation and disclosure* in the financial statement in terms of depreciation method employed and in terms of adherence to accounting standards;
- *Appropriate valuation* of the assets held and the stock;
- *Rights and obligations* of the organisation in terms of ownership and anything linked to that ownership, e.g. appropriate registration of vehicles in the name of the company;
- *Existence,* whereby the auditor can confirm that book entries are physically present.

Importance of information technology in the audit work plan

Computer-assisted audit techniques

Computer-assisted audit techniques (CAATs) are 'modern' audit tools which use IT facilities for investigative purposes. To some extent it could be argued that the use of CAATs has superseded the principles of sampling previously described earlier. However, there may be circumstances when CAATs cannot be used – perhaps the software is incompatible or maybe the client's system is manual and not computerised. There is always a place for sampling and whilst the traditional auditor will stick to their random or attribute-based approach, the young undergraduate or trainee accountant will want to operate in a computerised environment.

Examples of CAATs include test packs and general audit software, which includes both in-house and off-the-shelf designed specific audit software.

Test packs

The test pack is a technique that is designed to test the reliability of internal controls incorporated into the client's systems and programs. For example, computer programs can have an edit facility whereby items that don't meet the specific requirement are rejected or printed out on an exception sheet for investigation and resubmission. The use of test packs is straightforward and doesn't need a sophisticated knowledge of computing. From compliance test interviews, the auditor may have ascertained that data will be rejected if certain conditions are not met.

Consider the following conditions relating to payroll audit:

- personnel authorisation is set up and there is HR approval for the employee to be paid;
- all employees will have a National Insurance (NI) number and a tax code;
- all employees will have an employee number in an acceptable format;
- all employees to have proper banking facilities.

In this example the auditor will put together a dummy pack of information which will break all the above conditions. Soon the auditor will be in a position to look back and see whether the 'detective' internal controls have done their job.

When test packs are being used, it is essential for the auditor to obtain approval from their superiors and to alert senior management of the procedure. This is done for the auditor's own protection. It would be rather embarrassing to be seen to input data into the system to pay employees who simply do not exist. Secondly the auditor must be alert to the danger of contaminating the client's records and financial information systems. Sometimes if data is accepted, it will update the accounting records unless reversed.

General audit software

In contrast to test packs, here the auditor uses audit software known as computer audit programs. They do range in their degree of sophistication. At the top end they are bespoke programs designed by a specialist computer auditor or by consultants or a programmer engaged by the auditor to join the audit team. In this instance, the auditor designs the tests as part of the software and, when processed, they perform a wide range of procedures from analytical review to testing transactions or account balances.

The most common type of software is the retrieval package. Sometimes this software is part of the client's operating system but in other cases it is provided by the auditor. The functions provided include the reading of computer files, performing calculations if necessary, making comparisons or reading and selecting data that does not conform to a certain pattern. For example, when auditing a payroll system of a company that has 150,000 employees it is not possible to examine every record, and as an alternative to sampling the auditor may set a series of tests to interrogate the client's payroll system. These tests are as follows:

- all employees to be under the age of 65;
- all overtime levels to be less than £1,000 per month;
- all employees to have a proper tax code and NI number;
- all expenses to be less than £200 per month;
- no employees to have a duplicate pay number;
- all employees to have a bank sort code and account number.

In this example the auditor has built six tests or parameters into the software which interrogates the payroll system. All 150,000 employees therefore undergo these tests. Any record that fails one of these hurdles is known as a 'hit'. The auditor will receive a printout or a list of items on screen detailing the numbers of each employee and which test they have failed. This now allows the auditor the time to examine a realistic sample of employees who don't conform to the organisation's procedures. However, it is worth reflecting on the parameters set. If auditing a department of travelling representatives, the parameter of travel expenses will be set too low at £100 per month. All staff may fail the test and the auditor will then be faced with the choice of having to work with a very large sample or revising and re-running the program. This is where the auditor must exercise judgment when reviewing the outcome of the test.

There are also enquiry programs available on packages used to sort, total, check and retrieve data for audit purposes from analytical review to providing auditor records.

The enquiry package may be used for some basic tests. For example, in a payments system the enquiry package may compare supplier details and amounts. Two records that appear the same will be listed as the auditor enquires into the possibility of duplicate payments. The auditor is therefore provided with information that requires investigation. However, all 'hits' do not necessarily mean there are errors. In the case of periodical payments such as monthly rentals it is obvious that the supplier number and the payment amount will be the same.

In another example the auditor may want to use the enquiry software to provide a list of balances or to provide information on the provision of housing stock according to types and amounts of bedrooms.

Organisations rely heavily on computerised systems to process data and therefore audit software will be invaluable to the auditor.

Computer-assisted audit techniques enable the auditor to complete the audit in a manner that both increases efficiency and allows large volumes of data to be reviewed electronically. To summarise, the use of IT in audit can mean that examination of data is more rapid and more accurate and can often be the only practical means of examining large volumes of data. Once set up, the cost of the exercise is relatively low, and the audit becomes more credible in the eyes of the client. The use of computers to audit computerised systems means that the auditor is auditing throughout the computer and not around the computer. Computer packs become audit juniors to sift through data and undertake some of the mundane tasks.

Audit software such as IDEA (Interactive Data Extraction and Analysis), developed by the Canadian Institute of Accountants, is an example of interrogation software, providing access to client files that enables comparison and analysis of data held by various programs. Interactive software allows for interrogation of online systems while resident code software provides the ability to review transactions as they are processed.

On the down-side, computerised information systems lack visible evidence. Normal accounting systems have inputs, processes and outputs; these are often computerised transactions and are not always evident. Input documents may not exist, e.g. online ordering, while discounts may be generated by the computer without any visible authorisation. There may be a lack of an audit trail of evidence when transactions are processed, e.g. customer credit limits may only appear on an exception basis. In terms of physical evidence, output reports may not be produced by the system, and any printed reports may be in summary format only.

In collecting evidence the audit will itself generate evidence in the form of audit working papers, which can be in the form of hard copies or, increasingly, in electronic format. Whichever format they take, it is important that they should be sufficiently complete, detailed and clear. It is also important that, should another auditor not involved with the audit be required to take over the audit, they would be able to appreciate what the audit entailed and reach the same conclusions as the original auditor.

Structured audit documentation

Structured audit 'documentation', either a paper version or an electronic version, plays an important role in the audit. A 'typical' set of electronic audit working papers will have:

- information of continuing importance;
- audit planning information;
- the auditor's assessment of the accounting system;
- details of the audit work undertaken;
- evidence that audit staff work has been reviewed;
- a record of relevant balances/financial information;
- a summary of significant points and how they were dealt with;
- a draft copy of the management letter and the response from management, if applicable;
- recommendations and report to the Audit Committee.

Using the work of others

Using the work of others means that auditors are looking for expertise other than their own. Some aspects of audit will mean a reliance on professionals other than the auditor. These include asset verification, stock verification and valuation of certain assets. The 'others' may include surveyors, engineers, architects, contractors and specialists in the area of art. Auditors may also need to rely on other auditors when subsidiaries are located elsewhere, while findings of specialist auditors may need to be incorporated into the overall audit report, such as forensic audit activities.

Using the work of an expert

When considering whether to use the work of an expert, auditors should review the importance of the matter under consideration and assess the risk of misstatement, which will depend on the nature and complexity of the matter. In addition, the quantity and quality of other available relevant supporting audit evidence may need to be used to confirm the additional work undertaken by others. The competence of the expert will have to be considered in terms of the professional certification of the firm or individuals concerned in delivering the work to be relied upon. The experience and reputation will be assessed along with any related issues or impact on the subjectivity due to any relationship with the client that the expert may have.

The auditor will therefore need to review the work of the expert in terms of the source data used and assumptions made, bear in mind any inconsistencies with other audit evidence, and also confirm the qualifications of the expert. The auditor will need to assess the appropriateness of the expert's findings as audit evidence in relation to the assertions made. If the outcome of the expert's work does not give sufficient and appropriate audit evidence, or if the results are not in line with other audit evidence, the auditor will have to resolve the issue.

ISA (UK & Ireland) 620, Using the Work of an Auditor's Expert, defines an expert as:

■ an auditor's expert possessing expertise in fields other than accounting or auditing;
■ in possession of expertise including skills, knowledge and experience in a particular field;
■ a management expert representing expertise used by the entity in preparing the financial statements.

Although the auditor may use the work of an expert, the auditor has sole responsibility for the audit opinion. If auditors are unable to obtain sufficient appropriate audit evidence in relation to the work undertaken by the expert, they may need to consider modifying their report. When auditors issue an unqualified audit report, they should not refer to the work and evidence provided by the expert, as doing so might lead to a misunderstanding in terms of the qualification of the auditor's opinion, or give an indication of a division of responsibility.

Using the work of another auditor

ISA (UK & Ireland) 600, Special Considerations – Audits of Group Financial Statements (Including the Work of Component Auditors), states that when the principal auditor plans to use the work of other auditors, the principal auditor should consider the professional competence of the auditor in the context of the specific assignment. In the same way that using the work of an expert requires an assessment of the professional qualification of that expert, so must the qualifications of the other auditors be taken in account – including the professional qualification, experience and resources of the other component auditors in the context of the specific assignment. The principal auditor should consider the significant findings of the other component auditors.

ISA 600 states that:

■ the auditor of the group financial statements must communicate clearly with component auditors about the scope and timing of the work;
■ the auditor obtains sufficient appropriate evidence about the financial information of the components and consolidation process to form an opinion.

There are instances, however, when the division of responsibility in terms of the principal auditor and the other auditors can occur due to local regulations in some countries. These will permit a principal auditor to base the audit opinion on the financial statements taken as a whole solely upon the report of another auditor regarding the audit of one or more of the elements being audited. When the principal auditor follows this path, the principal auditor's opinion report needs to state this fact clearly and must indicate the magnitude of the portion of the financial statements that have been audited by the other auditor.

Use of internal audit work by the external auditor

The objectives of internal audit are different from those of the external auditor, but their audit work is very similar: they both adhere to international auditing standards, both have ethical codes of practice and both are expected to act in an independent manner. Often the areas audited are the same and for this reason it makes sense for the external auditor to use the expertise of the internal auditor. ISA (UK & Ireland) 610, Using the Work of Internal Auditors, outlines the situation for considering the work of internal audit from the point of view of the external auditor.

The external audit is required to review the work of the internal audit function, but before placing reliance on the work of the internal audit, the external audit will assess the independence of internal audit and the scope and objectives of internal audit. It will consider whether internal audit exercised due professional care, the technical competence of internal audit, the standard of reporting and how the resourcing of the internal audit function was achieved. External audit will also review the attitude of management towards internal audit.

The scope and objectives of internal auditing include monitoring of internal control, examination of financial operating information, review of value-for- money activities, review of compliance with legislation, regulations and other external requirements with management polices and directives, and provision of assurances to management on systems of control and risk management, plus special investigations into particular areas. The role of internal audit is determined by management, and as part of the organisation it cannot be as independent as the external auditor, but this independence is supported by independence of mind, commonly referred to as objectivity. ISA 610 states that the external auditor should obtain a sufficient understanding of internal audit activities to identify and assess the risk of material misstatements of the financial statements and to design and perform further audit procedures. When the external auditor intends to use specific work of internal auditing, the external auditor should evaluate and perform audit procedures on that work to confirm its adequacy for the external auditor's purpose.

Assessment of internal audit by the external auditor

The adequacy of internal audit is measured in terms of the number of internal audit staff within the department or entity and whether they are qualified auditors. In-house training and professional training programmes followed are also of relevance, e.g. internal audit (Institute of Internal Auditors) qualification or accounting qualification, Association of Accounting Technicians or other Consultative Committee of Accountancy Bodies qualifications. The job specifications and any non-audit work undertaken by internal audit should also be considered, as well as the audit manuals, audit programmes, questionnaires and instructions developed and used, and the level of computer knowledge and the use of CAATs by internal audit. The status of the chief internal auditor/head of internal audit function should be ascertained in terms of independence, responsibility and relationship with the Audit Committee.

External audit review of internal audit

The review of internal audit in terms of documents will include audit files, audit plans, progress records, audit programmes, systems, flowcharts, internal control questionnaires (ICQs) and sampling techniques.

External audit will assess the effectiveness of internal audit based on the reports produced and their content. It will identify the recipients of the reports, such as the Audit Committee and relevant managers, and the responses by management and any action on the recommendations suggested by internal audit. External audit will assess the depth of check tests on internal audit work based on risk assessment affecting the audit of financial statements.

ISA (UK & Ireland) 610 states that:

- The external auditor shall consider the nature and scope of specific work performed by internal audit.
- The assessed risk of material misstatement of transactions, balances and disclosures.
- The degree of subjectivity involved in the evaluation of audit evidence gathered by internal audit.

In summary, the issues to consider when assessing the level of reliance on internal auditors' work are as follows:

- the materiality of the areas/items tested or the information to be obtained;
- the level of audit risk inherent in the areas/items tested or of the information obtained;
- the level of judgment required;
- the sufficiency of complementary audit evidence;
- the specialist skills possessed by internal audit personnel.

The McKinsey 7-S framework

A benchmark for the effective utilisation of internal audit by external audit firms is the McKinsey 7-S framework. Developed by global management consultancy firm McKinsey from 'The art of Japanese management' and 'Search for excellence' theories based on the successful management of Japanese companies in the late 1970s, the framework contains seven factors: three hard factors (structure, systems and strategy) and four soft factors (style, staff, skills and shared values) (see Figure 8.1).

In terms of audit, it is anticipated that organisations with proper and objective interaction of executive management, internal audit, Audit Committees and external audit firms, in the context of the seven factors in the framework, will lend themselves to a better external audit process.

The seven factors in the framework can be explained as follows:

- *structure* – this factor represents the way the organisation's units relate to each other: centralised, decentralised, functional, matrix or networked;

Figure 8.1 **The McKinsey 7-S Framework**

Source: McKinsey & Company (UK).

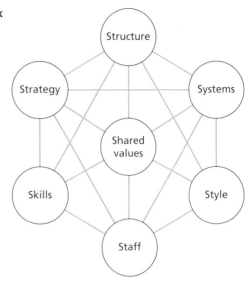

- *systems* – these are the procedures, processes and routines that characterise how the work should be done;
- *strategy* – plans for allocation of the organisation's scarce resources to reach the identified goals;
- *style* – represents the culture of the organisation and how management behave in achieving the organisation's goal;
- *staff* – represents the number and type of personnel within the organisation;
- *skill* – represents the distinctive capabilities of personnel or of the organisation as a whole;
- *shared values* – this factor represents what the organisation stands for and what it believes in.

Working effectively with other review and assurance agencies (external and internal)

When the audit function works with other review and assurance agencies, there are distinct quality benefits. Knowledge sharing allows a greater level of assurance and higher quality as there are more individuals involved, something that can be beneficial across the board. Cross-fertilisation of working practices can lead to greater synergy and understanding. There will be greater reliability of overall assurances due to increased volume of activity through non-duplication of effort and complementary review activity. The involvement of others will also enhance and widen the skills and experience base of the auditors. The cost benefits will mean that there will be more efficient and economic assurance activity due to the fact that assurance providers will not be duplicating their efforts, resulting in greater coverage with an increased opportunity for a variety of reporting and review.

There will be an opportunity to reduce staff numbers in some assurance functions if they are appropriately co-ordinated, although the role of the audit assurance function should not be regarded as something that can be replaced by others. There is an argument that if the internal assurance activity is being undertaken in a joined-up and holistic framework then there will be less demand for the external assurance function, or at least there will be a reduction in the amount of external activity.

The time benefits will include less time spent 'getting up to speed' on specialist subject areas when there are others with the appropriate expertise who can be relied upon. Less time will be spent within the business hosting poorly co-ordinated reviews, and systems and documents will not be reviewed by four or five different agencies, all looking at the same thing. This will do away with the confusion between internal and external audit where staff often think they are one and the same, frequently asking 'Weren't you just here?' ('No, that was external audit.') The merits of joint programmes will allow joint teams or task-based groups to be established to review areas of mutual interest and concern, saving time for all involved.

The scope benefits can be categorised in terms of risk assessment being co-ordinated and covered by one team rather than both, allowing more time to focus on assessing key risks not covered by the other assurance function, thereby increasing the reliability of the findings.

Outsourcing internal audit

In the above discussion, the assumption has been that the internal audit is an in-house department within the organisation; however, there are many organisations that employ an internal audit function that is outsourced. Many organisations find that the provision of an in-house internal audit function is not feasible due to the costs involved. Also the internal audit function has changed so considerably in the last decade that establishing a fully functional internal audit department would not only be costly but also time-consuming and possibly unproductive.

The solution, therefore, is to outsource the internal audit in order to capitalise on established skills and know-how. The scope of the audit work undertaken and the responsibilities are the same.

Advantages

One advantage of outsourcing internal audit mean is there will be access to a wide range of special knowledge and expertise which the entity may not be able to develop in-house, such as computer audit skills. Flexible resourcing will enable the internal audit function to meet peaks of audit activity as required without maintaining a fully staffed permanent function. There will also be a strategy in place to focus management's attention on the key business activities of the entity, which can reduce or eliminate non-core activities that have been formally undertaken by an in-house audit function. There is an argument that outsourcing can lead to cost savings due to economies of scale when the audit provider also provides internal audit services for similar organisations and the skills and knowledge gained elsewhere can be utilised to the advantage of the organisation. The tendering process can lead to good use of resources in terms of value for money through competitive tendering of the service provision.

Disadvantages

There are, however, some disadvantages to outsourcing internal audit which the organisation may have to bear in mind should it decide to do this. Conflicts of interest may arise when the service provider is reluctant to challenge senior management for fear of losing the business; the financial benefits will outweigh the audit role of questioning systems of the organisation. A reduction in organisational knowledge will be a feature during the initial period as will the lack of insider knowledge of what the grapevine might provide, and thus the effectiveness of the internal audit function may be lower than if it were in-house. A reduction in staffing stability and in the continuity and quality of service from an outsourced provider may occur due to turnover of staff or deployment in other organisations. The loss of in-house expertise can lead to over-dependence on the outsourced provider. Despite what may seem a reduction in cost in the short term, the organisation will be vulnerable to future cost increases, which may be the only option as there will not be an in-house provider.

Summary The audit work plan provides a sound framework to ensure that all aspects are considered during the audit. Appropriate documentation, evidence collection, maintenance of working papers and reliance on both internal audit and other experts all provide the basis for the auditor to complete the audit activity leading to the preparation of the audit report.

? PRACTICE QUESTION

What are the advantages and disadvantages of outsourcing the internal audit function?

Chapter 9

Internal control and systems audit

Objectives

After studying this chapter you should be able to:

- identify high-risk areas;
- link risk to control in relation to auditing;
- understand the importance of analytical review;
- define internal control and be aware of its relevance;
- link internal control to systems control objectives;
- identify key controls and how they relate to systems control objectives;
- understand the different types of audit testing;
- relate the concept of control to the business.

Introduction

Risk is a daily problem and cannot be ignored – it must therefore be managed. In the most extreme situations, risk can cause major financial embarrassment and severe financial hardship. It can even result in the bankruptcy of the corporation, just as Nick Leeson's unchecked wrongdoings resulted in the collapse of Barings Bank. Many risks faced by an organisation are small and will lead to losses which, although they may cause annoyance and customer complaint, will not result in any degree of hardship to the company and merely be grounds for management disappointment (if trade is lost) or disciplinary action.

Systems process transactions and within any system there has to be an element of control to prevent error, fraud or poor administration. The auditor in the 21st century is driven by a systems-based approach to audit. While professional accounting bodies long preached the wisdom of a systems-based approach, it was only after a succession of major financial scandals and outright fraud that the British government of the day realised it had to make some changes. It could easily have legislated but decided that financial institutions must put themselves in order, or at the very least be given that chance. A succession of corporate governance reports in the UK, discussed in detail in Chapter 5, moved organisations towards a control-based environment. In the USA The Sarbanes-Oxley Act 2002 moved the American model towards a harder control environment. In any event, the overriding conclusion in all of this is that systems must have controls and these controls must be identified and tested at regular intervals. It is the auditors' role to do this, acting as 'policeman', repeatedly identifying systems, identifying and measuring risks, highlighting and analysing controls and then testing them before finally reporting back to the highest level of management. This political shift towards a tighter control environment results from a greater awareness at boardroom level that the highest level of management bears ultimate responsibility for internal control and risk management. The various corporate governance committees advocated that an effective internal control system is an essential part of the efficient management of a company. They recommend that directors should report on the effectiveness of their system of internal control, and that auditors should report on their statement. The Financial Reporting Council (FRC) takes the leading role as follows:

- developing a set of criteria for assessing effectiveness;
- developing guidance for companies on the form in which directors should report;
- developing guidance for auditors on relevant audit procedures and the form in which auditors should report.

Risk

A good definition of risk is the possibility of meeting danger or suffering harm or loss. One thing is almost certain and that is that the worst thing that can happen to an entity will happen – and usually at the worst possible time. It is therefore

Figure 9.1 **Risk identification and management**

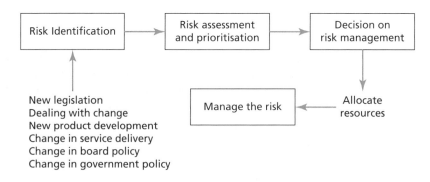

Figure 9.2 **Hierarchy of internal control**

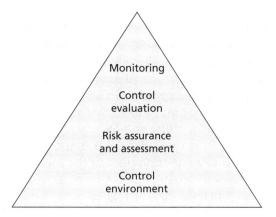

important that an organisation's control environment functions in a manner that will identify the risk it faces and ensure the management has a chance to deal with it. It is always essential for management to think through and identify risk as illustrated in Figure 9.1.

Internal audit can provide assurances that procedures are in place to support the risk assessment process. Risk management must therefore be as part of a control environment, as illustrated in Figure 9.2.

Internal control

Internal control is best defined on the whole range of controls, both financial and managerial, necessary to protect the organisation against waste, mismanagement and fraud. Management must ensure that proper records, systems, assets and personnel are in place as necessary for the adequate fulfilment of their responsibilities. Control means to regulate, check, constrain and limit, and auditors are interested in measures that perform these functions.

It is a management responsibility to determine the extent of internal control in an organisation's systems and they should not depend on internal audit as a substitute for effective controls. Internal audit, as a service to the organisation, contributes to internal control by examining, evaluating and reporting to management on its adequacy and effectiveness. Internal audit activity may lead to the strengthening of internal control as a result of management's response.

It is a management responsibility to maintain the internal control system and to ensure that an organisation's resources are properly applied in the manner, and to the activities, intended. This includes responsibility for the prevention and detection of fraud and other illegal acts.

The internal auditor should be aware of the possibility of such malpractice and should seek to identify serious defects in internal control which might permit the occurrence of such an event.

An internal auditor who discovers evidence of, or suspects, malpractice should report firm evidence, or reasonable suspicions, to the appropriate level of management. It is then a management responsibility to determine what further action to take.

It can be clearly seen, therefore, that the ultimate responsibility for controls, malpractice and fraud rests with the highest level of management. The directors must now provide an assurance to the shareholders that the organisation is a going concern and that all necessary internal controls are in place. Clearly they need the auditor's help in this matter, firstly, to advise them on controls and, secondly, to test them at regular intervals. The auditor within the organisation must therefore report to the highest level of management, unedited, in his or her own name. Unless this is done, audit independence is compromised and management is failing to make full use of a key resource.

Whilst internal control is enhanced by the corporate governance framework and management is ultimately accountable, it is unlikely that they will want to become involved in the operational duties. These are left to internal audit, who act as the internal watchdog for the organisation, and report to the Audit Committee, who in turn relay the outcome to the board. Hence the directors of the company rely heavily on the work of internal audit to provide assurance to management, shareholders and other stakeholders.

Internal control can be broken down as shown in Figure 9.3. Internal check involves a subdivision of duties, so that no one person processes the entire financial transaction through a system. In other words, the work of one person acts as a check on another. Of course, the risk of collusion always exists, but at least it is minimised. Consider the example of collection of income. A clerk sends out the invoice, while the cashier collects the money and arranges the banking. The accounts department then ensures that the ledger is posted and the bank statement is reconciled. Of course, if the debt is not paid, a debt-collecting officer will arrange recovery procedures, and ultimately it will be written off if it becomes uncollectable. If an internal check were not in place in the system, the customer would merely pay the invoice clerk and this would enhance the temptation for both parties to gain from the transactions. With internal check, one person

Figure 9.3 **The internal control model**

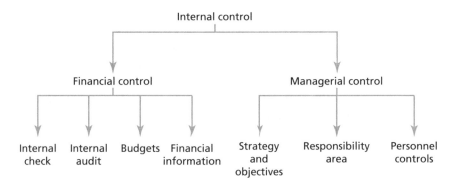

within the system simply checks the work of another on a regular basis. Hence a psychological process starts to work, often without people realising it. If an administrator is to gain from a transaction for fraudulent reasons, they must co-ordinate or collude with a colleague. This will fall apart if they or their colleague goes off sick or takes a holiday and somebody else becomes involved in the checking. Internal audit will without doubt review the degree of internal checking within the system. If it is weak, they will test it further than if it is strong, and vice versa. Internal check is one of the first warning indicators for auditors to concern themselves with.

Internal audit is also a control within an organisation. It is an appraisal function necessary to evaluate, monitor, test and report on the whole range of controls to the highest level of management unedited. Internal audit must not be used as a substitute for a control but as a vehicle to test which controls are in place.

All large organisations should have an internal audit section in place in order to comply with the Sarbanes-Oxley Act (2002) or the UK Combined Code of Corporate Governance (2003) to which London Stock Exchange listed companies and those applying for listing must adhere.

Controls, however, are expensive and must, clearly, be seen to work. To measure whether a control is effective it must have one or more of the following characteristics:

- It must be preventative.
- It must be detective.
- It must be corrective.

Controls are necessary so that unpredictable events are managed within the organisation. A control system defines areas of responsibility and ensures that the business is managed in the most appropriate way.

Each management accounting system will have in built layers of controls to deal with problems, both expected and unexpected, and to provide both feedback and feed-forward information. Some practitioners talk about cybernetic control systems, which identify system control objectives and key controls. They then test the control, identify any discrepancies and correct them, providing information to the responsible manager. This is known as management feedback. It can be compared and contrasted with feed-forward controls, which prevent a future deviation from occurring. Examples of this are the use of critical path analysis or a cash budget, used to plan for future cash discrepancies.

A large and complex business organisation should have the following important characteristics:

- roles and jobs are clearly defined and established; a structure of job specifications exists;
- stability – the climate is certain and clear to all who work within the company;
- an ability to manage change.

Within this framework the main concept is to put in place a system which enables the entity to adopt to a changing world by updating work-related practices to meet the modern competitor environment.

Control theory is best explained by a cybernetic control model, which is a well known and well used model (see Figure 9.4).In this model feedback must be related to the organisation's objectives. Feedback relates to past performance and may be negative or positive. Feeding forward relates to the future and may allow for predictive forecasts to be made. Within any control system there must be a clear strategy, laid down and communicated. A plan, rule book, financial regulations, targets and budgets should exist and be communicated.

ISA (UK & Ireland) 300, Planning an Audit of Financial Statements, requires auditors to:

- obtain an understanding of the accounting systems and internal control systems to plan the audit;

Figure 9.4 **The cybernetic control model**

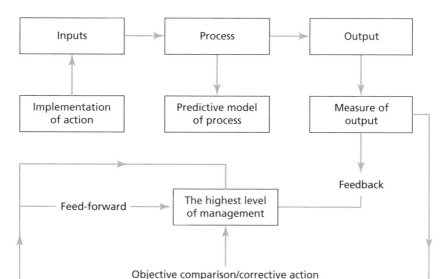

- when planning the audit, obtain and document the system and the control environment on which to determine their approach and form a judgment.

Internal control includes:

- ensuring separation of duties exists;
- approval and control of documents or online transactions;
- controls over computerised applications;
- reviewing and maintaining control accounts and trial balances;
- ensuring reconciliations exist as necessary;
- comparing internal to external data;
- limiting physical access to assets and records;
- ensuring security is paramount;
- ensuring organisational controls are present from a managerial perspective;
- ascertaining that figures add up;
- ensuring proper supervision and training exists;
- ensuring a personnel function is in place;
- ensuring management receive adequate feedback and feed-forward.

It is always easier to evaluate and document internal control when there is a clear strategy and when roles and responsibilities are well known.

Organisational scientists agree that organisations do not so much identify objectives as operate as a political process in which various interest groups seek to identify areas of agreement. Generally, it is easier to reach agreement on actions to be taken (means) rather than objectives (ends).

In addition, in this process of compromise, all stakeholders in the company have a role of play, including managers, employees, shareholders, customers and perhaps even the government. Figure 9.5 shows this diagrammatically.

Contingency theory states that organisations are influenced by their environment, history, ownership, competitiveness and management style. Each organisation is unique and has its own culture. The structure of control systems within

Figure 9.5 **The key players with the key objective that all parties can agree on**

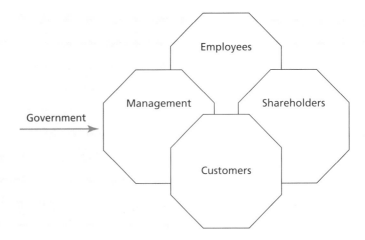

the management accounting system must therefore fit this culture. As a result, there is therefore no one system that can be prescribed for all organisations.

In order for control to exist, certain conditions are essential and must be met:

- Objectives must exist – if there are no objectives, control has no meaning.
- Output must be measurable.
- There must be a predictive model of the process being controlled. It should be possible to take corrective action so as to achieve the objectives.

The absence of any one of these conditions means there is a lack of control.

Questions to managers should be directly related to risks and objectives. The key aspects relating to control is that they are expensive and contribute to the constraint of freedom within the organisation. When recommending controls, the auditor should consider those that are simple, complete, intelligible, reasonable, strong and provide security and validity.

Systems-based auditing

A system is defined as a series of related procedures designed to achieve some overall objective. In essence, transactions are processed by systems. Controls ensure that only valid transactions are recognised, authorised, classified, summarised and reported within the objectives of the system. However, systems interact and need to be broken down into auditable units.

A systems-based approach would follow the procedures shown in Figure 9.6.

Figure 9.6 **A systems-based approach**

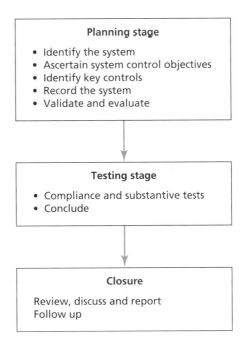

133

Planning

Auditors should use their personal experience and knowledge to plan the audit by identifying the key systems control objectives. The audit file will contain details of previous audits, minutes, flowcharts and correspondence. It is important that points of follow-up from the last audit are noted.

It is important to consider the control objectives within the system. These are clear statements about what the auditor thinks the controls within the system should be trying to achieve. For example, in a payroll system one systems control objective (amongst others) should be that the right people are paid the right amount at the right time. Another example in a payments to suppliers system is that goods and services paid for are used for authorised purposes only.

Once system's control objectives have been established, they need to be linked with key controls which ensure that:

- processing operates effectively;
- assets are safeguarded;
- records are complete, reliable and accurate;
- statutory requirements are met;
- management directives are met.

It must not be forgotten that whilst controls are necessary, they may need justification because they are expensive. However, once identified they will need to be cross-referenced to systems control objectives.

Internal control evaluation sheets should be used to document the evaluation process. Alongside each control objective the relevant control(s) should be recorded with the auditor's assessment as to whether the control meets the control objective; this must be cross-referenced to subsequent compliance or substantive tests.

Systems control objectives should cover the following areas:

- Segregation of duties is adequate.
- Payroll data is accurately processed.
- Permanent and temporary variations to the payroll are valid and properly authorised.

Evaluating a system

The steps to evaluating a systems are as follows:

1. Identify the systems control objectives.
2. Select the key controls that achieve these objectives, and upon which internal audit intends to rely.
3. Identify the control weaknesses of the system.
4. Identify the types of errors and irregularities that might occur and determine where audit tests should be focused.

Key controls

Key controls are important internal controls which are selected by the auditor and upon which it is intended to place reliance as part of the audit. They should:

- contribute significantly towards ensuring that a system produces reliable information or output;

- determine the degree of reliance internal audit can place on the system, in order to minimise the level of substantive testing;
- be capable of verification.

For example, in the case of a payroll audit, one systems control objective would be that all permanent staff added to the payroll are valid. Key controls to satisfy this objective would be:

- All additions (starters) to the payroll are supported by properly authorised documentation.
- All new staff brings with them a tax code and NI number.
- Staff on the payroll exist and are properly employed.

The auditor is then in a position to go out into the field and to ascertain and record the actual system as it exists. Of course, this may have been done already and appropriate details can be taken from the audit file. However, it may be appropriate to consider fully recording and documenting the system from scratch. This can be done in a variety of ways:

- *Interviews* are the most popular method of ascertaining the system. Of course, this means that auditors must make an appointment and not just turn up. They should explain the purpose and the remit of the audit and why it is being done. It is essential that the manager is given the chance to feed into the audit with any points or concerns they have. In such circumstances, the auditor in a future report should acknowledge the source of the comment and not take full credit for it in the report at the end. Any interview must be supported by observation and inspection.
- *Questionnaires.* These can take several formats: internal control checklists (ICCs) and internal control evaluation questionnaires (ICEQs) are probably the most common. Some auditors enjoy this approach as it enables them to learn quickly about the system. Other auditors feel that it stifles their initiative. It is advisable that if a questionnaire is used, it should be followed up by observation and inspection.
- *Flowcharting.* This means recording the system in diagram form. Modern software has brought this back into fashion.
- *Walkthrough.* This is sometimes called a 'Cardiff check' or 'cradle to the grave test'. It involves tracing a transaction through a system from start to finish to see how things work and how the transaction interacts with the manual staff.

Having documented the system, the auditor will be in a position to reflect. How do the actual key controls laid down meet the systems control objectives? Are the controls operating satisfactorily in the period which is being reviewed?

The auditor must now think of risk and potential sources for error or mistake. Concentrating on the key controls they must ask the following questions:

- Are the controls absent?
- Are the controls inadequate?
- Are the controls adequate?
- Are the controls working very well?

This is a professional judgment, which the auditor will need to make, and there is scope to do this on the working papers.

Testing

In this section four types of testing will be discussed, each of which has its part to play in audit (see Exhibit 9.1). The link between control evaluation and these test programmes is illustrated in Figure 9.7.

Compliance testing

This method of testing is one of the most effective to be applied and will determine whether the key controls are being properly applied. Compliance testing can be carried out in a number of ways but it is at its most effective when senior management determine the controls and safeguards in the system but at the operational level the employee actually does something totally differently. If key controls are not being applied, they have to be reclassified as weak. Therefore, with compliance testing the auditor reviews that operations are

Exhibit 9.1 Aims of different types of testing

- Compliance tests – determine whether the key controls have been properly applied
- Walkthrough tests – define whether the systems control objectives have been achieved
- Substantive tests – provide the evidence if a problem exists
- Weakness tests – provide a high intensity of substantive tests and will provide evidence of error, abuse or plain inefficiency

Figure 9.7 The link between evaluation and testing

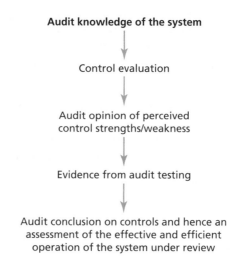

Audit knowledge of the system

↓

Control evaluation

↓

Audit opinion of perceived
control strengths/weakness

↓

Evidence from audit testing

↓

Audit conclusion on controls and hence an
assessment of the effective and efficient
operation of the system under review

consistent with established objectives. Direct evidence cannot be obtained by compliance testing; validity of output can only be determined by substantive testing.

Indirect evidence allows the auditor to assess the risk of errors arising in the output, i.e. the extent of operation of internal controls. This evidence is obtained by compliance testing.

Controls evaluated as ineffective should not be compliance tested. Techniques for compliance testing include:

- observation;
- interviews (conduct at different levels for best effect);
- computer-assisted audit techniques (CAATs).

All control failures should be investigated to identify the cause.

The second stage of the evaluation should take the results of compliance testing along with the control evaluation to enable further conclusions to be drawn on the strength of the systems. A substantive test programme can then be designed to assess the effect of perceived control weakness or strengths on output validity. Compliance testing therefore ensures that internal controls laid down have been applied.

Walkthrough tests

While auditors may conduct walkthrough tests to help them understand the system, the possibility exists that they will test out the key controls as well.

Substantive testing

This type of testing establishes whether individual transactions have been properly treated by the accounting procedures. This means inspecting the output (documentation).

The purpose of substantive testing is to gain direct evidence as to the completeness, accuracy and validity of transactions. The nature, extent of timing of substantive tests will be determined by the results of the compliance tests. Weak compliance test results will increase the degree of substantive testing. Substantive testing leads itself to sampling. The Auditor should concentrate on material items and audit to 90–95% confidence limits.

Substantive testing is therefore concerned with the quality of output and with direct evidence of error. Two key considerations of substantive testing are:

- to test the effect of specific areas of concern;
- to test the general quality of output.

There are several types of substantive tests, including:

- inspection, e.g. stock check;
- reperformance, e.g. check calculations by carrying out the task again to prove it is done properly;
- vouching, e.g. examination of supporting evidence to a transaction;
- analytical review, e.g. comparative data, trends and the like.

Weakness testing

When a substantive test shows an unacceptable level of weakness, errors and mistakes, the auditor must widen the sample considerably to ascertain just how bad the problem really is. Weakness testing takes a considerable degree of time but if it is considered necessary then the auditor leading the team may want to delegate this to a junior member of staff but will want to monitor the work carefully because eventually they will want to present the evidence to senior management.

Evaluation and closure

After obtaining the test results, the auditor will want to analyse and evaluate the outcome of the exercise and put together a draft report. In evaluating control and compliance test results, the following guidance may be useful:

- *Excellent* – controls are satisfactory and found to be working effectively
- *Good* – controls are satisfactory but found to have very minor failures
- *Fair, but retest using substantive testing* – controls are satisfactory but have several control failures
- *Poor* – controls are unsatisfactory
- *Poor* – controls are not in existence.

Once the audit report is in draft form, it is advisable to discuss the findings with senior management. In this discussion, which takes the form of a post-audit interview, it is important to concentrate on the risks that the organisation faces rather than simply on the controls themselves. If at this stage management accepts the recommendations then clearly implementation will be much easier and the report will be readily accepted, welcomed and acted upon. In any event, major systems audits and their findings will need to be reported to the Audit Committee of the organisation and management called to account. In this way, audit really does report to the highest level of management unedited.

Example of control evaluation: a staff restaurant

Consider as an illustration the audit of a staff restaurant, where the remit is to concentrate solely on income. The financial details are as follows:

		£000	£000
Income			800
Less:	Expenditure:		
	Labour	328	
	Cost of materials	290	
	Overheads	230	848
Loss			48

The focus of the audit is solely on income. This defines your task and what you will concentrate on in the first instance. It is therefore pointless to discuss stock, labour cost or overheads as they are not part of your remit.

The following are the systems control objectives for restaurant income:

■ to ensure that there is adequate separation of duties;
■ all sources of income are initialised;
■ to ensure that appropriate prices for goods and services are applied;
■ all receipts are collected and banked promptly, properly and in full;
■ there is adequate physical security.

The following key controls and actual controls are identified during the audit with appropriate comments illustrating the evaluation of the controls.

Control objective: To ensure that there is adequate separation of duties

Key control	Actual control	W/P*	Comments
1. Separation of duties is formalised.	1. Cashier's instructions maintained, to which all cashiers have access and there is supervision.		Full instructions all procedures
2. Adequate separation between collecting cash and banking.	1. Cash collected by end cashier.		Satisfactory
	2. Admin. officer checks cash for banking. There is bank reconciliation.		
3. Adequate separation between collecting cash and reconciling cash due with that banked.	1. Cash collected by cashier and admin. officer maintains Collection & Deposit Register.		Satisfactory
4. Adequate separation between collecting cash and preparing management information.	1. Cash collected by cashier and admin. officer prepares management information, which is received by restaurant manager.		Satisfactory

Auditor's conclusion	Reviewer's comments
Generally satisfactory, however formal procedures do not exist for the admin. officer's role. This needs to be highlighted.	1. Admin. officer has access to cash and also all controls. This is a serious weakness. 2. Lack of separation of duties in absence of admin. officer. Check this.

*W/P = working paper number.

139

Control objective: All sources of income are initialised

Key control	Actual control	WIP	Comments
To ensure: 1. Appropriate documentation of existing systems, so that management may review income-generating opportunities.			Not really appropriate within restaurant environment, although systems notes are not available in full anyway.
2. Appropriate channels exist to enable suggestions to be considered.	Staff suggestion box		This is not really used.

Auditor's conclusion		Reviewer's comments	
There are no formal channels but, within the restaurant environment, this may be entirely appropriate. I conclude that current arrangements are sufficient.		Agreed.	

Control objective: To ensure that appropriate prices for goods and services are applied

Key control	Actual control	WIP	Comments
To ensure that: 1. Prices are displayed.	Prices are displayed.		Satisfactory
2. Price amendments are made by an authorised officer.	1. Restaurant manager signs new price list.		Satisfactory
3. Price amendments are in accordance with charging policy.	1. Price list clearly on view to customers. 2. Prices are monitored on the monthly financial statement.		Satisfactory

Auditor's conclusion		Reviewer's comments	
Satisfactory.		Agreed.	

Control objective: All receipts are collected and banked promptly, properly and in full

Key control	Actual control	WIP	Comments
To ensure:			
1. That cashiers are aware of procedure notes and use them.	1. Procedure notes are available.		Satisfactory
2. That all cash collected by cashiers is subject to reconciliation by another member of staff.	1. Clearance of till by admin. officer – separation of duties. 2. Daily reconciliation by admin. officer of till roll and cashing-up statement. 3. Collection & Deposit Book maintained and reconciled monthly. 4. Cashiers use unique cashier letter key. 5. Bank reconciliation exists.		Satisfactory
3. Adequate records are maintained to identify all items issued for sale, in order to ensure all money due is received.	1. Stock records maintained by independent staff (catering staff). 2. Financial statement prepared.		Satisfactory
Auditor's conclusion		Reviewer's comments	
The control objective is being satisfactorily achieved.		Admin. officer having access to cash and records is a serious weakness.	

Control objective: There is adequate physical security

Key control	Actual control	WIP	Comments
1. That safes and tills are suitable and adequate for the purpose.	1. Safe is controlled by combination and key. 2. Safe is insured to sufficient value. 3. Safe is secured to floor. 4. Tills are secured to counter. 5. Tills and safe are kept locked.		Tills are not in an enclosed cashier's office. Need to check insurance limits here with cash collected.
2. Proper controls exist over keys to tills and safe.	1. All key issues are recorded in key register, maintained by admin. officer.		Satisfactory
3. That cashing-up and banking arrangements provide adequate security for cash and personnel involved.	1. Cashing up takes place. 2. Security company is responsible for transferring cash to bank (Group 4 Securicor).		Satisfactory
Auditor's conclusion		Review's comments	
Level of physical security is adequate, given the amount of cash held at any one time.		Admin. officer and manager have access to the safe.	

Summary

A system is a series of interrelated procedures, composed of processes and controls designed to operate together to achieve a planned objective. The auditor should always be aware of risks that need to be managed. What can go wrong will go wrong at some point in time. The auditor is therefore part of the internal control mechanism. Controls are expensive and in order to be justified must have one of the following characteristics: they must be either preventative, detective or corrective.

When conducting a systems-based audit the auditor will run through a series of procedures, as follows:

1. Be clear about the system to be audited. Draw boundaries around it so that your work is focused.
2. Document the system as your preparation.
3. Form an initial evaluation.
4. Establish from the initial evaluation the systems control objectives.
5. Establish from your preparation what key controls should be present to satisfy the systems control objectives.
6. Test the system by firstly using compliance testing.
7. Compliance testing determines the degree of substantive testing.

8. If substantive testing yields weak results, then increase substantially the level of substantive testing because the system is probably poor.
9. Evaluate the testing results.
10. Draw appropriate conclusions and prepare your report to management.
11. Discuss your report with management. This post-audit interview helps to sell the results.
12. Issue report.
13. Evaluate your own work by verifying how many of your recommendations have been implemented.
14. If the system is poor, then clearly a follow-up audit is required.

In conclusion, systems-based auditing is an effective tool for management as it takes an overview of the system and looks at controls. It is more effective than probity auditing, which has a very high volume of testing. At a time when the board must certify that the organisation has a proper system of internal control, they can have the assurance that it is the auditor who can give them that degree of confidence.

 PRACTICE QUESTION

Compare and contrast the differences between compliance, substantive and weakness testing.

Chapter 10

Key systems audits

Objectives After reading this chapter you should be able to:

- carry out or write an audit programme for stock and procurement;
- carry out or write an audit programme for a payroll system;
- carry out or write an audit programme for payments;
- carry out or write an audit programme for sales and receipts;
- carry out a computer audit systems review.

Introduction

This chapter deals with systems common to most organisations. These systems are by nature very large and process a high number of transactions. They will need regular audit to assure the board of directors of the integrity of the organisation's systems of financial control. While management must take full responsibility for internal control and fraud within the organisation, they must be satisfied that these key systems are subject to rigorous internal audit.

Stock and procurement

Stock is valued at the lower of cost and sale price. There is a need to differentiate between a perpetual inventory and a periodic inventory. A proper set of records must be kept as a perpetual basis. A periodic inventory is an end-of-year stock-take of what items remain unsold at the balance sheet date. There are many variations of perpetual stock records, but one example is shown in Figure 10.1. The online page in this figure details the procurement of stock as it comes into receipt. It moves on to the issue of the stock when it is purchased and then provides an updated balance. Large organisations will use optical character readers to scan the purchase or issue at the point of sale. This will immediately update the stock records, providing a new balance. The administrator and auditor will therefore have up-to-date information on the balance of stock at any point in time.

Figure 10.1 **Perpetual stock inventory record**

COMMODITY								
RECEIPTS			ISSUES			BALANCE		
Date	Number	Value	Date	Number	Value	Date	Number	Value

Potential risks

- Incorrect additions and calculations.
- Incorrect prices.
- The inclusion of goods in stock, the invoices for which have not been passed through the purchases ledger.
- The inclusion of goods in stock that have already been sold and entered as sales, prior to the date of the balance sheet.
- The omission of stock in the hands of agents, at docks, in warehouses, etc.
- The omission to provide for diminution in value in the case of damaged, out-of-fashion or obsolete stock, or slow-moving stock.
- The valuation of stock on the basis of incorrect principles.
- The inclusion of stock which, in fact, does not exist.
- The omission or suppression of some of the stock sheets.
- Inflation of closing stock on a temporary basis.
- To provide a temporary false position with regard to profitability.

Systems control objectives

- All stock is used for organisational purposes.
- All stock belongs to the company and is properly valued and classified.
- All items are priced at the lower of cost or realisable value.
- Stock in the inventory is reconciled with the stock on the shelf.
- Stocktaking procedures are in existence.
- Proper information is kept for goods coming into stock and goods issued from stock.
- Slow-moving or obsolete stock is identified and reported.
- There is a proper system for stock write-offs.

Questions about the system

- How often is stocktaking carried out and when was it last done?
- What is the system of security for valuable stock?
- Which personnel carry out the stocktaking?
- To whom are stocktaking personnel responsible?
- Do the stocktaking personnel render formal reports, and to whom?
- Are the stocktaking personnel independent of those responsible for stock records and stock custody?
- What is the procedure for stock reconciliation?
- What is the method of stocktaking?
- Value of stock under observation at the previous year-end.
- Is the section/location arranged in a manner suitable for counting, measuring etc., and generally in good order?
- Is each section/location subdivided so that each area is easy to count?
- What is the method of identifying items?
- How is the quantity/volume established (e.g. weighed or measured)?

- Does the stocktaking or other records of work in progress include sufficient detail to enable the degree of completion to be properly assessed and valued?
- Are damaged or defective goods identified during stocktaking?
- Is slow-moving or obsolete stock identified during stocktaking?
- Is such stock segregated?
- To whom is the information reported?
- Are descriptions pre-printed or are there stock lists?
- Are standard units prescribed for measurement of all stock items?
- Are any of the items owned by third parties?
- Where items are stored in more than one area, what is the procedure for collating information to agree the total stock?
- If the staff who are taking stock are collating the information themselves, do they provide sufficient detail so that the totals can be checked?
- Is the stock counted or checked by staff who are not responsible for the custody of the stock?
- Is there a separate check count by another person or team? How is this evidenced?
- When goods have been counted/check counted, how are they marked to avoid duplicated counts?
- After the location/department has been counted, is the section inspected to ensure that all items are marked as having been taken into stock?
- When are stock items reported to management for write-off?
- Who takes responsibility for approving write-offs?
- Who do they report?

When the auditor has learnt the system hopefully from this list of points they can identify a number of key controls which can be cross-referenced to the systems control objectives.

Substantive tests

- Consider whether stocks are valued:
  - on an appropriate basis;
  - in accordance with disclosed accounting policies;
  - on a basis consistent with the previous year.
- Test that stocks have been valued correctly by reference to cost records, purchase invoices and other source data.
- Ascertain the stock records and verify with the stock on the shelf.
- Inspect security of valuable items.
- Check authorisation for write-off obsolete stock.
- Sample check invoices of purchases for items coming into stock and verify with the goods received note.
- Note slow-moving stock and question company policy on its possible future write-off.
- Attend end-of-year stock-take or ensure it is carried out by qualified stock-takers and that the auditor can place reliance on their integrity.

It is now important to draw conclusions on the client's prescribed procedures for holding stock.

Payroll

Payroll systems vary from company to company. In this example it is assumed that all employees are paid per calendar month directly into their bank accounts. That is the most efficient, effective and economic method of payroll. However, there are variations to this method. Some companies pay by the lunar month (i.e. every 28 days), others pay by cheque and there are cases where some staff are paid weekly in cash. This is a very expensive practice not only because insurance costs are high but also because cash-handling agents need to be used. Clearly the auditor quickly needs to be aware of the system that is in place and which part of it they are inspecting. For major companies, payroll systems are large.

Potential risks

- People are admitted onto the payroll but don't work for the organisation.
- Staff leave the company but continue to remain on the payroll.
- Employees are paid an incorrect amount.
- Deductions are incorrectly calculated.
- Employees are paid for work not carried out.

Systems control objectives (SCOs) and key controls

(Note that in the following the key controls are the questions/points listed beneath each SCO.)

SCO.1 Are the correct people paid?
- Check the authorisation for putting people onto the payroll.
- Check the procedure for deleting staff from the payroll.
- Is there adequate separation of duties between the personnel and the payroll divisions?

SCO.2 Are people paid the right amount?
- Who authorises the contract?
- Who inputs the data and what are the control procedures?
- Is there reconciliation?
- Are the correct rates applied?

SCO.3 Are people paid at the right time and at the right place?
- Who releases the banking data?
- Verify that all staff are paid by the Bankers Automated Clearing System (BACS).
- Who controls the release of BACS data to the banks?
- Is there a system of cover for payroll staff who are sick or absent?

SCO.4 Are all variations to salary authorised?
- Check the procedure for authorisation.
- Who inputs data if done online?
- Is there adequate reconciliation?

SCO.5 Is timely management information produced?
- Is payroll reconciled to personnel records?
- Is there monthly cash reconciliation?
- Is there proper budgetary control of salaries?

SCO.6 Are salary deductions made correctly?
- Do all employees have a NI number and a tax code?
- Are calculations correctly made?
- Are deductions made for trade union membership?
- Is car parking authorised by the employee?
- Are deductions paid over to the relevant authorities?

Within the above framework there is considerable scope for both compliance and substantive testing. Analytical reviews of payroll normally involve comparisons with previous years adjusted for pay increases and possible changes in employee numbers. In large payroll systems computer-assisted audit techniques (CAATs) come into their own.

Employees who prepare or administer payroll documents or payroll master files should be subject to individual tests on their own salaried remuneration.

Tests on whether employees are genuine are an area of ongoing enquiry. It is important that personnel records are cross-checked and verified. Independent checks can be made with the internal telephone directory and also with their line manager.

Payments to suppliers

Payments to trade creditors or suppliers is another core system to any organisation. The volume of transactions is once again likely to be very high. The auditor should ascertain whether all payments to suppliers are prefixed by an order and subsequently a goods received note. Payments to creditors should be made promptly and completed by either a cheque or by an electronic medium.

Potential risks

- Suppliers are paid who don't exist. Third party companies are set up and subsequently paid.
- Suppliers are paid an incorrect amount.
- The wrong supplier is paid.
- Payment is made in the wrong financial year.
- Goods have not been received but have been invoiced.
- Payment is made twice.

Systems control objectives (SCOs) and key controls

(Note that in the following the key controls are the questions/points listed beneath each SCO.)

SCO.1 Is the correct supplier paid the correct amount at the right time.
- Is there a payment registry which is checked?
- Is there a reconciliation with orders?
- Are invoices authorised by a responsible officer?
- What computer controls should be in place to ensure the correct supplier number is inserted?

SCO.2 Are there adequate checking procedures?
- Is the amount paid included in the budget?
- Does the authorised officer have budgetary authority?
- Who checks the accuracy of the price paid?
- Is there reconciliation with the order and goods received note?

SCO.3 Are goods received used for legitimate purposes?
- Is there a list of approved authorising officers?
- Goods are received into stock and are in line with the company's business.

SCO.4 Does proper management information exist?
- Is this information up to date?
- Is this information supplied to the authorising officer?

SCO.5 Are all suppliers legitimate.
- Are payments made on the basis of a properly headed invoice?
- Does the purchasing officer verify supplier details?

Substantive tests

There are numerous substantive tests which the auditor can carry out as follows:

- Verify supplier details with rating records, telephone listings or directly with the Registrar for companies.
- Cross-check the double entry with the ledger accounts.
- Examine old outstanding balances and enquire about why there is a delay in payment.
- Check that invoices are authorised by the proper responsible officer.
- Examine payments close to the year-end to ascertain that they have been debited to the correct financial year.
- Consider circulation of suppliers to ensure records agree.
- Test check to ensure duplicate payments have not been made (CAATs can do this check effectively).
- Where data is submitted online, verify the system of hash totals and ensure that there is proper reconciliation.
- Enquire into the systems input controls which ensure that the correct supplier is paid. Check digit verification is probably the most effective.

The above framework provides a basis for independent examination of this system.

Sales and receipts

This system can vary considerably from company to company. In some cases, such as restaurants and canteens, income is inevitably in cash which presents its own control problems. Storing cash on the premises and its eventual transportation to the local bank provide the auditor with all sorts of worries. In other cases, such as mail order sales, payment is often made by credit or debit card. This can give rise to customer security problems, particularly if transactions are made over the internet. Many retail organisations refuse to accept payment by cheque because of the risks of checking signatures. They prefer the system of debit or credit cards supported by a chip and pin number. Clearly the auditor will want to find out details of the system before commencing work.

Potential risks

- Offering goods for sale at prices which are too high to be competitive. The reverse also applies because customers will be unhappy if items are seen as too cheap. Suspicion will inevitably be aroused.
- Sales promotion may be badly targeted and ineffective.
- Attractive goods for sale may be stolen.
- Cash may be stolen or pilfered and cheques could be dishonoured.
- Goods are faulty and hence are returned.
- Employees may misappropriate some income or alternatively borrow from takings.

Systems control objectives (SCOs) and key controls

(Note that in the following the key controls are the questions/points listed beneath each SCO.)

SCO.1 All cash takings are reconciled and banked promptly intact.
- Each cashier should be subject to cash reconciliation procedures.
- A collection and deposit register should be kept and maintained.
- Balanced cash should be reconciled with receipts issued.
- Receipts should be reconciled with bankings.
- Banks should be made daily.

SCO.2 Is cash securely held?
- Arc cash-handling agents used for large amounts of cash banked?
- Cash held on the premises should be in a secure (fixed) safe.
- The insurance limits must exceed the cash held.

SCO.3 Are prices appropriate?
- Are prices for goods displayed?
- Are prices for goods competitive?

SCO.4 Is there a policy for dealing with slow-moving stock?
- Are there write-off procedures in place?
- Is there a policy to offer sales discounts?

SCO.5 Are all despatched goods invoiced?
- Are despatch notes reconciled with the debtors account?
- Is there reconciliation with control accounts?
- Is the right price charged?
- Is VAT correctly dealt with?

SCO.6 Are returned goods returned to stock?
- Is a record kept of the return, and why?
- Is there a returns inward account kept?

Test of income will vary depending on the type of organisation and the medium used for payment. Analytical review procedures work well here because trends of income between branches, shops and income collected per cashier will all be revealing. An accounting ratio approach will also be very useful in these circumstances.

Computer systems

Most systems in any organisation, apart from the very smallest, are computerised. Organisations are very dependent on their hardware and software so it is important for the auditor to take a thorough look at them.

Potential risks

- Alteration of input to the advantage of a third party.
- Hacking into secure systems.
- Virus infection spreading in to corrupt the company's systems.
- Sabotage by employees.
- Theft of data programs and hardware.
- Identity theft from staff or customer records.

Information is the mainstay of any organisation and it is important to direct management's attention on how to protect it. Nobody fully knows the losses suffered as a result of computer crime. The Audit Commission has undertaken surveys on computer fraud yet many organisations such as banks do not want to admit to losses because of weaknesses in their systems. The Home Office produces statistics on crime but it does not go into any detail with respect to computer crime. Computer fraud is defined as fraudulent behaviour connected with the intention of gaining dishonest advantage and can occur because of:

- inadequate division of duties;
- transactions that are not properly authorised;
- inadequate control over access;
- poor system development controls;
- poor or non-existent reconciliation procedures;
- passwords not being regularly changed, easy to guess or widely known.

Some of the computer fraud surveys show an even spread of perpetrators among clerical, supervisory, managerial and manual workers and an even split on gender. One significant fact to come from the Audit Commission surveys over several years is that computer fraud is committed by users and not by computer or IT staff. In most instances of computer fraud, people see an opportunity and try to get away with it. Many frauds are discovered by accident, presumably because the perpetrators have committed several so it is likely that sooner or later they will be caught out. However, many frauds are discovered because the control procedures that have been put into place actually work. The sad truth is that fairly few computer frauds are discovered by the auditors. Perhaps the lesson to be learnt from this is to confirm that the internal controls are in place and are effective. If management want to reduce risk then they must be prepared to pay attention to basic controls with an emphasis on division of duties as well as access controls.

Computer systems are at their most vulnerable when they crash. The organisation should have adequate back-up systems in place, perhaps from other local companies. Insurance arrangements should be in place if the organisation suffers losses from a breakdown. Most computer systems have five elements of control:

- input
- processing
- storage
- output
- access.

Input controls

Input controls are online but they should provide hash total checks and check digit verification. It is important to verify that the right person is paid the right amount. Hash totals provide a check on this. Consider the following payment to a supplier:

Payment due:	A.E. Green & Co. Ltd	9,053.25
Payment made:	A.E. Green & Co. Ltd	90,053.25

Can you see the difference? Only one zero in the wrong place and it will cost £81,000 or will you rely on A.E. Green & Co. being honest and making a refund.

Check digit verification provides us with a written assurance that the supplier number on the invoice or the employee number on the timesheet is correct. Otherwise the wrong person will be paid. A worked example of a system of check digit verification known as modulus 97, as used by HM Revenue & Customs (HMRC) is shown below.

Worked example:
Check digit verification – HMRC

The HMRC VAT office has an account with the Chester Hotel, Westcliff Gardens, Bournemouth. The number is 423799228 as shown on the top of the invoice.

CHESTER HOTEL
CENTRAL GARDENS
WESTCLIFF, WC2 5HL.
VAT No. 423799228

2 nights' accommodation 25/9/07 to 27/9/07: amount due £230

How can the HMRC control any manipulation or error in the VAT number (by accident or by design)?

Answer   The system of check digit verification used here is known as modulus 97. The last two digits, 28, are the check digit and the computer is programmed to carry out the following control:

Step 1   Recognise the main number   4237992

Step 2   Sum up the number of digits and
         add 1   8

Step 3   Multiply the numbers as follows:

4	2	3	7	9	9	2
×8	×7	×6	×5	×4	×3	×2
32	14	18	35	36	27	4

Step 4   Sum up the results   166

Step 5   Deduct the modulus until a
         negative is reached

$$\begin{array}{r} 166 \\ -97 \\ \hline 69 \end{array} \qquad \begin{array}{r} 69 \\ -97 \\ \hline -28 \end{array}$$

Step 6   If the number is correct it will
         agree with the check digit (28)

Another example of an input control is the machine-readable passport (Figure 10.2). Not all input controls are quite so dynamic e.g.:

■ format checks (check the input field for alpha or numeric data);
■ range checks (check data or values are within a particular range or limit);
■ logic checks (check data in one field is often correlated with data in another).

Processing controls

These controls check the reasonableness of data and present an exception or edit report if data is not as expected, e.g. negative stock balances, or store balances that don't change.

Storage controls

Firstly there should be proper control of computer files. Standing data which is permanent or semi-permanent must be held on the master file. Here records can be amended, added to or deleted. Authorisation must be restricted to the user department and approval to update master files must be restricted.

Transaction data such as pay rates, hours worked, overtime and, deductions are best subjected to the normal input controls. However, there must be appropriate access controls so no more people than necessary have access to input transaction data.

Most organisations have back-up files which are kept externally from the master file and hard drive. Fireproof cabinets should be used to store files with a file library kept. Computer systems are not perfect and technical hardware problems can result in the loss of important data. Back-up files are therefore essential. Given their importance, security of files is paramount. There are too many examples of sensitive data, particularly from government departments, going missing

Figure 10.2 **Annotated example of a machine readable passport**

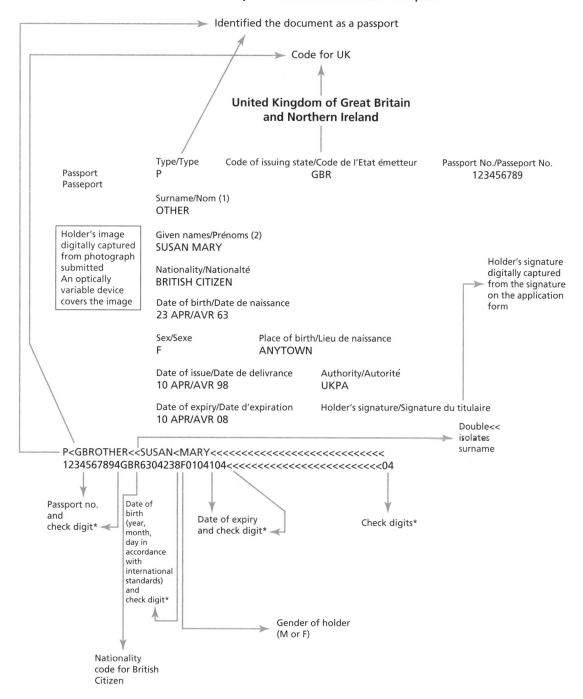

Annotated Example of a Machine Readable Passport

*Check digits enable the machine to check that it has correctly read the passport.

(Source: Adapted from Passport Office)

or being left on trains or planes. Not only does this cause considerable embarrassment, but the clients and customers lose confidence very quickly.

Output controls

Information consists of data shown on screen which can, if required, be printed off so that a hard copy is obtained. Large or unusual items should be subject to an exception or edit report for checking by administrators within the system.

The auditor will want to ensure that there are proper reconciliation controls. These could be in the form of control accounts or totals where the output can be reconciled with the receiving system.

Access controls

Within all large organisations, sensitive data is held on file. Staff who are allowed access to the system must register a computer identification number and a password. These passwords must not be related to addresses, ages or dates of birth, and they should be regularly changed and kept secretly. The Audit Commission in its surveys on computer fraud criticised many organisations whose staff had passwords that were widely known and rarely changed. 'I've forgotten my password, can I borrow yours?' is an unacceptable course of action. Some organisations have, in addition to the password, another piece of predetermined recognition such as a place location. As an alternative to password control, some systems can use voice recognition, retina recognition or fingerprint recognition. Such is the technical age in which we live.

Staff access to systems should be divided into three:

- no access allowed;
- read-only access;
- read and write access.

In the first instance, employees and members of the public should be restricted from having any access to confidential information. This can be achieved through the password control or user ID.

Secondly, responsible employees who need access to confidential files should be granted read only access. They have the responsibility to make decisions from the information they see on the screen.

In the third instance the number of employees who can update or input data should be carefully restricted and controlled. They require supervision and some degree of control.

Summary This chapter takes the reader through some of the most common types of systems being audited. Stores, payroll, payments to suppliers and sales are areas which should be constantly reviewed and examined. They are large in size and process a considerable volume of transactions. For that reason both internal audit and external audit will want to ensure that they are working effectively and efficiently.

As most systems today are computerised, the auditor will want to pay particular attention to computer controls and ensure that they work effectively. Areas of risk to computer systems have changed over the years. Today identity theft, a fraud from e-commerce, is a major issue which will be in the news for some considerable time. It remains one of our biggest challenges in modern times.

? PRACTICE QUESTION

You are required to carry out a systems-based audit for the organisation's payroll.

Prepare six systems control objectives linked to key controls which you would expect to find in place as part of your audit.

Chapter 11

Revenue and capital expenditure

Objectives

After studying this chapter you should be able to:

- illustrate the internal controls to ensure protection of assets and employees;
- ascertain information by questionnaires;
- document the system by flowcharting;
- identify the system for capital construction contracts;
- identify the system controls for service contracts.

Introduction

Capital expenditure can be defined as expenditure on the assets of the company whether they are current or non-current. By implication this is likely to be a significant sum of money, which will have a degree of materiality about it. Revenue expenditure is annual month-by-month expenditure charged to the income statement or profit and loss account. Some items will be minor by nature while others will be material. All stakeholders within the organisation will have a common vested interest to ensure that the entity achieves value for money. Waste and extravagance are difficult to explain whichever level of the organisation you work or whatever your role is.

This chapter focuses on capital construction expenditure, as this is an area where many problems occur.

Asset security

Clearly some assets are more secure than others. Some may, by their physical size, only be prone to serious damage due to fire or terrorism, while other, moveable assets may be considered a target for pilfering. For fixed assets the auditor will want to ensure that proper insurance cover is in place for all major risks which will result in significant loss or damage. A detailed breakdown will need to be kept of all assets in ownership. For that reason an asset register must be kept, with the cost of the asset recorded together with the book valuation. In the case of depreciating assets the auditor will quickly want to be fully satisfied that the depreciation policy is consistent with previous years and displays prudent financial management. Sometimes depreciation is referred to as a capital charge or as a capital allowance. In some circumstances, the rate of capital allowance is prescribed by the Income and Corporation Taxes Act. For example, in the case of plant or vehicles the current rate is set at 25% on a reducing balance basis and this will feed into the financial statements. Asset registers will record both the cost of the asset and the depreciation charged. The difference between the two is known as the book value and the auditor will want to ensure that it bears some resemblance to reality. When assets are sold, the loss or profit on disposal must be transferred into the profit and loss account. There will always be instances where the asset appreciates in value. In these circumstances, the revised value of the asset needs to be restated in the balance sheet and a capital reserve created. Once again the auditor will want to ensure that the value is realistic. This can be done by requesting independent valuation in the case of land or premises, or by the use of insurance indices.

Some assets are moveable, such as desktop computers or audio-visual equipment. Many of these items are highly desirable and are subject to pilferage. It is essential that these items are recorded either in an asset register or an inventory. These documents should be kept in duplicate and at least one copy kept in a fireproof cabinet. This is probably an insurance requirement in any event but it makes sense for management to be aware of what assets it owns. Moveable assets are subject to theft and it is important to record their identity number in the inventory or asset register as proof that the asset belongs to the company. It may be sensible to mark the asset in some way with security paint or security marking. A volumetric pen marks the asset in such a way that the marking cannot be seen by the naked eye but will show up clearly under ultraviolet light. In the case of a company such as Hughes plc trading from Ealing, London W13 9JR, the asset might be marked as follows:

Hug plc W13 9JR.

Alternatively the asset could be marked with bright yellow Camrex paint visible to all. This type of security paint cannot be washed off and has a habit of getting into each nook and cranny. The police with their powers of stop and search have a greater success rate finding stolen assets in the wrong possession than they do catching employees in the act of stealing them. Of course, management can be proactive by ensuring that pilferable assets are kept under lock and key or in a locked office or, if in a public place, under the scrutiny of CCTV cameras.

Safety of employees and members of the public

The law requires employers to assess and manage health and safety risks. This involves once again an exercise of risk management, looking at the risks that may arise in the workplace and then putting sensible measures in place to control them. Most managers regard their employees as their most highly valued assets. Yet in spite of this, according to the Health and Safety Executive (www.hse.gov.uk/risk) 'During 2004/05, 220 people were killed and over 150,000 were injured at work because of a failure to manage risk'. Of course, if managers regard employees as their most valuable asset then they will consider the customer or members of the public to be pivotal to their success. Likewise the public or the customer must feature in the risk assessment.

In many instances, it is a question of common sense, e.g. ensuring spillages are cleaned up promptly so that people do not slip over. The law does not expect businesses to eliminate all risks but protection of the public should always involve what is reasonably possible.

There are five steps of risk management recommended by the Health and Safety Executive:

1. Identify possible hazards.
2. Decide who might be harmed and how.
3. Evaluate the risks and decide on precaution.
4. Record your findings and implement them.
5. Review your assessment and if necessary update.

This process may involve consultation with trade union officials, supervisors and managers and should be a matter of common sense because in most organisations the risks involved are usually very well known and therefore the necessary control measures are easy to apply. When considering risk assessment, it is important to consider that a hazard is anything that could harm or cause injury and may range from electricity to ladders, dangerous substances to open desk drawers. One employer required some of its employees to carry vast amounts of cash, up to many thousands of pounds, from the bank to their offices in order to pay staff. This involved walking about a quarter of a mile, partly along a busy street and partly down a dark narrow lane. This risk could have been easily eliminated by paying staff electronically or by cheque. If vast amounts of cash had to be carried then it should have been done by cash-handling agents such as Group 4 Securicor who are the market leaders. In this case the inevitable happened and a loyal employee was beaten up and robbed. After a lengthy spell in hospital he never worked again.

Employers have a duty of care not only to employees but also to their customers. Many take out insurance to cover themselves from public liability, employee liability and employer liability. When dealing with claims, insurance companies will want to see that employers have acted with all due care and have not been negligent in any way. There are regrettably many examples of accidents which could not be foreseen and where negligence of the employer could not be proved. Examples include children hurt on the rugby pitch or on a skiing holiday or a member of the public falling down a hole in the pavement and suffering broken bones. In one such case the local authority had taken all reasonable steps to display warning signs, boarding off the area and lighting it. However, somebody wishing to cause mischief stole the warning signs, boards and lighting and hid them. Moments later the accident happened. In this case it is hard to see what more the local authority could have done. The auditor has a key role to help and ensure management carry out their responsibilities in full.

Control of revenue expenditure

This is often referred to as 'vouching' or 'probity audit'. The auditor's role is to confirm the integrity of revenue transactions. This means confirming the honesty, soundness and legality of individual transactions. This approach involves a high volume of test checking one transaction after another looking for error or fraud. It is repetitive and boring and unlikely to achieve very much success; however, many managers require the integrity of their work to be checked and it is right and proper that the auditor should oblige. Revenue expenditure transactions are charged to the profit and loss account or income statement. In large organisations the sheer volume of transactions means that sampling is a necessity and the task tends to be done by low-grade staff. If this is the case, an acceptable level of supervision is necessary, otherwise nothing tends to happen due to the boredom of the task.

Analytical review involves the use of mathematical procedures to make comparisons of recorded accounting data. This is done ensure a form of consistency with two variants. It is a form of benchmarking and may reveal a distinct trend of where something is going wrong. Types of data are listed as follows:

- accounting ratios
- percentages
- financial data compared with different periods
- production or employment statistics
- performance indicators
- industry statistics
- employee comparisons.

Employee comparisons are useful indicators not only of efficiency but also of integrity. For example, comparisons between cashiers working equal hours or at different branches of the same store may yield interesting results.

Probity audit is often referred to as *vouching* or 'tick and turn', to give it the trade name. Vouching involves selecting a transaction from within the accounting system and then carrying out an inspection of the documentation which supports the record entry. Vouching is carried out with the intention of finding error, fraud, waste, overstatements or simply detecting illegal and questionable payments. Vouching can be used as part of substantive testing in systems-based auditing to obtain documentary evidence. It may also be used as part of a fraud investigation to accumulate documents, which may later be used in evidence. The process of vouching, if carried out correctly, means selecting entries in the accounting records and then inspecting the relevant documentation. It is the opposite of tracing, where the auditor carries out an examination of documentary output and then ascertains that the documents are properly recorded in the accounting system. Hence, although tracing and vouching are technically opposite in practice, they are interchangeable.

In the audit of organisations with a significant turnover, the auditor is advised to use the following tips:

- Review the previous year and compare with current year and then identify areas of significant variation without immediate explanation.
- Examine significant budgetary overspends.
- If the audit risk is low and the internal control is very good then keep testing to a minimum.
- If the audit risk is high, concentrate audit effort.
- When internal controls are weak then concentrate the audit effort.
- Use analytical review to good purpose.
- Concentrate, if possible, on materiality. Look at high-cost items.
- Use sampling to good purpose in a logical and scientific manner.

These principles certainly relate to large organisations. In small organisations, and particularly those who choose to have an annual audit, very large samples of documents need to be inspected. This is because, in these types of entity, internal control often doesn't exist because of a trust culture that is in place.

The method of vouching or tracing revenue expenditure transactions involves checking the following:

- The invoice or order should be addressed to the organisation.
- It must appear authentic and display all the expected details.
- The goods or services must relate to the business and be charged to the correct budget.
- The document must be authorised by the relevant manager. To pre-empt this necessary check, the auditor will want to ask for a list of signatories prior to commencing the audit.
- In the case of calculations, the auditor will want to ensure that everything adds together and items such as VAT are correctly calculated.

Clearly these tests are a matter of time-consuming routine and may yield very little apart from some irritating minor errors. Audit managers will want to concentrate on a systems-based approach to audit, which is likely to yield more significant findings. To that end, vouching, tracing and analytical review should form part of substantive testing, which is why it is described in some detail here. Nevertheless, clients will still want the integrity of their department, division or subsidiary tested and for that reason there will always be a place for probity audit.

Questionnaires

Questionnaires are a formal survey to extract and record data to aid the audit process. They may be in a loose-leaf form designed by the auditor or purchased from a professional accounting body and are used to find out how the system is operating or to help the auditor gain an understanding of how things work. Their purpose is to assist in the evaluation of the various types of internal controls that are in operation.

Questionnaires are thought by many auditors to be a useful device in gathering data. They are certainly helpful in an area where the auditor has limited expertise and if the questionnaires are prepared in advance by a third party then they provide a device which brings the auditor up to speed. However they are not universally popular. There are several different types of questionnaire, which will be discussed and analysed next.

Internal control questionnaires (ICQs)

These are questionnaires applied to a particular operation or system, which provide an overview of the controls within the system. ICQs call for direct answers and are good at establishing who is responsible for particular operations. The questions are generally 'closed' by design in that they call for 'yes' or 'no' answers. A cross-referencing system is used to cross-check the control with the audit programme or flowchart (see Figure 11.1).

Figure 11.1 **Example of an internal control questionnaire (ICQ)**

ICQ System: Payment of Suppliers Auditor J. Jones			Reviewed by C. Williams Interview with R. Davies Date: 15/1/201X		
QUESTIONS	YES	NO	REF	COMMENTS	
1. Are invoices checked against orders?	✓				
2. Do you check them?	✓				
3. Are invoices checked against budgetary provision?	✓				
4. Are invoices checked with the goods received note?		✓			
5. Do you authorise invoices for payment?	✓				
6. Are statements checked regularly each month?		✓			

In the example in Figure 11.1 the questions are very direct. Weaknesses are usually reflected with a 'no' answer and this is clearly illustrated. The questionnaire is best used by the auditor at the time of the interview with the auditee; they should never be left until later to be filled out. The auditor should not understate the value of body language, as auditees have a way of showing discomfort if they have something to hide and the auditor will clearly want to watch out for that. ICQs provide a record of evaluation and can be held on file. They help supervisors understand the system and provide a sense of direction. They are simple to use and particularly good for junior staff who are learning the trade. ICQs promote a systems-based approach, which the accountancy profession recommends as the best approach for internal audit.

However, critics say they are mechanical and can lead to a stereotypical approach. Many an auditor has claimed that they don't aid creativity and imagination and some of the professionally prepared ICQs are not always geared to a particular client. It is dangerous for questionnaires to be left with the auditee to complete, as this may result in them giving the answers the auditor would want to hear rather than the reality. The biggest criticism of ICQs is that they encourage too many closed questions, resulting in yes or no answers that are not very revealing.

Internal control evaluation questionnaires (ICEQs)

The key distinction between ICQs and ICEQs is that, whereas ICQs concentrate on controls, ICEQs focus on other types of poor administration and mismanagement. Opinion seems to suggest that a combination of the two will provide the best results.

An example of an ICEQ is shown in Figure 11.2 and it can be seen that the auditor will ascertain a far greater degree of information than from the ICQ

Figure 11.2 **Example of an internal control evaluation questionnaire (ICEQ)**

ICEQ			
System	Payment of Suppliers	Reviewed by	
Auditee	....	Interview with:	
		Date:	
Question		Answer	Comments
1. How often do you check suppliers' statements?			
2. Where are goods received notes filed?			
3. Where are orders filed?			
4. Do you check these against the supplier's invoice?			
5. Do you check the price?			
6. How do you do this?			
7. When do you pass invoices for payment?			
8. Can you personally guarantee the accuracy before passing for payment?			
9. Who is the authorised signatory?			
10. What happens if they are absent?			

Figure 11.3 **Example of a separation of duties questionnaire**

System: Payment of Suppliers		
Operation	Responsible officer	S/W
Order despatch	Mrs Holman	W
Invoice check	Mrs Holman	W
Invoice authorisation	Mrs Holman	W
Payment of invoice	Mr Chapman	S
Posting in the accounts	Mr Singh	S

S = strength; W = weakness.

because many of the questions are open, thus allowing the auditee the freedom to talk and discuss. The auditor's job is to listen and note possible weaknesses which will influence the testing process.

A further questionnaire that isn't mentioned in many textbooks is a separation of duties questionnaire (see Figure 11.3 for an example). It can be given out at the early stages of the audit. The questionnaire in Figure 11.3 can be used as a device to assess the system of internal check or separation of duties.

Flowcharting

One of the main options available to the auditor for documenting a system is flowcharting. This is an alternative to questionnaires or narrative notes. Flowcharting means showing a system diagrammatically in the form of a drawing. It is used in engineering and by IT systems analysts who design the system and put it into the form of a diagram before the programmer turns it into machine code. For the auditor, flowcharting works like a map of related operations within systems.

Detailed narratives are replaced by symbols connected by lines, which indicate the flow direction. Flowcharts will not normally show the movement of money or goods as the assumption is that they flow with the documentation. For example, money will flow into the bank account but it is the bank paying slip which is shown in the flowchart. If the system displays a goods received note then the assumption is that the goods have been received into stock. Only at the testing stage will it be shown if this is not the case, in which case something serious is going wrong.

Flowcharts are an invaluable aid in systems-based auditing as they provide information for managers as well as being a guide to the new auditor. They represent a way of highlighting strengths and weaknesses of internal check and internal control. Modern computer packages have meant that flowcharting can be completed relatively quickly compared with the days when they were constructed by hand. Care must be taken, however, to ensure that the flowchart adds value to the audit and that time is taken to evaluate the system.

The flowchart shows people or departments who administer the documentation displayed horizontally across the top of the chart from left to right. The start of the flowchart is always at the top left and the chart is read from left to right. If more than seven people or departments are involved then it may be necessary to produce two charts, but this is a matter for the auditor to consider. The physical movement is shown by a continuous line. If one document is produced from another then that will be shown as a dotted line.

When preparing flowcharts there are some basic guidelines that need to be followed. Always head up the flowchart with the name of the system and always produce a key or legend to explain the symbols. This is important, as there is more than one system of symbols. In any event, managers and clients need to be reminded what these symbols mean, as they will be forgotten. A narrative column on the left-hand side of the flowchart may be used as an option but the auditor should take care to use words sparingly. Always describe briefly the name or the number of the document. Reverse flows usually relate to control information, so when seen they should be studied carefully. Always work with perpendicular lines at 90° angles. Avoid lines that are drawn at 45° angles. A complicated flowchart may be drawn over several pages.

Figure 11.4 presents some of the flowchart symbols used in several different systems. With such a wide range of symbols in operation it is essential that the constructor of the flowchart has a key.

Capital construction contracts

Capital construction involves very high amounts of capital expenditure and has a propensity to go wrong. It is an area that becomes extremely costly when things do not go to plan. There are many examples in the public domain of this happening. The delay, known as slippage, and the subsequent project overrun of the national football stadium at Wembley is well documented. The construction of the Millennium Dome in time to mark the year 2000 produced a building with an interesting and unusual design, but by 2001 nobody knew what to do with it. Subsequently it became a national embarrassment. History is full of 'white elephant' projects and the public sector has had more than its fair share.

The basic audit approach must be to follow the system audit methodology with the project broken down into the following stages:

- need and feasibility study
- options
- capital programme (or capital budget)
- design
- construction of a bill of quantities
- tendering
- issue of a contract
- construction work
- final account
- post-project appraisal.

Each of these stages is explored in a little more detail in the following pages.

Figure 11.4 **Examples of flowchart symbols**

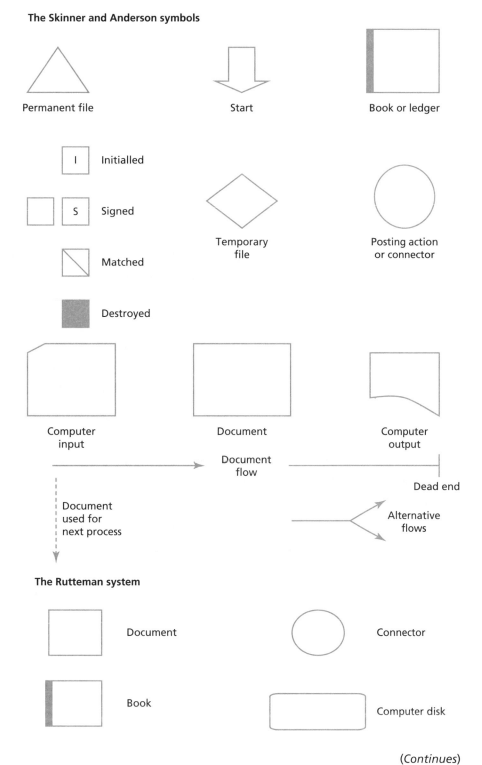

The Skinner and Anderson symbols

Permanent file

Start

Book or ledger

I   Initialled

S   Signed

Matched

Destroyed

Temporary file

Posting action or connector

Computer input

Document

Computer output

Document flow

Dead end

Document used for next process

Alternative flows

The Rutteman system

Document

Connector

Book

Computer disk

(*Continues*)

Figure 11.4 *Continued*

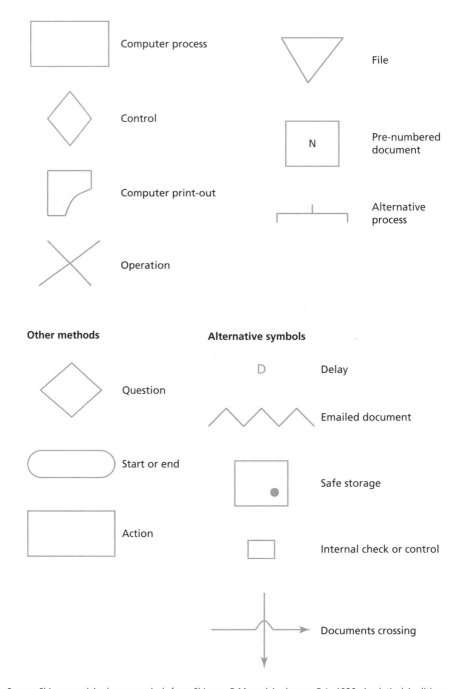

Source: Skinner and Anderson symbols from Skinner, R.M. and Anderson, R.J., 1996, *Analytical Auditing*, Pitman, Pearson Education Ltd (Harlow). Also from Rutteman, P.J., 'Flowcharting for Auditors', *Accountants' Digest*, no. 32 (1976) (ICAEW).

Need and feasibility study

The first stage is to establish that a problem exists which will warrant a large capital spend. It must be firmly established that there is a demand for the project, and the decision to go ahead must be made by the highest level of management if the project is above a specified size. Key questions, which the auditor will want to ask, are as follows:

- Why is the project really necessary?
- What will it achieve?
- What will it cost?
- Will it meet the solution to the problem and provide value for money?
- What are the assumptions, which are built into the investment appraisal stage?
- How will the project be financed?

These questions should, of course, be built into the feasibility study right from the start with the financial officers working to pull the figures into an investment appraisal. Some projects may in fact generate savings or positive cash flows, e.g. a bridge financed from tolls or new offices that save rental costs. Sometimes capital projects will have negative cash flows. In such circumstances the traditional investment appraisal techniques such as net present value (NPV), internal rate of return (IRR), accounting rate of return (ARR), profitability index (PI) and payback are not so meaningful. Instead the project should be justified on the benefits that it brings. Clearly an initial examination must be completed as part of the feasibility study where all the salient features are pulled out. The report must explain the problem and what kind of solution is needed. Of course the estimates of the cost are fairly basic at this stage and can be as much as 50% above or below the actual cost. Overspends costing several times their original estimate are unacceptable.

Option appraisals

Where there is more than one way of solving the problem, a second feasibility study is required. Whilst the first study is weighted towards settling a need, a further study will be required it there are several possible solutions to be considered. Sometimes the option of doing nothing must also be weighed up as an alternative. Key questions the auditor will want to focus on are:

- How can the problem be solved with this project?
- What are the options available?
- When should the project be undertaken?
- What are the likely costs of the options?
- What are the benefits of the options?
- Is appropriate financial data supplied to management/decision makers?

Option appraisal addresses the evaluation of the alternatives, sometimes using sensitivity analysis. It should produce costings to a higher level of accuracy, which as a broad-brush estimate should be within 30% of the final cost. The second study should have better information on the cost–benefit analysis, and should probably reflect market research into the public's perception of the benefits, weighted on a sale of 1 (the lowest) to 10 (the highest). An economic analysis and environmental impacts should also feed through into the study. Outline designs, construction options, land and planning requirements should be available to influence the choice. The decision-making process must therefore be in place to choose the best solution because, once chosen, changes of mind can result in changes of design, and if there are time delays this will add to the cost. Once the design brief has been produced, it will provide a basis for construction drawings.

Capital programme (or capital budget)

Organisations that have several capital expenditure projects on the go at once will want to put them into a capital programme. Projects that go into the capital programme must have been given the go-ahead by management. They must be therefore ranked into priority order, with projects where construction work has already started given priority over projects where work has not started. An example of a capital programme is given in Figure 11.5.

The capital programme provides a clear focus for approved projects. The example in Figure 11.5 shows the project description, priority key, start and end dates and total cost phased across financial years. For smaller companies, which have far fewer capital projects, a simple capital budget will suffice. The capital programme provides a working document for professionals. Company solicitors will want to ensure that planning permission is obtained together with any conveyancing activities. Accountants will want to arrange financing, surveyors will

Figure 11.5 **A capital programme**

				Capital programme				
Project	Category	Start	End	2008/09	2009/10	2010/11	Subsequent years	Total
				£000	£000	£000	£000	£000
1. North East regional offices	A	03/07	09/10	7,000	3,000	–	–	12,000
2. Staff social club refurbishment	B	02/10	06/10	–	1,500	–	–	1,500
3. Factory in Singapore	B	04/10	11/12	–	4,000	6,000	5,000	15,000
4. Asian offices	C	01/11	12/12			10,000	9,000	19,000

Note: A, committed scheme (work has started); B, NOT committed (work due to start); C, NOT committed (further design work to be completed).

want to estimate quality and quantity of building materials, and architects will want to produce the final design, from which the bill of quantities can be produced.

The key question for the auditor to ask is this: is the budgetary data in place to support professional decision-making?

Design stage

Detailed design calculations must cover all aspects of the project and be supported by construction drawings. While this is proceeding, it is normal practice to allow a site investigation to check ground conditions. Towards the end of this stage, specifications, contracts and bills of contract will be drawn up. Estimates of cost can now be revised but they should be within 10% of the final cost. If there are any possible problems, an immediate report must be generated. It may be that the project is costing significantly more than envisaged and management may want to revisit the design brief to reduce costs, e.g. by cutting down the size of the building. Companies who defer projects or cancel them after the tendering stage will subsequently pay a far higher price. The decision to proceed at this stage or not is critical. Time delays will ultimately cost money and there are many examples in the public domain of this happening.

Key questions for the auditor to consider are:

- Does the design brief meet the original brief?
- Have management approved all major changes to the design?
- Does the design provide good value for money?
- If design work is contracted out, how are consultants appointed, what are their terms of reference, is this in a legal contract and how is their performance appraised?

Construction of the bill of quantities

A bill of quantities is a specification of client requirements measured by amount and type of material. It forms the basis on which construction companies will price their tender. This is very much a technical matter between the architect and the surveyor. The auditor may want to check that it is consistent with the earlier design and construction plans. Items missing from the bill of quantities or changes of mind will prove to be very costly. All parties should be aware of this. An example of a Bill of Quantities is shown in Figure 11.6. It involves mains, drains and fences, and is just one of 50 pages.

Once completed, the bill of quantities becomes the basis for tenders from selected or invited companies. Some organisations have a select list of contractors who have been vetted and are known to be reliable in their work. There is much merit in this approach. Some bodies in the public sector invite allcomers to bid for work. Clearly, in this instance, the vetting procedure is vital. It must not be forgotten here that tendering costs are typically at least 1% of the value of the contract for each tenderer. The costs should only be incurred if the project is expected to go forward to the construction phase. Many organisations

Figure 11.6 **Sample page of a bill of quantities**

RISING MAINS – BILL NO.3

Item no.	Description	Qty	Unit	Rate	Amount £
	Fences etc. Allow for all additional costs in rising main construction in passing under or through the items detailed hereinafter, including all reinstatement				
1	Post and rail fence	1	No.	14.50	14.50
2	Hedge	1	No.	10.90	10.90
3	Post and wire fence	3	No.	7.75	23.25
4	Stile	1	No.	8.10	8.10
5	Ditch	1	No.	4.15	4.15
6	GPO telephone cable	1	No.	15.07	15.07
7	800 dia. water main	1	No.	245.00	245.00
8	200 dia. water main	1	No.	95.00	95.00
9	Electricity cable (m.v.)	1	No.	14.50	14.50
10	Mole ploughed land drains	11	No.	20.00	220.00
	Concrete				
11	Class 'C' concrete in thrust blocks	6	cu.m	30.25	181.50
12	150 thick Class 'C' concrete slab over pipe for full width of trench at stream including all rough shuttering, etc.	7	lin.m	11.05	77.35
13	Excavate for, provide and lay sand bags filled with Class 'F' concrete to profile of stream bank (slope approximately 1 in 1). Include for forming fill to slope and compacting and disposal of surplus excavated material	8	sq.m	7.75	62.00

Total of Page Carried to Summary of Bill   £   971.34

have regulations in place which determine whether or not services above a particular value are to go out to tender, together with the procedure for awarding contracts and a supporting policy on the use of subcontractors. There are several types of tendering:

■ *Competitive tendering.* No restrictions are placed on contractors and their work and reputation. Once the list is completed, only these companies are invited to tender.

■ *Negotiated tendering.* Competitive or selected tendering may take place but the preferred choice of contractor is approached and the tender price is negotiated in line with the lower to average bids of the other contractors. In some parts of the public service, this may be considered unacceptable.

■ *Single tenders.* Only one company is invited to tender because of the size and specialist nature of the contract. This is used, for example, with Ministry of Defence contracts for military equipment.

Key questions the auditor will want to ask with respect to tendering are as follows:

■ Does the system allow the best contractor to be selected at the most advantageous price?
■ Is the form of tendering adopted in accordance with the organisation's policy and procedures?
■ Is there a proper procedure for the vetting of contractors?
■ Is there a full technical evaluation of the tenders?
■ Is there a system for opening and evaluation of tenders which leads to the selection of the most appropriate bid?

The worst things that can go wrong in the tendering process are firstly that the decision-makers for the award of contract receive a bribe or inducement so that they favour one of the bids. Operational procedures usually require two or three staff to be present in the tender-opening process, one of whom should be chief officer or at director level. It is probably best to be independent from the other operational procedures. Other problems can arise when the contract is awarded to an artificially low bid, resulting in substandard workmanship or an unacceptable level of service. Lastly, if the contractor is financially unstable they may go into liquidation during the execution of the contract. This may result in time delays while the organisation re-tenders and produce a significant increase in costs. For that reason the auditor will want to ensure that proper vetting procedures are in place for the selection of the most appropriate contractor. This will include a financial assessment, trade references and a technical assurance that the procedures to be used will not result in substandard work. Financial vetting usually involves accounting ratios to measure solvency, activity, profitability and gearing. Under no circumstances should a contract be awarded if it is larger than 20% of the contractor's turnover. It is unacceptable and would probably result in excessive subcontracting. If there are financial concerns about the health of a company then the contractor can always be asked to lodge a performance bond with a bank or building society. If the contract is completed satisfactorily then the bond is repaid to the contractor with interest. If not, it is used by the client to offset the likely cost increase. The examination of trade references is vital. Past performance provides a suitable yardstick for selection. Recommendations and a good reputation are very important factors for contractor selection and this must not be understated.

Tenders can be grouped into three categories:

■ *Low.* Experience tells us that the lowest bids are not necessarily the best and there must be some concern about the quality of the work. Despite this, some organisations have a policy of always accepting the lowest bid. If this is the case it should be rigorously evaluated from a technical perspective in order to ascertain that delivery is possible.

- *High.* Often companies don't really want the work and will only undertake it at a premium price. But they do want to be considered for future contracts.
- *Medium.* Tendering is a competitive business and a good form of market testing. Tenders that fall in the mid-range fully supported by good trade references and reputation are likely to be the best. Experienced companies do not want to be bothered with cheap work and will not undertake such contracts.

Contract stage

For major capital construction work, a contract is legally advisable as litigation can be expensive. There are standard forms of contract put together by professional bodies. The auditor will probably be happy to leave the form and issue of a contract to the company solicitors, well aware that it will follow the law of contract. The auditor will probably want to check the start and end dates and also to see if any performance targets are included. Particularly important are liquidated damages. These are predetermined damages built into the contract which will become payable if the work is finished late or if there are major problems of the contractor's own making.

The contract will probably consider the use of consultants or the organisation's policy on subcontracting. Consultants or sub-contractors can be used extensively or occasionally for specialist input.

Construction phase

The company will have a clerk of works or project manager on site who will perform the role as the client's or the company's representative. The major role involved here is the payment of the contractor. Usually payments are made in stages in proportion to the completion rate of the contract. There may be instances where payment is made in advance of the work starting or when it has finished. This is fairly rare because it is not the contractor's role to finance the work; this must be done by the client company. Therefore, payment to contractors is usually made monthly as you go in proportion to the work completed, which is signed and verified by the clerk of works or project manager. A contract register is also kept, an example of which can be seen in Figure 11.7.

Among the main concerns for the auditor are changes of mind, changes to the contract or extenuating circumstances. Extenuating circumstances such as poor weather or contaminated land are not the fault of the contractor and they should not be penalised for it. Changes to the contract are made by a variation order and this results in a contractor's claim, i.e. an additional payment. Variation orders and claims will want to be avoided at all costs as they can be expensive. The auditor will want to scrutinise these very carefully. Many contractors who are seeking to win the contract price the tender bid competitively, often working on profit margins of between 1 and 2%. But many contractors expect the client company to change their mind on design issues and materials. When this happens they tend to over-price the variation as they know it will be difficult for the client

Figure 11.7 **Example of a contract register**

CONTRACTOR: Blackwood Construction plc   CONTRACT: Hinton Road Offices
ADDRESS: Old Drive, Nottingham   Tarmac and Landscape

CONSULTANTS: Kent, Alyn & Fisher, Surbiton, Surrey
CAPITAL PROGRAMME REF. 09/07
CONTRACT SIZE: £250,000   Bond Issued: No.

DATE COMMENCED 1.6.07		COMPLETION TIME 7 MONTHS	COMPLETION DATE 31.12.07	LIQUIDATED DAMAGES £5,000 p.w.	
Date	No.	Cumulative value of work £	Less retention £	Stages payment £	Remarks
8.7.07	1	30,200	906	29,294	
6.8.07	2	48,750	1,463	17,993	
9.9.07	3	88,500	2,655	38,558	
	4				
	5				
	6				
	7				

company to re-tender. The auditor will certainly want to consider the following questions:

- Is there a good system of project management in place?
- Is there an adequate system of financial management information in place?
- Are materials delivered to the site at the right time?
- Are building materials properly secured?
- Is site security adequate?
- Is the work being carried out in accordance with the bill of quantities and the terms of the contract?

Final account stage

It has been stated that payments are made in stages on a pro rata basis with a specified retention sum deducted. When the project is completed, a final invoice will be provided so that the final payment can be made. Traditionally auditors have spent considerable time and effort checking the final account. This is considered within the profession to be misplaced. The auditor must ensure that a systems-based approach is taken with capital construction work. If the project goes wrong in the early stages, it is likely to continue to cause problems, slippage, overruns and will ultimately cost well in excess of the tender price. Key questions for the auditor to consider include:

- Was the project completed on time and within the tender price?
- Was the end product completed to a satisfactory standard?
- Have all variation orders and contractor's claims been dealt with properly and professionally?

Post-project appraisal

This is sometimes known as post-completion review or post-completion audit. The aim and value of post-project appraisal are to learn from the experience. Once the lessons are learnt and the mistakes noted, they can be used to improve financial control in future projects. The lessons learnt from the national football stadium at Wembley can be applied to the 2012 London Olympic Games Project, and the lessons from the Olympic project can be applied, for example, to a Football World Cup festival in the future.

It may be best to split the project review into two areas. Firstly, project reviews are undertaken by technical staff and secondly the appraisal is undertaken independently. Neither of these functions is an audit task but that doesn't stop the auditor becoming involved. It is essential that the project review examines the consultant and contractor performance. The question needs to be asked whether you would use them again. The project appraisal stage reviews the whole project and compares outcomes with the initial objectives. It asks: what do we now have that is not needed, and have we really satisfied the need or the problem and at the same time obtained value for money?

The project contract must be examined, particularly the causes of any overrun. The liquidated damages, which are based on predetermined conditions set out in the contract, must be considered and pursued if these conditions are not met. A good example of this is that roadworks or office building are finished by a certain date. If that fails to happen, then the client company suffers additional costs when making contingency plans. In practice, they are best worked out on a daily basis, but if they are clearly stated in the contract documents then the organisation has every chance of being successful. Auditors have the responsibility to vet the contract and the performance of the contractor. If they feel that the contractor has underperformed on a multi-million-pound contract, they should report this to the highest level of management. The implications of this may mean removing the contractor from any further work for the organisation.

Post-completion reviews often reveal errors in the early stages. For example, the need or the problem is not clearly identified, nor is it ranked in terms of priority. Perhaps public and staff consultations were poor and so is the resulting impact on the population, the customers and the staff. It is pointless saving 5% on a £1 million contract that wasn't necessary in the first place.

Taking this a stage further, history teaches us that frequently not all the options have been appraised and that the outcome is often driven rather than planned. The effectiveness of the design stage can be judged by the number of contractor claims. A high number of variation orders results in a high number of claims, which in turn shows a lack of design. Key errors revealed in the tendering stage include tenders being received when the organisation is not ready to tender; contractor vetting is an area where there is room for improvement. The construction stage often reveals pressure to accelerate the contract and there is still too much audit time involved in checking the final account when that is the responsibility of the architect and quantity surveyor. Auditors rarely review the select list of contractors, which can become too long and cumbersome. In practice, architects and surveyors have their favourite contractors and often use only less than half the firms on the list. In conclusion the post-completion view is a very valuable exercise – but only if the organisation is prepared to learn from its mistakes.

Service contracts

Many organisations now have a policy of externalisation or outsourcing of work to a third party under 'facilities management' contracts. These traditionally involved 'blue collar', services such as cleaning, catering, transport maintenance, grounds maintenance and printing. However, the 1990s witnessed a spread of outsourcing of the so-called 'white collar areas', such as IT, payroll and human resources. This has increased in recent years and now includes some of the accounting functions, customer support and call centres. There is nothing wrong in market testing as long as it achieves value for money. However, if outsourcing is expedited simply to save money without any concern for the customer then the alarm bells should start to ring and the auditor has a duty to comment. Service (revenue) contracts are subject to a similar basic audit approach as applied to construction contracts, namely:

- feasibility study
- options
- budget
- specification
- tender
- issue of contract
- monitoring process for duration of contract
- payments in respect of service level agreements
- contract appraisal for renewal.

The systems-based approach in service contracts has some similarities and some differences compared with capital construction contracts. Firstly, the service contracted out must be identified and then a specification for the tasks to be completed must be drawn up. The specification is the most important document and must consider the tasks to be done all individually broken down, with the frequency, times, method of delivery and the service standard. Some type of performance testing may be included. The specification becomes the document upon which the tender is based. Tendering procedures have already been discussed in this chapter but the in-house team, if invited to tender, will base their bid on staff requirements and equipment needed, plus any back-up which is needed as cover.

The tenders are assessed and tenderers vetted. Management may want to favour the in-house bid if the figures are close. They will be aware of the distinct possibility of redundancy costs and other fixed costs, which would not be saved. However, in areas such as IT they will be influenced by the standard of service. A contract must be drawn up for the winning tenderer. It must overtly cover performance standards and penalties. Liquidated damages are once again an important part of the contract. Poor performance is difficult to prove in law unless service standards are clearly laid down. Financial penalties are to be included in the contract, with higher penalties for non-delivery of service and higher still for subsequent non-delivery. A point of contract termination must be stated if poor performance and non-delivery are repeated. It must be remembered the management may outsource the service but it cannot outsource the ultimate responsibility for it. As that remains with the company, monitoring of the contract and supervision are essential factors to be in place. When the contract comes towards its end, the procedures will start again.

The auditor's role is to ensure a systems-based approach is undertaken and that market testing is fair. The standard of service must achieve value for money in the customer's eyes and must not be seen as a cheap option operated by low-paid staff without adequate knowledge or training. If that is the case then business will be lost.

Summary

The auditor is a master of techniques and will recognise the different approaches required to audit revenue and capital expenditure. The auditor should concentrate on issues of materiality and must always be aware of security issues, particularly the security of assets and of staff.

The use of probity audit must be demonstrated when it is required but the auditor will be aware of its limitations.

A systems-based approach is the recommended one for internal audit. The auditor should be comfortable with the use of questionnaires and flowcharts to help document the system.

Capital expenditure contracts involve large amounts of money. It is essential that it is determined at the outset that the project is really necessary. The auditor will want to take a systems-based approach to the audit and must not become preoccupied with making arithmetical checks of the contract final account.

The examination of service contracts again requires a systems-based approach. Such contracts must ensure value for money and must not merely be used as a means of cost-cutting.

? PRACTICE QUESTION

Your company has a number of capital construction contracts, some of which have started and others that are about to start. Outline the different stages of the capital contract process the auditor would expect to find in place.

Audit risk assessment and sampling

Objectives

After studying this chapter you should be able to:

- appreciate the different degrees of risk and be able to measure them;
- understand the importance of an insurance policy;
- understand the differences between audit risk, detection risk, control risk and inherent risk;
- recognise of the risks in an IT environment;
- understand how to apply and use statistical sampling to determine sample size and sample chosen;
- use IT techniques to assist the audit;
- understand the importance of security of data.

Introduction

Risk is defined as the possibility of meeting danger and as a result suffering damage, harm or loss. Clearly this is a very general overview because risks that threaten an organisation come in all shapes and sizes. Some are neatly packaged while others wait to cause maximum disruption and inconvenience. The worst-case scenario is that some risks have a fatal ring to them from the point of view of human life while others of a business nature threaten termination and liquidation. What is certain from experience is that the worst thing will happen to the organisation at the worst possible time.

The auditor will be forced to think at an early stage about the likely impact of risk. Figure 12.1 shows the component parts of risk. Clearly risk presents a series of challenges to be met but this must be viewed in the light of the firm's aims and objectives, which should be kept firmly in mind.

The Turnbull Report states that management must provide a balanced assessment of the significant risks and the effectiveness of the internal control systems for measuring, detecting, correcting and preventing the risks from occurring. All reports should identify the impact on the organisation if the risk were to occur. It is a clear fact that risk, control and fraud are management's responsibility. The establishment of a system of risk management is critical to an organisation's success. However, research tells us that not all organisations have taken this seriously despite the tightening up of corporate governance over the last decade. One recent example was Société-Générale, the second largest bank in France, where Jerome Kerviel caused five times the financial damage caused by Nick Leeson, who was responsible for the collapse of Barings Bank with losses in the region of £800 million. In 2007 Jerome Kerviel spun an elaborate web of fake transactions from his desk costing €4.9 billion. When a disaster like this happens, management has a habit of undergoing a Damascene-like conversion to become disciples of control. However, the damage to Société Générale's 22.5 million customers plus a loss of confidence in the banking systems by the public and financial markets was considerable. The intervention of French Prime Minister, Francois Fillon, failed to

Figure 12.1 **Risk and its component parts**

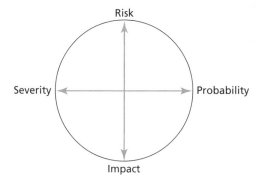

stop share prices falling across Europe by 7%. In the mid-1990s Baltimore-based trader John Rusnak was jailed after hiding trading losses in Allied Irish Bank. In 1995 Toshihide Iguchi, one of Japanese Daiwa Bank's most senior executives, confessed that he had lost $1.1 billion through bond trading that was unauthorised. These illustrations are examples of fraud within one industry. They don't include examples of the mismanagement of business risk due to poor quality lending as experienced in 2007 with Northern Rock Bank. What all these organisations have in common is that they have all paid lip service to the management risk. Regrettably the price paid has been very high, not only to the organisations but also to the managers involved. Not only will they lose their jobs and go to prison but they render themselves virtually unemployable.

Control risk self-assessment takes time to develop in a large company. However, whether it is due to the impetus of the Turnbull Report or the Sarbanes-Oxley Act in 2002 there is now an awareness among top management. The systems-based approach to audit using non-executive director involvement through the Audit Committee, which in turn feeds into the board, is all part of an integrated control risk assessment. Many auditors undertaking such a task will ascertain the risks the organisation faces by questionnaire, and subsequent follow-up procedures with departments and divisions, such as a top-down or bottom-up approach, acts as a good servant to the communication process.

Risk management

Risk management involves making decisions on which risks to bear in-house and which ones to lay off (that is, to externalise). It is thus, self-evidently, an activity of major importance to the company. There are five elements to managing risk within a company (see also Figure 12.2):

- identification
- measurement
- avoidance (if possible!)
- reduction
- accommodation.

Identification of risk

Decisions about insurance matters are concerned with the identification of risk and its financial consequences. The art of minimising the cost of risk is to weigh the cost of insurance cover against the likelihood of loss if no insurance were taken out. This technique is known as risk management. It requires an assessment to be made of:

- risks involved – What is at stake? What can go wrong?
- the degree of probability of something happening;
- the degree of severity of cost in the event of that happening.

Figure 12.2 **The five elements of business risk management**

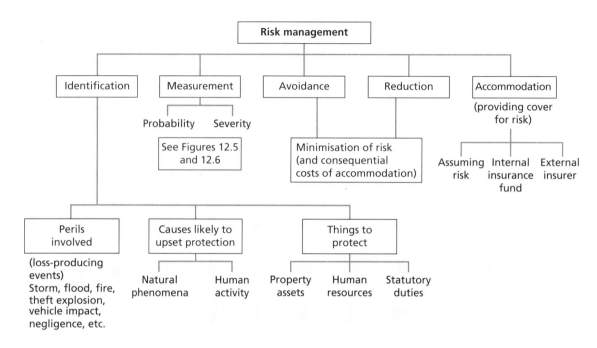

Against these assessments it is necessary to:

- investigate methods and ways of avoiding or reducing the risks identified;
- investigate ways of avoiding or reducing the associated costs of the insured risk happening;
- judge the best ways of accommodating those risks that remain.

For example, one way of reducing the risk of the theft of cash is to remove as much cash as possible from the system and encourage payment by electronic means.

The identification of risk really involves three elements. The first is an identification of things which require protection, e.g. property, buildings, mechanical equipment. Secondly one must identify what can go wrong, e.g. natural phenomena such as storms, floods and hurricanes, or those things arising from human activity such as theft, negligence, vehicle impact, libel or slander. Thirdly, there is a business risk, which might involve either the loss of a major customer or a major competitor setting up very close to your region.

Some project managers will categorise risk in relation to the project. The different categories of risk are itemised in Exhibit 12.1.

Historically risk management has been concerned with all those events that a business considers to be undesirable. Undesirable events that destroy, reduce or devalue the company's assets result in expenditure and/or loss of income that impacts on the profit and loss account. This in turn leads to lower profit or even losses and adversely affects the company's balance sheet and financial position.

Exhibit 12.1 **Risk identification in a project management environment**

- **Environmental risks** – main risk area related to the project: uncertainty and high dynamism of market, industry and competition
- **Operational risks** – may negatively affect the project: speed and responsiveness are crucial in a competitive environment. Delays and slippage.
- **Financial risks** – due to the dynamism of the environment, a sensitivity analysis will assess this area of risk
- **People risks** – main asset of the project, people skills are fundamental for its success: carefully plan, recruit and skill key staff at least 1 year in advance
- **Technology risks** – same infrastructure of IT: need of having a good competitive database
- **Organisational risks** – rigidity of sale processes: team needs to act and react in a very flexible way in order to be effective within industry markets

It is clear that risk is concerned with negative impacts for the most part and it would not be prudent to suggest that organisations should not look at risk from this viewpoint. However, over the past few years thinking has also evolved into considering the positive side of risk-taking and acknowledging that in order to capitalise on business opportunities there will always be an element of risk.

One major insurance company comments that risk management means acting and thinking in a systematic way to manage risks and is an explicit part of the management of a business.

The goal is to minimise costs resulting from undesirable events and to safeguard income. This is therefore the traditional down-side approach. However, it is worth stating that in the hands of the company management, it is a tool which can be used to secure profits and the profitability of invested capital, and to protect the company's balance sheet.

In the modern environment, this down-side and up-side approach is critical for most organisations. Put simply, sound management of 'down-side' risk enables the freeing up of capital for investment in projects and activities, which can result in increased profits and long-term business continuity. The ability to have resources to capitalise on these opportunities is effectively therefore the 'up-side' of risk. Further categories of risk are shown in Exhibit 12.2 and Table 12.1.

It is a fact that business and operational risks threaten the tangible and intangible assets of a company and that comprehensive risk management creates the basis by which a company can protect its tangible and intangible assets. Tangible assets are generally persons, property, environmental and money/capital and intangible assets are items such as image, trust, goodwill, information, intellectual capital, patents and licences.

As previously stated, solid risk management practice helps to safeguard profits and protect the balance sheet by avoiding or reducing the additional expenses and reductions in income caused by undesirable events. In turn, resources are kept free for other uses.

This can only really be achieved by having identified, assessed and determined how best to manage all those risks that exist in any given business situation. Risk management is therefore a discipline that spans the entire organisation

Exhibit 12.2 **Risk identification by category**

Business risks
Strategic risks
- Products, services
- Markets
- Mergers and acquisitions

- Management skills
- Major competition

Market risks
- Inflation
- Market access (barriers)
- Price war

Financial risks
- Interest rates
- Liquidity
- Investments

- Financing
- Credit/receivables
- Currency risk

Operational risks
- Product liability
- Fire
- Perils
- Business interruption
- Computer system failure

- Accident
- Health
- Environment
- Plant breakdown

Phenomena
- Flooding
- Storm
- Hurricane
- Earthquake

- Civil unrest
- Industrial action
- Sabotage
- Terrorism

Table 12.1 **Internal and external risks**

Internal risks		External risks	
Technical (pure or speculative)	Non-technical (speculative)	Predictable/uncertain (speculative)	Unpredictable (pure)
Technology	Resources	Currency	Acts of God
Work	Human	Taxation	Natural hazards
Design	Material	Inflation	Weather
Construction	Financial	Economic	Government
Change		Social	Third parties
Performance			

and this is demonstrated in Charles Handy's (1993) functional model shown in Figure 12.3.

Risk management needs to be considered in every aspect of the business from the welfare of staff to the protection of assets and the risks involved in exporting goods overseas. For example, the marketing director may want to develop a new product; this has monetary implications for the finance director and, in turn, human and plant resource concerns for the manufacturing director. All areas

Figure 12.3 **Simple functional organisation model**

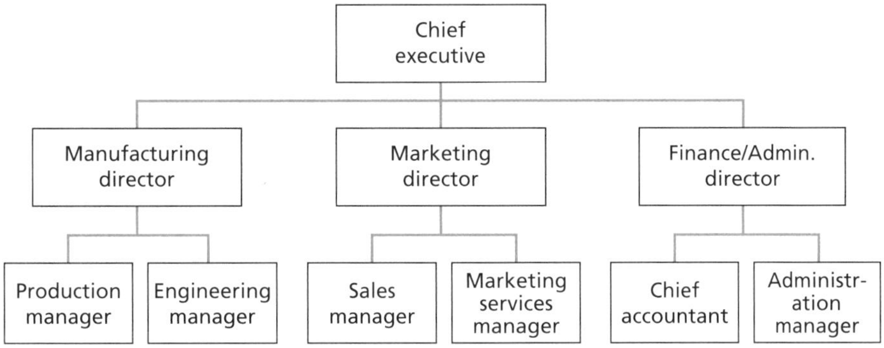

Source: From Handy C (1993) *Understanding Organizations*, 4th edn, Penguin.

have risks to consider and it is therefore critical that an integrated understanding and management of risk across the organisation takes place.

Again this echoes the requirements of the Turnbull Report, in that an organisation must have a 'sound system of control' and that risk management sits squarely with the company's directors. Responsible risk-taking means a culture in which controlled gambles enhance the business in some way and avoiding detriment as far as possible. Risk does not mean not taking gambles, even controlled ones, in areas such as health and safety and the environment.

The key message here is that organisations need to take stock of all incidents that happen, not just those that result in a defined outcome. Analysis of near misses can be used to prevent or control future incidents where the outcome may be less fortunate. Quite simply, firms need to learn from experience.

A summary of the types of risk a company faces are shown in Figure 12.4.

Risk measurement

Once identified it is important to prioritise the risk by assessing the significance of each risk using a likelihood versus impact matrix (see Figure 12.5). Each quadrant in the matrix has an associated implication in terms of management actions to be taken to manage the risk. Some managers prefer to use the five-by-five probability matrix (see Figure 12.6).

The first measurement of risk is an assessment of the probability of a loss-producing event occurring. This assessment is often based on a five-point scale giving varying degrees of probability. Whilst the degree of probability gives some measure of the risk involved, of equal importance is the need to assess the severity, in terms of financial costs, of a loss-producing event. This assessment, too, is often measured on a five-point scale.

The five-by-five matrix illustrates these dual aspects of risk measurement, and why both elements need to be recognised at the same time in decisions concerned with what to insure and for how much. The interconnection of probability and severity is of fundamental importance to these decisions.

Figure 12.4 **Classification of risk types**

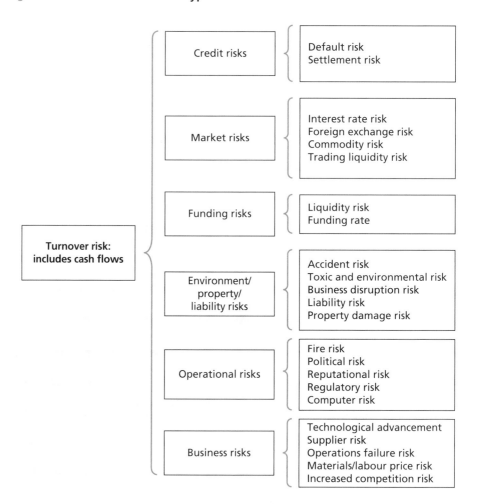

Assessments of the degree of probability of the occurrence of a peril will be reasonably standard, regardless of the type or size of company involved. For example, there are no differences in the chances of a small company suffering from an earthquake compared with those of a public limited company. In both cases the odds are fairly remote (the probability is 'unlikely') and, although these odds may vary in relation to the geographical location of the company, size and type of company have no bearing on the degree of probability.

However, assessments concerning the degree of severity will vary in relation to type and size of organisation. For example, a loss of £1 million may be catastrophic for a small company. However, for a large multinational conglomerate it would be a mere drop in the ocean. In practice, materiality can be measured using materiality tables, which recognise the correlation between turnover and materiality.

The lower areas on the five-by-five matrix are very likely to warrant insurance, particularly from three to five on the severity scale.

Figure 12.5 **Impact/likelihood matrix**

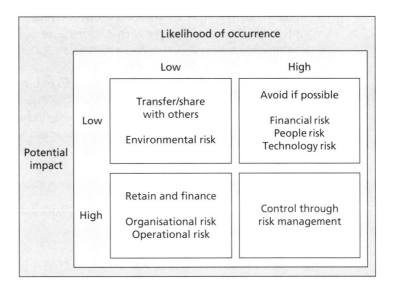

Figure 12.6 **The five-by-five probability matrix**

		Degrees of probability				
		1. Unlikely	2. Slight	3. Fair	4. Probable	5. Very likely
Degrees of severity in financial cost terms	1. Insignificant				Theft of Petty Cash	Damage to office equipment
	2. Low			Theft	Minor cash defalcations	Minor injury to employees
	3. Medium		Minor Fraud	Vandalism	Vehicle damage	
	4. High	Flooding	Fire	Public liability claim		
	5. Catastrophic	Earthquake	Tempest	Terrorism		

Avoidance of risk

It is possible to deal with the question of risk by simple avoidance; in other words, eliminate risk by eliminating the activity that creates the potential loss-making event. This may be a suitable strategy if an unacceptably high rating is given to certain loss-making events. Examples would be the closure of facilities owing to high levels of vandalism, or the use of cash-handling agents to avoid the risk of cash (i.e. bank notes) transmission.

Avoidance, however, is a somewhat blunt method of reducing risk. Nor is it always a feasible means of dealing with risk, because in many areas it is a question of 'the show must go on'. A company could not, for example, cease to pay wages in cash to its workforce because of the risk of robbery or injury to those involved. However, in this instance, it could take action to reduce the level of risk involved, which is the next category in our survey of the elements of risk management. Some of our leading supermarkets have recently refused to take cheques from their customers. This is because, in the event of fraud, it is they who suffer all the loss. So by refusing to take cheques, the risk is eliminated.

Reduction of risk

Reduction of risk is concerned with creating circumstances that have the effect of limiting either (or both):

- the probability of a happening
- the cost associated with that happening, should it occur.

Many examples of risk reduction are seen in the management of insurance policies, and are often conditions imposed by insurance companies before they will accept responsibility for the risks involved. In the above example concerning the payment of wages in cash, a prerequisite condition may be the employment of a security firm for the transportation of cash from the bank and/or to the various payout locations. Here risk reduction involves the employment of additional safeguards in the day-to-day operation of the particular activity involved. Other examples are the use of security alarm systems, proper employment and practice of fire drills, and, more generally, the system of internal control, including internal check, intended to safeguard an organisation's assets and ensure their proper use.

These additional safeguards do, however, have a cost and must be seen to be cost-effective in relation to the amount of risk eliminated by their installation. It may, for example, be economic to pay higher insurance premiums than go to the expense of buying additional equipment; or incurring costs on a more sophisticated system of stock control to eliminate any possible losses from a stores depot.

Accommodation of risk

It is important that all identified risks are 'accommodated', i.e. provision is made in some way to cover the costs of a happening, or the losses involved in an insurable event. Risk may be accommodated in three ways, the first of which is by assuming one's own risk. This involves building into normal budgets an allowance to cover insurance losses, in the same way that provision is made for normal repairs and maintenance, or employee costs. This method of accommodating risk is perhaps ideally suited to those risks that are measured in the very likely/insignificant and probable/low categories.

The remaining categories of accommodation of risk are both concerned with transferring the risk to somewhere else: internally through an insurance fund, and externally by buying cover from an insurance company. The transfer of risk in either way naturally involves a cost – the insurance premium. The fund may be established initially by a lump-sum contribution from income. The income of the fund will comprise premiums paid by those departments' activities that are relying on the fund to cover liabilities, and also from interest, which will be earned on the unused balance of the fund.

It is unlikely that any organisation will accommodate all its risks internally – even the largest organisations would be unhappy covering risks measured in the catastrophic/unlikely and catastrophic/slight categories. In fact, a company may consider it prudent to cover risk, other than in the medium probability range, internally, rather than rely on external insurance for other categories. By operating one's own insurance, in theory one saves only the element of the insurance company's profit, as administrative costs of managing in-house claims and possible litigation will need to be borne directly, plus an average year's claims, balanced by annual premiums charged to user accounts.

Often, however, insurance companies assess small claims risks as high in terms of their own administrative costs, so significant premium savings can be achieved by agreeing to restrict these small claims – known as taking an excess. The excess amount could be covered internally.

Duties of the insurance officer

In some organisations, insurance comes under the direct control of the finance manager, but this is not always the case. Insurance should be regarded as an important element in financial management, recognised as such by identifying a senior officer within the organisation as having special responsibilities for insurance matters.

Ideally the responsibility should be held centrally; at least the organisation should make sure that any separate activities regarding insurance are properly co-ordinated to obtain any benefits of operating on an organisation-wide basis and to ensure that equal standards apply to covering the many risks involved.

The functions of the person (or people) charged with responsibilities regarding insurance matters may be stated as follows (these matters might ideally be referred to in financial standing orders and regulations). The designated officer should:

- regularly review the organisation's insurable risks, deciding:
  - whether insurance cover is appropriate;
  - how best this cover might be obtained (e.g. by assumption, internal/external transfer);
- ensure proper competition is obtained for externally insured risks;
- ensure that any risks covered by an internal fund are properly identified and that the fund is maintained at an appropriate level to meet potential claims;
- impose proper procedures in dealing with insurance reviews, so that
  - all changes in risks, acquisitions and disposal of assets are duly notified to the insurance officer;
  - all claims procedures are dealt with by the duly appointed officer;
  - proper historical records of claims are maintained – this may be required in any subsequent review involving a change in insurance company or of the premium rates charged.

There are two types of insurance, which the auditor will want to reflect on:

- Reinstatement insurance – the full cost of the damage will be reimbursed plus a premium for replacement. In other words, if equipment is stolen it will be replaced at replacement cost. Insurance premiums here are more expensive.
- Indemnity cover – if equipment is stolen, the written-down (depreciated) value will be reimbursed. Insurance premiums here are cheaper.

Auditors are experts at dealing with risk but it is important that they understand the principles of insurance and can ensure that, in their judgment, all risks are dealt with.

Audit risk

Audit risk is defined clearly by ISA 330, which defines it as 'the risk that auditors may give an inappropriate audit opinion on financial statement'. ISA 330 recognises and evaluates that audit risk has several components: inherent risk, control risk (this would have been mentioned as internal control risk) and detection risk or sampling risk. This is summarised in Figure 12.7.

For the external auditor, the main overall audit risk is to give an audit opinion which states that the financial statements give a true and fair view when the opposite is the case, i.e. they contain a significant material error. Of course, the opposite is also true: the external auditor might state that the financial statements contain a significant material error when clearly they don't. For the internal auditor the main overall audit risk is that after testing a system they are prepared to issue a clean audit report concluding that all controls are working as intended when clearly they are not. Subsequently a major fraud occurs which causes the organisation and the auditor great embarrassment. Such issues often lead to a loss of confidence, a lack of trust and a loss of business.

In large organisations it is not possible for the auditor to examine every item. Therefore, there must be an acceptable level of risk, which the auditor must accept as a prerequisite of sampling. Auditors will always be more assured when they see strong internal control systems and, in particular, strong internal checks. When auditors see strong key controls in place then they can be a little more assured that the degree of loss is minimal. However, they will need to keep in mind the issue of

Figure 12.7 **The audit risk components**

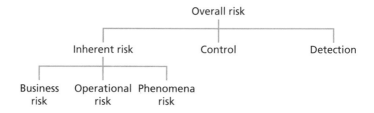

Figure 12.8 **Risk scoring**

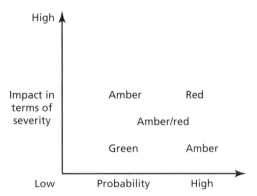

materiality and test and examine items of high value. The 'audit nose' will 'smell' and see indicators where the overall audit risk increases, for example:

- a new client;
- a new audit;
- poor accounting systems;
- poor book-keeping and a lack of records;
- an autocratic manager who rules in a single-handed manner;
- problems which are inherent in the nature of the business;
- a difficult or fiercely competitive market place.

The auditor will want to consider the severity in terms of materiality against the probability of the integrated risks (see Figure 12.8).

Inherent risk

Internal risk is the risk or error that may arise from the environment in which the company does its business. It may be due to high technology or the complexity of the business, which the layman wouldn't understand. It could arise because the company does business with a developing country and/or a country led by a dictator where policy is unreliable or oppressive. While some businesses are risk-free, others will be affected by economic conditions or technological advancements. Difficult trading conditions will also put management integrity under pressure.

Control risk

Control risks are errors that will not be prevented until after they have taken place. Hence the error is not prevented because of the weaknesses or limitations in the internal control system.

Detection risk

Detection risk can occur when the auditor misses the obvious. The internal controls have worked correctly but the message is missed by the auditor, due to error, distraction, inexperience, poor supervision or simply negligence. Detection risk can also be present due to a sampling error. One can never be 100% confident unless every record is examined. Even sheer boredom is likely to increase the risk of detection error.

Overall audit risk

Overall audit risk (OAR) is the product of internal risk (IR), control risk (CR) and detection risk (DR), i.e.:

$$OAR = IR \times CR \times DR$$

Concluding this section auditors are advised to concentrate on systems that have too much trust placed in them. They must not assume anything and take nothing for granted. The general advice is that they should concentrate on areas of greatest risk, on sizeable or material items and on controls that only detect errors after they have occurred.

Sampling

Sampling is defined as an application designed to test a sample that is less than 100% of the population, but which is representative of the population. The objective is that you can form a meaningful conclusion. Given the size of organisations and the number of transactions processed, sampling is often inevitable unless the auditor makes use of IT packages, which will be discussed later. Of course, sampling does bring with it a degree of risk. There is the risk that the auditor fails to recognise any errors in the sample selected and there is also the risk of sampling error. A biased sample may not be representative of the population and so the items inspected will fail to reveal any errors.

There are particular instances when it is advisable not to sample, as follows:

■ there is a major enquiry;
■ in a fraud investigation;
■ there are very few transactions;
■ there is a small population;
■ a statutory disclosure has to be made.

There are two factors to be decided upon before sampling starts: the approach or selection and the sample size. Although a lot of this may be down to judgment, the auditor will want to demonstrate a degree of scientific application.

Sample selection

There are a number of different approaches, which can be used here:

■ random
■ internal
■ cluster
■ attribute

- monetary unit sampling
- statistical.

Random selection technique

Random sampling is often preferred in practice although auditors must base their opinion on the assumption that the sample is representative. Tables can be used here, so can basic computer packages or the auditor can simply apply a policy of 'take your pick'. However, the key feature of random sampling is that each item has an equal chance of selection.

Interval sampling

Here the auditor selects at random a fixed starting point and then a fixed interval between selections. This policy will result in the selection of every nth item. Here n is determined by dividing the population by the sample size.

Cluster sampling

This method of sampling will involve identifying clusters of records from the population as opposed to individual items. The first item in each cluster is often determined at random. For example, in the case of purchase orders, a sample size of 150 items may be selected in clusters of 10, i.e. 15 clusters or 10 items at a time.

Attribute sampling

The aim of attribute sampling is to select a sample that is representative of the population but includes items that either require special attention or have a particular characteristic. An example of this is a selection of items when the supervisor is away on annual leave or sick. Another example is when the computer system crashed and a back-up system came into operation. Of course, one problem with this type of judgment sampling is that the results cannot always be evaluated objectively in order for the auditor to express an opinion on the total population. However, a significant advantage is that it allows the auditor's judgment to be focused on unique circumstances. However, should the sample ever be challenged, it would be easier to defend a random sample as being more representative of the population.

Monetary unit sampling (MUS)

There are some auditors who select a level of materiality from the materiality tables. If checking involves, for example, a materiality approach, they will examine all items above a certain amount and then that will be a slight variation to pure MUS which has developed over time. MUS tends to look at monetary intervals taking into account confidence levels, materiality and precision:

- *Confidence level.* Any test of less than 100% of the population contains a degree of risk. The level or degree of risk is expressed in terms of confidence in the results. Therefore, if the sample is selected on the basis of a 90% confidence level, there is a 10% sampling risk that the sample is not representative of the population.

■ *Materiality (R)*. Clearly, size is a major factor in determining materiality. A large error is likely to be more significant. However, this must be placed into the context of the size of the organisation. What is material to a company the size of IBM, with its multi-billion-dollar turnover, will be considerably more than a sole trader who has a turnover of £50,000 per annum.

■ *Precision (P)*. The projection of sample results across a large population will cause a loss of precision. This is quoted not as a specific figure but often as a range. Precision is closely related to confidence; for example, a high degree of precision and a low degree of confidence, or alternatively a low degree of precision with a high degree of confidence. Thus the result may be expressed as giving a 90% confidence level within a range of ±2%, or 95% confidence ±5%. Sometimes precision may also be expressed in monetary terms. For example, the auditor may wish a precision limit to be £10,000 at a 95% confidence level. This means that on 5% of occasions the auditor is prepared to accept an error rate of over £10,000. Hence 5% of the results falling outside the precision limits is referred to as the sampling risk.

Worked example: MUS

Precision, *P*	£10,000
Confidence limit	95%
Materiality factor, *R*	3

The sampling interval is 10,000/3 = £3,333.33. The auditor will look at monetary units of £3,333.33 as follows:

Invoice no.	Amount (£)	Cumulative amount	Inspect
1	250	250	
2	2,500	2,750	
3	1,000	3,750	✓
4	5,800	9,550	✓
5	120	9,670	
6	75	9,745	
7	6,100	15,845	✓
8	2,000	17,845	✓
9	150	18,995	✓
10	700	19,695	
11	500	20,195	✓
12	90	20,285	
13	50	20,335	
14	30	20,365	
15	175	20,540	
16	80	20,620	
17	4,525	25,145	✓

Hence from this example the following seven monetary units are passed:

1	3333.33	Invoice 3
2	6666.66	Invoice 4
3	9999.99	Invoice 7
4	13,333.32	Invoice 8
5	16,666.65	Invoice 9
6	19,999.98	Invoice 11
7	23,333.31	Invoice 17

Statistical sampling

This approach uses probability theory to determine sample size and to measure sampling risk. It therefore uses some of the terminology discussed under MUS. One great advantage of statistical sampling is that it defends the auditor against charges of bias or favouritism. Of course, with this method of sampling the auditor still has to set confidence levels, but a sample size will be determined.

The bell-shaped curve in Figure 12.9 indicates a normal distribution. An average or mean shown as x can be calculated, as can the standard deviations (i.e. measures of dispersion).

Hence what this tells us is that 68.3% of the data is $\pm$ one standard deviation from the mean; 95.4% of the data is $\pm$ two standard deviations from the mean; and 99.7% of the data $\pm$ three standard deviations from the mean.

Auditors may then be wise to look closely at all data that falls more than one standard deviation from the mean. They would certainly be strongly advised to look closely at all data falling two or three standard deviations from the mean.

Statistical sampling is based on rigorous mathematical theory. Given required values for the materiality limit (or for the monetary precision) and the level of confidence, the application of the statistical method specifies how the sampling should be undertaken.

To this extent, statistical sampling is objective. However, the setting of materiality limits and confidence levels is a matter of judgment which is inherently subjective. There is no satisfactory alternative to the use of judgment. As a result, although the

Figure 12.9 **Statistical sampling with a normal distribution**

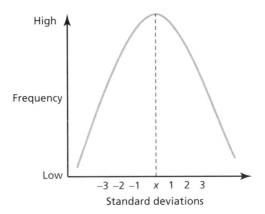

sampling cannot be regarded as objective, it does separately identify those elements requiring judgment, making them more clearly defined matters for examination. Further, it encourages the setting of materiality before sampling commences.

Worked example: Statistical sampling

Range of turnover (£000)	Materiality limit (%)
0–50	4.0
50–100	3.0
100–200	2.0
200–500	1.5
500–1,500	1.0
1,500–3,000	0.5
3,000–10,000	0.2

Confidence level (%)	39	63	78	86	95	99
R	0.5	1.9	1.5	2.0	2.5	3.0

N.B. The materiality limit determines the monetary precision required.

Turnover in this company is £1,400,000. The auditor sets a 95% confidence level ±2.5.

$$\text{Sample size} = \frac{R}{P}$$

$$\frac{R}{P} = \frac{2.5}{1.0} \times 100$$

$$= 250 \text{ items}$$

$$1.0\% \text{ of } £1,400,000 = 14,000$$

Everything above £14,000 is material for this company.

If MUS is used, use £1,400,000/250 = £5,600 sample points.

Summary

In this chapter the reader will be aware that risk is a part of everyday life. However, to the company, it must be managed as part of a control risk assessment. Risk must be identified, measured and managed. This chapter shows the link between risk and insurance. This is an issue all too often forgotten by auditors.

The auditor should be aware of the purpose of statistical and non-statistical sampling and be able to distinguish between the different approaches. The importance of sample size and sampling approach must also be considered.

In addition the use of computer-assisted audit techniques (CAATs) it is essential for understanding the purpose of IT to undertake data mining and data retrieval. See Chapter 8 for further details.

? PRACTICE QUESTION

Critically evaluate the different approaches to sampling that the auditor would be prepared to adopt.

Chapter 13

Financial statement audit

Objectives

After this chapter you should be able to:

- describe financial statement assertions;
- understand the debate of auditor independence;
- distinguish between the interim and final audits;
- appreciate the problems and issues associated with the audit of estimates;
- make a link between planning and preparation of the audit and the records to be kept.

Introduction

The United Kingdom requires all companies with a turnover of greater than £5.6 million to produce annual audited financial statements. The external audit is therefore a statutory requirement under company law and for public limited companies produces major business for the UK's top four accountancy firms. The regulation of stock market listed companies is a key cornerstone of the British financial services market. Users of the financial statements need to rely on their accuracy.

The word audit comes from the Latin *audire*, which means to hear. Its origins date back to Egypt, Greek and Roman times when accounts were presented by word of mouth and a responsible official who was the auditor had to provide an oral report of the proceedings.

Financial

Today auditors add value to the financial reporting process. They provide an opinion that the financial statements themselves are reliable indicators for directors, shareholders and potential investors. Auditing is therefore a process of analysing, evaluating and testing evidence that the profit and loss account or income statement and the balance sheet provide a 'true and fair view' in accordance with international financial reporting standards (IFRSs) or national accounting standards at the balance sheet date. The auditor must confirm that all information given in the directors' report is consistent with the financial statements. The directors are responsible for preparing the annual report, the directors' remuneration report and the financial statements in accordance with applicable law and regulations. Company law requires that directors prepare financial statements for each financial year. Financial statements are required by law to give a true and fair view of the state of affairs of the company and of the profit and loss for the period.

In preparing the financial statements, the directors are required to:

- select suitable and proper accounting policies and then apply them consistently;
- make judgments that are prudent;
- state that the statements comply with applicable UK accounting standards or, if a public limited company, with the IFRSs as adopted by the European Union.

The directors confirm that they have complied with these requirements in the annual report. It is worth stating that they are responsible for keeping proper accounting records that disclose with reasonable accuracy at any time the financial position of the company. They are also responsible for safeguarding the assets of the company and therefore taking all reasonable steps for the prevention and detection of fraud and any other irregularities. Lastly, the directors are responsible for the maintenance and integrity of the company's website. It is the duty of the external auditors to help them discharge their responsibilities whilst being ultimately accountable to shareholders. This relationship is shown in Figure 13.1.

Figure 13.1 **Responsibility flows in the 'eternal triangle'**

Based on the primary audit objectives, the following main categories of work are established:

- financial statement verification
- compliance auditing
- other audit work.

The financial verification work is the main aspect of the external auditor's work, providing shareholders and other interested parties with an opinion as to whether or not the statements provide a true and fair view. This is illustrated in Figure 13.2.

Compliance auditing, on the other hand, is carried out to determine that the organisation has acted in accordance with the law, its own strategic objectives and any applicable regulations. Many compliance audits will ensure that company staff are complying with the internal controls laid down by management. In many companies, internal audit deal with this task and therefore all external audit has to do is to establish the effectiveness of the internal audit department and to ensure that its work can be relied on.

Figure 13.2 **The features of the verification audit**

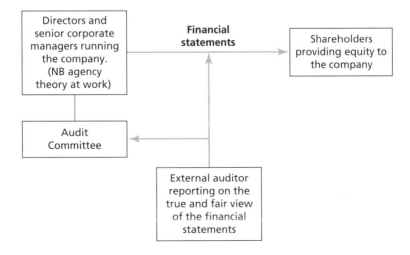

Other audit work may involve additional duties requested by senior management at the pre-audit meeting and confirmed with the letter of engagement. This can involve the examination of the company's operations to ensure or improve value for money or a review of a system which may have recently changed or been updated.

Non-audit services

Many companies will require the auditor to carry out non-audit services. There is considerable debate in the profession as to whether this compromises the independence of the auditor.

The increasing complexities within the business environment coupled with the shift in primary objectives of the auditing profession resulted in auditors needing to attain an in-depth understanding of their audit clients, their businesses and their industries. These changes gave auditors new avenues for providing additional services to their audit clients. Such additional services include additional management and advisory services relating to tax, financial planning, management information systems and other aspects of operations. These additional services are classified as NAS (non-audit services) and are services other than the financial statement audit provided by a company's auditor. Over time the fees generated by NAS have risen more rapidly than audit fees. This led some to question whether and to what extent the provision of these NAS influence auditor independence see Table 13.1.

Clearly the determining factor for the auditor to take on non-audit work must be the desire to increase their fee income and hence their own profitability. However, there is a fear that auditors will feel that the benefits from keeping their clients content outweigh the costs of sacrificing their independence.

Despite the systems of regulation in place, these did not hinder the extremely close working relationship between Enron and its auditor Arthur Andersen, who allowed substandard practices to go undetected within the firm. Arthur Andersen functioned as both Enron's internal and external auditor, while also providing consultancy services. Enron had been the audit partner's only client for a number of years and was also the main client for Arthur Andersen's Houston office. Hence, Arthur Andersen's Houston office was economically dependent on retaining Enron.

It is not really known if Arthur Andersen compromised independence in 'fact', but the 'appearance' given is that independence was severely compromised. As a result of the Enron–Andersen scandal, to address the audit–client relationship and to also restore investor confidence the US hastily introduced the Sarbanes-Oxley Act in 2006, requiring the mandatory rotation of the audit partner after every 5 years and prohibiting the provision of certain NAS by the auditor. Following the US scandal, the UK also set up the Co-ordinating Group on Audit and Accounting Issues (CGAA) in 2002 to review the UK's independence framework. In the same year, the UK also agreed to adopt the European Commission's (EC) recommendations. Similarly to the US Sarbanes-Oxley Act requirement, it is recommended that the audit partner be rotated every 5 years. The UK government

Table 13.1 **Impact of non-audit services (NAS) on auditor independence – some empirical studies**

Studies	Effect of NAS on auditor independence		
	Negative effect	Positive effect	No effect
NAS and Earnings Conservatism	Threat of litigation not enough to increase independence in 'fact'	Independence in 'appearance' may be improved	
Professionalism vs. Commercialism: The Association between NAS and Auditor Independence	Damage to reputation if there are problems	Increase in fee income	Independence not impaired
Enron and Worldcom experience	Independence totally compromised		
Are Auditors Compromised by NAS? Assessing the Evidence	Effect on independence in 'appearance' Stock prices lower for companies with high NAS fees		No links between NAS and audit failure
Do NAS fees impair Auditor Independence? Evidence from Going Concern Audit Opinions		Irrespective of high NAS fees, threat of litigation and reputational loss promote independence	
Compatibility of Management and Consulting	Many respondents suggest conflict of interest		
Audit Conflict: An empirical Study of the Perceived Ability of Auditors to Resist Management Pressures	The richer the client company, the competition in the market and the higher the provision of NAS increase the likelihood of a favourable outcome for the client, hence independence is impaired		

also requires the disclosure by auditors of fees in excess of 5% received from any one client.

The increasingly high level of market competition is likely to increase the auditors' dependence on the client. Based on audit fees, the so-called 'Big Four' firms held well over 90% of the world market. In some years the Big Four audited all the FTSE 100 companies in the UK and the vast majority of other listed companies.

Audit failures can weaken the stability of capital markets if confidence in the audit process is lost. Hence the auditing profession and governments work continuously to ensure regulatory safeguards are in place to protect investors and maintain perceived auditor independence. The following key aspects of audit regulation have been cited as promoting auditor independence: the existence of unlimited legal liability for auditors' strong enforcement of standards and effective discipline of companies and auditors.

The interim audit

If the external audit is to be undertaken in an efficient and effective manner, both the client and the auditor must plan their work. The process usually commences with a pre-audit interview between the partner leading the audit and the finance director of the firm to be audited. These plans will document the following points:

- the overall audit timetable, agreeing a set of dates for the commencement and completion of the work;
- the main audit tasks to be undertaken;
- company resources that may be required, i.e. an area to work and interview rooms needed to interview staff;
- client requirements – any directed areas from the Audit Committee to consider;
- a review of the internal audit section (if applicable);
- a summary of staff involved and any budgetary constraints;
- an agreement on the level of audit fees.

A letter of engagement will formalise these details (see Figure 13.3).

The interim audit is generally associated with the evaluation of the client's systems followed by an assessment and subsequent testing of internal control. This will involve a significant degree of substantive testing of transactions using a scientific sampling technique or a computer-assisted auditing package. Taking the example of a very large client, interim audit work may involve several similar visits during the course of the year, or even a continuous audit presence. In the case of a small company that is just over the audit threshold, the interim visit may be fairly brief and in some instances, if the company is a closed company (i.e. the directors and the shareholders are the same people), may not happen at all.

The interim audit can be differentiated from the final audit, which is largely confined to the verification of the financial statements and a review of the draft annual report.

Figure 13.3 Specimen letter of engagement for a company. This example is intended as a guide only and should be varied as circumstances require

To the Chairman, Managing Director or Secretary (as appropriate)

....Company Limited.

Dear Sir,

In accordance with normal professional practice we have pleasure in setting out below our understanding of the services you require us to perform.

1. Audit

   a. We have appointed auditors of your company at the annual general meeting on .... and as such will be responsible for the audit of the first year's accounts to .... in accordance with the Companies Acts 1985 to 2006. Our duties as auditors are to examine the accounts presented to us by the directors.

   b. We shall report, as required by law, to the members whether in our opinion the accounts so presented give a true and fair view of the state of the company's affairs at the date of the balance sheet and of the profit or loss for the year or other period ended on that date and whether those accounts comply with the Companies Acts 1985 to 2006. We shall in addition be obliged under the requirements of our professional body to state whether the accounts are in accordance with the statements of standard accounting practice approved by the profession and, if not, to mention significant departures therefrom and to explain them. Should the financial effects of such departures not be disclosed in the accounts at the request of the board of directors then the reason for that request would have to be stated in the accounts.

   c. In arriving at our opinion we are required by law to report on any of the under-mentioned matters in respect of which we are not satisfied:

      i. whether proper books of account have been kept by the company and proper returns adequate for our audit have been received from branches not visited by us;

      ii. whether the company's balance sheet and profit and loss account are in agreement with the books of account and returns;

      iii. whether we have obtained all the information and explanations which we think necessary for the purposes of our audit;

      iv. completing the writing up of your books and records in so far as they are incomplete when presented to us.

      (See below*)

      In dealing with such work we shall not perform a statutory audit, but will bring your records to a standard whereby an audit can be performed subject only to the information being available and the agreement of your board to our recommendations on accepted statements of standard accounting practice.

2. Taxation

   You have agreed that your staff will be responsible for:

   a. PAYE matters and the completion of all related returns to the Revenue;

   b. Completion and submission of Forms P.11D covering directors' and employees' expenses;

   c. Preparation and submission of monthly/quarterly VAT returns.

   (See below*)

   (*Continues*)

Figure 13.3 *Continued*

We have agreed that we will be responsible for:

preparation of tax computations and submission to and agreement with the Inland Revenue subject only to your instructions as to whether matters should be taken to appeal should circumstances so warrant.

(See below*)

3. Other services

We have also agreed ....

(See below*)

4. Fees

Our fees are based on the time occupied in carrying out the work having regard to the degree of responsibility and skill involved. It is contrary to our code of professional ethics to request or accept fees on a contingency basis.

We would like to conclude by adding that there could well be from time to time further matters in which we could assist you, such as insurance and other claims, management accounting and advisory financial or investment services, mergers and general tax planning, including estate planning. Our fee for the external audit itself is £500,000.

If our understanding of your requirements is correct, perhaps you would be kind enough to sign a copy of this letter and return it to us.

Yours faithfully,

Contents noted and agreed

Date ....   Signature of client ....

*These portions of the letter of engagement should be added to or varied according to the circumstances.

Auditing of accounting estimates

Auditors should be a master of analytical review techniques drawing on trends of figures, which will influence their approach to the conduct of the audit. Estimates will cause some problems and will be of one of three types:

- review estimates
- capital estimates
- financial statement objectives.

Auditors will always discuss the budgetary process as part of their familiarisation with the financial information systems of the company. They will be reassured if they know that the estimates are soundly based and not merely rough-and-ready manufactured figures, sometimes known as 'guestimates'.

It must always be remembered that budgeting and budgetary control systems are part of the organisation's systems of budgetary control. They represent information on which future management decisions are based. The data provided must always be reliable and up to date.

Worked example:
Using estimated information

Consider this problem regarding estimate information. Following an audit visit to a yachting marina the following facts were noted:

■ The main source of revenue was the receipt of mooring fees from privately owned boats.
■ Debtor accounts to boat owners are sent from HQ and income goes direct to HQ.
■ The marina is under the day-to-day control of a manager who lives on site.
■ The income budget for the year is £300,000 and for the half-year is £150,000. Actual income for the half-year period is £60,000 and there are accounts unpaid of £12,000.

As the auditor you are asked to deal with this situation.

When you get to grips with the data, you quickly realise that something is going wrong here. The problem is who is responsible?

It is easy to suspect that there is the possibility of fraud at the marina or income not banked. Income received plus income banked is far less than half the budget. If the auditor investigates this, they will want to make comparisons with previous years and they will want to know the rationale behind the setting of the budget and the assumptions that go to underpin it. It is quite feasible that there is an error in the way the estimates are put together. It is quite feasible that income is being credited to the wrong account. It would be regrettable if the auditor immediately conducted a fraud investigation without eliminating the other possibilities. That is the problem of auditing estimates.

Uncertainty and risk

Of course, when the capital budgeting system is entered into the equation there is the issue of uncertainty and risk. This is illustrated in Tables 13.2 and 13.3.

Table 13.2 **Investment in oil exploration**

Initial investment in oil exploration			−20
Expected cost of production facilities		Likelihood:	PWA
Cost scenario 1, low	−55	0.4	−22.0
Cost scenario 2, medium	−90	0.6	−54.0
Cost scenario 3, high	−175	0	0.0
PWA cost, sum:		1.0	−76.0
Expected value of revenues:		Likelihood:	PWA
Value scenario 1, low	85	0	0.0
Value scenario 2, medium	105	0.4	42.0
Value scenario 3, high	120	0.6	72.0
PWA revenues, sum:		1.0	114.0
Expected value of operating profit:			83.0
NPV incl. R&D			18.0

All numbers are NPV in £m.
PWA = probability-weighted average

Table 13.3 **Valuation of a strategic business unit**

				Valuation of SBA unit computation				
	2009	*2010*	*2011*	*2012*	*2013*	*2014*	*2015*	*Beyond 2015*
Operating profit	12,806	13,713	14,588	15,394	16,250	17,506	18,868	18,868
Taxation	−3,184	−3,512	−3,815	−4,117	−4,450	−4,852	−5,315	−5,315
Depreciation	7,234	7,725	8,039	8,407	8,812	8,980	9,170	
Cash generated from trading	16,856	17,926	18,812	19,684	20,612	21,634	22,723	13,553
Fixed asset investment	−8,410	−8,150	−8,400	−8,830	−9,260	−9,480	−9,710	
Working capital investment	−1,684	−1,678	−1,591	−1,508	−1,599	−1,849	−2,032	193,621*
Free cash flow	6,762	8,098	8,821	9,346	9,753	10,305	10,081	
Discounted at 12%	6,037	6,456	6,279	5,940	5,534	5,221	4,967	87,584
Business value	182,018							
Less net borrowings	−25,568							
Shareholders' value	102,450							
No. shares	40,000							
Per share valuation	256p							

*£193,621 is the value of the cash flow of £13,553 in perpetuity allowing for 5% per year growth. The calculation is: 13,553/(0.12 − 0.05)

Here are two examples of some capital predictions, one relating to oil exploration with data delivered in a manner that senior management is unlikely to understand (Table 13.2) and the other relating to the valuation of a strategic business unit (Table 13.3). Given the fact that the figures go beyond 2015, how much reliance can be put on the estimates? The problem of capital estimates for the auditor is even greater.

An accounting estimate in the financial statements is an approximation in the absence of precise information. Examples that impact on the company are:

■ provisions for bad or doubtful debts;
■ obsolete stock that cannot be sold;
■ provisions for depreciation of fixed assets;
■ contingent liabilities that may arise.

Very often estimates are based on judgment and historical experience. The auditor will want to ensure that management periodically reviews the formula and basis for the process, applying the concepts of prudence and conservation.

The auditor must understand the uncertainty behind the process of estimation and conclude that the estimates are:

■ reasonable
■ prudent
■ necessary
■ disclosed properly
■ where necessary, supported by data or paperwork.

Summary

This chapter highlights the auditor's responsibility for the preparation of financial statements. It is a key role for the external auditor. The early part of this chapter highlights a triangular relationship, which is a feature of the verification audit. The role of the Audit Committee is a critical feature in the system.

A contemporary issue to be considered is the undertaking of non-audit work by the auditor. The literature examines the issue and its impact on auditor independence. This is an area of much discussion.

The importance of the interim audit is put into perspective and linked with some of the early preparation, which must be undertaken.

Estimates can present a problem to auditors unless they are sure of the rationale and assumptions behind them.

? PRACTICE QUESTION

Should external auditors carry out non-audit duties as part of their ongoing audit service?

Asset verification

Contents

Objectives

After studying this chapter you should be able to:

■ describe the procedures involved in the audit of fixed assets;

■ describe the procedures involved in the audit of current assets;

■ explain the use and significance of analytical review.

Introduction

The balance sheet is not merely a statement of assets and liabilities but a document showing a classified summary of all balances appearing in the ledger. These balances, whether they are assets or liabilities, are shown at a particular date. The balance sheet is therefore a company photograph of balances at a point in time known as the end of the financial year.

Every large or medium-sized company must have its accounts audited by a professionally qualified accountant. The appointment is ratified by the shareholders at their annual general meeting (AGM), and while auditors are constantly in contact with the directors and senior managers, they are not acting for them. The shareholders will receive the auditors report at the AGM and will either confirm their re-appointment or replacement.

Most audits are of the annual financial statements of limited companies prepared by management for presentation to the members under the Companies Acts 1985 and 2006. Section 235 of the Act provides that an auditor is required to report whether:

- the balance sheet gives a true and fair view of the state of the company's affairs;
- the profit and loss account gives a true and fair view of the profit or loss for the year;
- in the case of group financial statements, the group financial statements give a true and fair view of the state of affairs and the profit or loss of the undertakings included in the consolidation as a whole, so far as concerns the members of the company;
- the financial statements have been properly prepared in accordance with the Companies Act 1985.

In addition, the auditor is required by section 237 of the Act to report whether:

- proper accounting records have been kept by the company and proper returns adequate for the audit have been received from branches not visited by the auditor;
- the company's individual accounts are in agreement with the accounting records and returns.

If the auditor fails to obtain all the information and explanations considered necessary for the audit, the fact should be stated in the report. Also, if the requirements of schedule 6 to the Act (disclosure of information: emoluments and other benefits of directors and others) have not been complied with in the financial statements, the auditor must, as far as possible, include the necessary information for the shareholders' benefit.

There are specific audit objectives when auditing assets. It is important to obtain evidence, which satisfies beyond all reasonable doubt the following objectives:

- completeness
- accuracy

- existence and ownership
- correct period
- valuation.

In this situation completeness means: does the organisation have the authority to purchase, and are all assets recorded and classified properly in line with company law or international accounting standards? Accuracy means that book value of the asset must reconcile with the ledger accounts. If depreciation has been calculated then the accounting principles must reconcile with one of the generally accepted methods. Existence and ownership are self-explanatory and any additions or disposals must be recorded in the correct financial year. Re-valued assets must be supported by professional evidence to support the new valuation. These tests underpin the audit objectives and should be applied across the board as part of the verification audit.

Pre-audit preparation

Planning and preparing to audit a company's balance sheet are necessary and important and should be undertaken prior to the work being done. Much of the information should be held on the audit file. It should include a description and history of the business, its location, and addresses of its HQ, other offices and branches.

Auditors will need to study an organisational chart and note the key personnel and their areas of responsibility. They will also want to see a copy of the memorandum of association, the letter of engagement, the contract and the pre-audit interview notes. It will be important to be aware of the company structure and whether it is a single company or a group that is being audited.

The audit file should contain details of the company systems, the internal financial regulations and the standing orders. Details of the company's financial history, previous annual reports, banking terms and conditions, insurance details and policies are useful to retain for future reference. So too are copies of specimen signatures for major authorisations.

It is highly recommended that the auditor reviews the previous year's accounts and management letter, noting those areas of weakness which arose from the previous audit together with the audit recommendations. Before setting out to start the verification audit, it is suggested that the auditor asks to read the minutes of both the board meetings and the Audit Committee. This then brings you up to speed to commencing the work on the verification of assets.

Verification of tangible fixed assets

This section will provide guidance on the series of substantive tests for fixed assets (or non-current assets if international accounting standards are used). It will take the reader through the different types of tangible fixed assets and the approach to be adopted in their verification.

Land and buildings

This is generally not an earning asset but it is one whose value may appreciate over time. Many of these assets will be freehold, in which case verification can be confirmed with an inspection of the title deeds and the dates of the conveyance. If independent or further verification is required then the auditor can contact the Land Registry. One of the biggest problems the auditor faces with this type of asset is valuation. Many premises in the UK have enjoyed considerable capital gains and the balance sheet must reflect this. Current re-valuations can be supported by either a chartered surveyor's report or, for cheapness, the use of an insurance company index. They can tell you the percentage increase in property values between given dates. Whatever basis is used, the auditor must ensure that the figure in the balance sheet reflects a realistic, albeit conservative, estimate. Of course, the difference between the book value and the re-valued figure must appear as a capital reserve and the auditor will want to verify this.

Leasehold property will be verified by the examination of the lease whose Terms and Conditions should be noted. It is worth taking a little time on this as the legal jargon can be an area of no concern for some people. Insurance and ground rent are often areas, which are overlooked. The rental of the lease is charged to the Profit and Loss Account but the auditor needs to be aware of clauses about dilapidation which lease holders tend to be very sensitive about either in the period towards the expiry date of the lease or if the property is left empty. The auditor should take note as to whether the lease is a tenants repairing lease or a landlords repairing lease. This can be cross-referenced to any subsequent costs appearing in the Revenue Account.

Plant and machinery

Plant and machinery is not generally valued upon the basis of its realisable or replacement value but on the basis of its value to the particular business as a going concern; in other words, the value is based upon its earning capacity.

The cost price of plant and machinery, less any 'scrap' or residual value, should be written off to revenue over the period of the estimated working life of the asset. The estimated life is, of course, the unknown factor, and it requires technical knowledge to fix this period.

The realisable or replacement values of similar machinery are commonly disregarded, for the plant of a manufacturing company is employed solely for the purpose of manufacturing for the whole of such an asset's working life, and this period is unaffected by fluctuations in the realisable and replacement values. The 'break-up' values are also disregarded, for this asset is not held with a view to resale. A portion of the plant machinery has, as a rule, very little realisable value. For example, machinery specially manufactured for a patent process might be of no value to any other concern. New machinery which has been just installed immediately becomes 'secondhand', and the realisable value is often considerably less than the cost.

All these circumstances, therefore, are disregarded, and the cost price is written off to revenue by means of depreciation over the period of the asset's working life.

In some cases, plant and machinery is re-valued for balance sheet purposes, in which case the certified valuations should be produced to the auditor, but this practice is not yet common. However, it is a very good plan indeed to have plant re-valued occasionally, in order that the proprietors of the business may see whether or not the insurance cover seems likely to provide sufficient capital to replace the fixed assets concerned.

Insurance valuation is good way to check the realistic valuation of plant and machinery, just as the capital allowances computations (tax statements) will be a good way to reconcile depreciation policy. Efficient organisations keep asset registers, which the auditor will want to cross-reference with the insurance records.

Vehicles

Most organisations of size will keep an asset register or inventory. This will be used as a basis for capital allowances tax computations. Proof of ownership can easily be cross-checked to the vehicle registration document or insurance documentation. Company vehicles are a depreciating asset and, in the main, details can easily be cross-checked from the ledger to the balance sheet. Problems that can arise with company vehicles are, firstly, that home or private use sometimes isn't covered with the company insurance policy, and secondly, that all companies will want to have a replacement policy that vehicles are sold on when reaching a certain age or mileage.

Furniture, fitting and equipment

Some of these items are fairly fixed by nature but others can be easily moved and may be seen as rather attractive to steal. Once again, an asset register or inventory should be kept and used for depreciation calculations and capital allowances computations. New purchases of equipment and furniture can be cross-referenced to the invoice and the subsequent account entry in the ledger. Employees may see certain items as easy to pilfer, and such items should be marked with security paint or by pen, which shows up under ultraviolet light. This provides proof of ownership in the event of theft and allows the police to contact the company if stolen articles are found later. In addition, the company should have a policy of keeping certain items of equipment under lock and key. The auditor will certainly want to check this out.

Investments

Most companies will keep an investment register which will give details of each investment. Quoted investments usually come with a share certificate or proof of the investment and the auditor will want to have sight of these. Investments are usually shown at the lower of cost or market price, based on the prudence concept of accounting. However, if quoted investments are shown at market value, this needs to be explained in the notes to the accounts.

Auditors will prove ownership of the investments by cross-checking to see if the dividends have been received in the revenue account. They will take careful note of any script or bonus issues. Valuation can easily be checked with the financial newspapers. Investments in developing countries must be verified for their correct valuation.

Goodwill

This will be classed as an intangible asset and the auditor should study FRS 10 and IAS 38, depending on which applies. The asset can be subdivided between internally generated goodwill, i.e. brand valuation, and externally generated goodwill, i.e. the price paid on acquisition. The key issue, which will always be of concern, is the valuation and measurement of internally generated goodwill and whether it, in itself, breaks the money measurement concept. For externally generated goodwill, the policy of measurement is such an issue. It is therefore sound financial policy to write the cost down against profits or reserves. The auditor should ascertain exactly how the balance on the goodwill account is built up and no improper items can be debited to it without proper justification.

Certification of current assets

This section will discuss the verification of current assets excluding stock, which is dealt with at length in Chapter 10.

Debtors

The auditor will commence work by asking for a statement of balances and will reconcile these from the ledger to the balance sheet. This should already have been done. It is useful at this stage to look at the age of the debt and to form an opinion as to whether it is good, bad or doubtful.

It is worth restating the audit objectives applied to debtors, which form part of the audit programme.

- *Completeness.* Check the personal accounts and ascertain that all debtor balances are included in the balance sheet total.
- *Accuracy.* Control accounts should be in operation to ensure regular reconciliation. There must be proper reconciliation with the accounting records and the balance sheet. This should be done prior to the audit by the ledger clerk.
- *Existence.* The auditor usually, in this instance, will want to check title and ownership of the debt. This is usually done by direct confirmation with debtors themselves. The auditor will write to the debtor and ask them to confirm the balance by reply in a pre-paid envelope.
- *Correct period.* By applying year-end cut-off tests, the auditor will endeavour to ensure that accounting entries appear in the correct accounting year.

■ *Valuation.* The issue for the auditor is to ensure that all debtors in the balance sheet are collectable, in theory at least. The company should have appropriate procedures in place for debt recovery and those debts that prove to be uncollectable should be written off. It would be useful for the auditor to ascertain the company write-off policy and verify that it is being effectively and properly applied.

A significant part of the verification work in this area is the circulation of confirmation letters to debtors, which seeks to verify the accuracy of the balances held on the debtors' accounts. The selection may be a result of random sampling procedures or according to a particular attribute based on size and type. Alternatively, computing software may extract those debtors that are outside a pre-set parameter. Confirmation requests should be clear and concise and sent out on headed stationery. A reply-paid envelope is always enclosed with return to the auditor's independent address and not the organisation's post room. The important thing to watch out for is the failure to respond. It may be necessary in such circumstances to take positive steps to speak to or visit the debtor personally. Follow-up is important with this type of audit. Debtors' personal names can be verified with the electoral roll, telephone directory or the local authority voting records.

The auditor should carefully watch out for debtors who fail to respond, disputes with the company, a high number of posting errors, the posting of remittances to the wrong account and customers who are in financial difficulty.

Bank and cash balances

It is the client's responsibility to provide proper bank reconciliation details so that the bank balances are reconciled with the accounting records. The bank statements themselves provide independent verification for the auditor. However, it is usual practice to request a certificate of balances independently from the bank.

Many cash balances should not be material and therefore carry a fairly low risk. However, cash is a sensitive area and the auditor may want to call for a list of petty cash holders and visit them on the balance sheet date. If this proves difficult then the auditor will want to inspect all petty cash records and vouch them to the appropriate documentation.

Analytical procedures

ISA (UK & Ireland) 520, Analytical Procedures, describes analytical procedures, which include the consideration of comparisons and trends of the organisation's financial information. This will include, for example:

■ comparisons with previous accounting periods;
■ comparisons with the industry average;
■ comparisons with the market leader or a competitor;
■ significant variations from the budget, either anticipated or unanticipated;
■ output data for what the company has achieved over the period and how it compares with previous accounting years.

Table 14.1 **Application of analytical review**

Audit stage	Audit objective	Analytical procedure used
Planning stage	To be aware of the business: ■ To plan approach and allocate time ■ Identify risk ■ Set materiality limits ■ Understand problems as a basis for error detection	■ Ratio analysis ■ Comparisons with previous periods ■ Benchmarking with other organisations ■ Provide a trend analysis ■ Measure outputs and outcomes
During the audit	Confirm ledger account balances or highlight errors	Consider the reasonableness of the ledger account balances
Final review	Confirm the honesty or integrity of the: ■ Profit and Loss Account ■ Balance Sheet ■ Cash Flow Statement ■ Directors Report ■ Corporate Governance requirements	■ Ratio analysis ■ Trend analysis ■ Benchmarking

Analytical procedures and analytical review are regarded as highly effective audit tests. They give a feel for areas which have gone well or badly within the business. They provide a platform to ask appropriate questions. When used as part of the planning stage, they give the auditor a greater understanding of the client's business and shape the course of the audit. Also when the audit is coming to its end and the partner in charge is considering the management letter, they help to provide information to confirm conclusions. This is set out in the Table 14.1.

Computer-assisted audit techniques (CAATs)

A computer-assisted audit technique involves either using a package or application or a test pack. CAATs usually involve professionally developed software for use in the audit of different clients. CAATs are often called retrieval applications because they can be used to identify unusual items or to apply re-performance analysis. They are incredibly useful because they can test vast amounts of data and provide a greater degree of reassurance than traditional statistical sampling. They are effective in the testing of data that does not conform to a particular pattern. An example would be payroll records of staff who have no tax code or National Insurance number or whose overtime is above a certain level. The auditor sets the parameter test within the package, and data that falls outside that parameter is highlighted. Some of the key functions of CAATs are as follows:

■ data above or below a certain parameter;
■ stock older than a certain date;
■ summaries of data obtained from a file;

- date from a file, which has duplicate characteristics (NB The auditor may be testing the system for duplicate payments, for example);
- age analysis of debtors and creditors.

In some cases, the audit facility is part of the client's operating system. In other cases, a package is purchased which allows the auditor to adjust the application. This task is often given to a computer specialist who, with audit training, becomes a valuable member of the audit team.

Some clients have exception reports as part of their system and this can provide audit trial evidence, but others do not, so the CAAT provides the material needed. Large clients have systems that produce vast volumes of data and transactions, making manual checking time-consuming and probably unproductive. The real strength of CAATs is that they identify unusual items which auditors can use as the basis of their investigation. Examples are as follows:

- slow-moving stock
- negative stock balances
- payments of overtime or salaries above a certain limit
- overdue loans or payments due
- employees above or below a certain age
- payments a very low or very high levels.

An alternative type of CAAT is known as the test pack. Test data is prepared by the auditor to test the client's system controls (see Chapter 7). By its very nature, a test pack provides information that is expected to be rejected or at least appear on the client's exception report. The procedure is used to gather evidence of the effectiveness of the client's internal control procedures.

It is recommended that auditors obtain clearance and approval before using a test pack. Otherwise it can be difficult to justify why they are, for example, trying to input data paying unauthorised personnel large sums of money. Another problem with test packs is that, should the data be accepted, it immediately has to be reversed, otherwise it inadvertently falsifies the ledger balances.

Auditors can no longer rely on manual tools. Information technology continues to grow at a considerable pace, electronic transactions are commonplace, data is entered online and there isn't always a paper audit trail. Auditors must go with the IT revolution. The sensible use of CAATs provides an efficient and effective analytical review tool for the auditor.

Summary

This chapter deals with the procedures for the audit of financial statements, commencing with the audit objectives and pre-audit preparation. The objectives are important to be kept in mind because they provide a basis for audit whatever the type of fixed asset and inspection.

The main thrust of this chapter is to take the reader through the approach of verifying both fixed assets and current assets in the balance sheet.

The use and purpose of analytical procedures are of importance in any financial statement audit. They should be used at the planning stage during the audit itself and as part of the final review. They not only provide a sound basis for learning the client's business for the junior auditor but are also an indicator to the audit partner of what has gone well or badly for the client organisation. The use of CAATs provides a modern efficient tool for the auditor to achieve effective results.

? PRACTICE QUESTION

You are required to carry out a verification audit of a company's freehold land and buildings, investments and debtors. Prepare your plan highlighting your approach to the audit.

Chapter 15

Liabilities and accruals

Objectives

After reading this chapter you should be able to:

- apply verification tests to long-term liabilities;

- apply substantive tests to current liabilities;

- appreciate the importance of analytical review.

Introduction

This chapter builds on the previous chapter dealing with the audit of assets. It looks at the other element of balance sheet by providing a basis for the audit of liabilities, both long-term and current. The types of test and the auditor approach are considered, as are comments relating to the significance and importance of analytical review.

Long-term liabilities

This section is designed to provide the reader with a series of substantive testing procedures to be used as part of the verification audit. It is worth repeating the key audit objectives in verifying component parts of the balance sheet:

- completeness
- accuracy
- existence and ownership
- correct period
- valuation.

If you have seen this list before then you will recall the chapters on asset verification. Just as there is ownership of an asset, there is a responsibility to pay for it. Long-term assets should always be financed by long-term liabilities. In effect, this is share capital, loans and reserves. This is the long-term finance used and the auditor has a duty to verify its existence and ownership. Keeping this type of debt off the balance sheet in order to show an untrue financial position is an example of company fraud.

Share capital

This is often split between ordinary and preference shares and also between authorised and issued share capital. The registrar keeps a register of the shareholding and as shares are bought and sold, the register will be updated. Shares can only be sold on production of a valid share certificate. Copies will not suffice in this instance. The registrar will provide the auditor with an analysis that reconciles with the balance sheet. The auditor will reconcile the authorised share capital with the company articles of association.

The rights of respective shareholders are dependent on the articles. Generally preference shareholders are entitled to a fixed dividend paid from profit after tax. The remaining profits are available for distribution to the ordinary shareholders based on directors' recommendation and subsequent approval at the AGM. The directors must make a decision on how much of the profit after tax they will commit to the ordinary shareholders and what percentage of the profit after tax they will want to retain in the business as reserves. They must be prudent with the dividend decision because excessive dividends meanless money re-invested back into the business. It is this level of re-investment which makes the business grow and hence is known as organic growth.

In addition to ordinary and preference shares, the auditor will want to know whether there have been any rights issues or bonus issues during the year. The registrar will confirm this, but of course it can be independently checked with the minutes of the board meetings. Registrars are usually independent of the company and many are affiliated to the major banks. Details of shareholding can be reconciled with the dividends paid, which will be held in the dividend register.

If there is an issue of shares during the year, the auditor will want to see the authority from the minutes of the board meeting approving the issue. The second point to be ascertained is whether the shares have been issued at a premium or a discount. If the shares have been issued at a premium then the balance between the nominal value and the market value must be credited to the balance sheet as a capital reserve, known as the share premium account. In such circumstances, the auditor should apply the following substantive tests:

■ Vouch preliminary expenses associated with the issue and consider their reasonableness.
■ Check the issue with the minutes and prospectus.
■ Verify that cash is received.
■ Independently verify title of the shareholder with its independent records such as the electoral roll.

Lastly, the auditor will want to verify the payment of dividends. These may be distributed by the company registrar independently or by the company itself. In the latter case, a check should be made between the share register, the dividend account and the payment less tax verified with the bank account.

In the case of the final dividend accrued but not yet approved or paid, the auditor will want to verify the accrual by re-computation and cross-comparison with the current liability.

Provisions and reserves

The word reserve means an appropriation of profit that is free for reinvestment for the redistribution for any nominated purpose. This is different from provisions, which is an appropriation of profit set aside for a known or a specific purpose. For example, this can be for bad debts or for depreciation. Reserves tend to be subdivided into capital reserves and revenue reserves.

Capital reserves are related to capital items which are not free for distribution unless the item to which they relate is sold. An example is a reserve that arises from the revaluation of premises. This cannot be spent unless the premises are sold. Another form of capital reserve is the share premium account.

Revenue reserves are amounts set aside for investment or distribution. The auditor will look at the previous year's balance sheet and then ask for a reconciliation statement, which reconciles each type of capital movement between the two financial years.

Loans and debentures

Upon an issue of debentures and loans, the allotments will be checked in exactly the same way as an allotment of shares. The auditor must see that the articles give the directors power to borrow money in this way, and should examine the directors' minute to verify authorisation. The actual debenture or trust deed should be examined, in order that the terms of the issue may be ascertained. It must further be seen that any charge given upon the assets of the company is entered in the register of charges in accordance with company law.

The entries in the financial books should be checked, and if debentures or loans are issued at a discount, the full nominal amount must be credited to the liability account, as that is the actual amount of the liability which will have to be repaid, and the amount of the discount must be debited to a separate account and then written off to the profit and loss account. The discount should be written off to revenue as soon as possible, but, subject to the provisions of the articles of the particular company, an auditor could raise no objection if the discount were written off over the period of the debentures or loan.

If debentures or loans are issued at a premium, the nominal amount again must be credited to the liability account, and the amount of the premium itself must be credited to a premium account.

If debentures or loans are issued at par and repayable at the end of a period at a premium, then they should appear in the books and on the balance sheet at the nominal amount, with a note that they are repayable at a certain date at a premium. The premium is in the nature of a payment of deferred interest, which should be provided for out of revenue over the period of the debentures or loans, as otherwise the whole amount of the premium will have to be charged to the profit and loss account of the year in which they are redeemed.

Debentures are usually issued as fixed or floating or, very rarely, unsecured. This means they are secured against a particular asset or against a range of assets. There is usually a stipulation in the accounts or notes to the accounts of the period when debentures are to be repaid. For example, 8% debentures 13–15 means that debentures can be repaid from the beginning of January 2013 to the end of December 2015. Interest on the debenture is 8% and the company will have to take a view on interest rates at that time. It may be that if interest rates are low, i.e. between 5% and 6%, then it would be cheaper to pay off the loan and, if further finance is needed, borrow at the lower interest rates. Alternatively, if interest rates are relatively high in 2013, i.e. about 11–12%, then the company will be well advised to repay the debt at the end of 2015, assuming of course that it needs the finance.

The auditor will want to apply the following substantive tests in order to achieve the objectives:

- Verify issues and redemptions of loans with board minutes.
- Look at the impact of issues and redemptions:
  - the loan account
  - the debenture account.

- Calculate by re-performance the interest to be paid and verify this with the revenue account.
- Ascertain whether a register of loans or a register of loan charges exists. Examine whether debentures are fixed, floating or unsecured, and whether loans are secured on assets.
- Examine the deeds or other documentation relating to debentures or loans.
- Enquire whether the company has a borrowing policy, a gearing policy or a strategy about its long-term financing. If a policy exists, check it is laid down, communicated and complied with.
- Cross-check the balance outstanding with the bank or the lending institution. Direct confirmation has many advantages.
- From a valuation perspective, are loans valued at a premium or a discount?

Current liabilities

In accounting the word current means short-term, i.e. less than a year. Hence short-term liabilities should be used to finance short-term assets. They form part of the working capital cycle. The audit objectives which apply to asset verification and long-term liability verification are the same for current liabilities but are worth re-stating:

- completeness
- accuracy
- existence and ownership
- correct period
- valuation.

Creditors

This section deals specifically with trade creditors, which are short-term liabilities that relate to the client's business. They relate to goods or services which have been received but not yet paid for, as the invoice has not been received at the year-end date. Alternatively, the invoice may have been received but has not yet been paid.

The auditor will be very much aware that profits can be inflated if invoices are not processed. The audit should be aware that cut-off testing has an important part to play here. Auditors should examine some of the company orders and check these with the dates of the goods received notes so that they can draw conclusions as to whether the creditors have been correctly set up in the accounts and that the accounting entries are in the correct financial year.

In order that auditors may be satisfied that all invoices have been included, their clients should arrange that, at the date of the balance sheet, a notice should be sent to every supplier requesting them to provide direct to the auditor a statement showing the balance due to them at that date, or if there is nothing owing, a notification to that effect. These statements should be compared with the ledger accounts, having seen that such statements bear the date on which the financial period ends. If all these agree, it is proof that the individual creditors' books agree with the books of the company, and therefore that, as regards these accounts at any rate, no invoices have been omitted.

In some cases, such statements may not agree, as goods may have been debited by the creditors on or before the date of the balance sheet, but they may not have been received and credited in the client's books until the following period. In such cases the auditor should carefully trace such goods through the goods received note, confirming the dates, and should see that these goods have not been included in stock. On the other hand, goods may not have been debited by the creditor until after the date on which they were delivered and the auditor must make similar checks to ensure that the goods have been included in stock. It may be found that certain accounts are in dispute, and therefore the statements disagree. In these circumstances, careful inquiries should be made to see that adequate provision is made in the accounts for all estimated liabilities.

This section deals with trade creditors but other creditors arise from utility bills and from employees. Utility bills are usually submitted quarterly in the instance of telephone, gas and electricity. It will be worthwhile for the auditor to test check that in these instances four bills are debited to the overhead account. The same procedure can be applied to other utility bills that are paid to a pattern. Business rates, for example, could be paid in one lump sum payment. If that happens, the auditor would expect to be able to trace one payment in the overhead account for the premises in question. It can happen that the next year's business rates are paid early and that two transactions sit in the overhead account rather than one of them being moved to a prepayments account. In other instances, business rates can be paid in 10 instalments. In such circumstances, the auditor will want to test check that 10 items appear in the overhead account and not 9 or 11, which can sometimes happen.

Of course, when it comes to staff expenses, a test check is useful to ensure that these expenses fall in the correct financial year. Some company employees can be a little lax when it comes to submitting claims. Others choose to build them up to have a 'savings account effect'. Late expenses claims beyond a certain cut-off point should not be paid.

Other late accruals that may be forgotten include the audit fee for the accounting period. Provision must be made for this.

The auditor will want to also ensure that all interest payable on any loans or debentures is included as an accrual.

The auditor will want to apply some substantive tests to ensure that they are satisfied with the figures stated in the balance sheet, as follows:

- Ensure all trade creditor balances are accurately summarised.
- Ascertain that control account reconciliation is in place.
- Test check the reconciliation procedures on the control account.
- Test that those creditors included in the reconciliation do, in effect, exist.
- Cut-off testing is important here. The auditor will want to ensure that proper account has been taken for all goods and services provided around the year-end date.

- Circulation of suppliers to confirm balances is useful.
- Test check that proper authorisation procedures are in place.
- Examine creditors' accounts for any debit balances and ascertain the reason for its existence.

Cut-off testing and proper reconciliation through control accounts are essential ingredients which the auditor will be watching carefully. If the client is unable to demonstrate proper systems of control and has difficulty in reconciliation then the auditor will be left with doubts as to whether the records are reliable and must therefore report on this fact accordingly.

Dividends

The articles usually provide that the directors shall recommend dividends to be paid to the shareholders who have no power to vote dividends in excess of those recommended.

During the year the directors may recommend the payment of an interim dividend, which the will be shown in the minutes at the board meeting for the auditor to inspect. Of course, by recommending this dividend the directors must be able to justify it. The final dividend is to be included in the financial statements as an accrual and approved by shareholders' vote at the AGM. Details of all dividends paid to shareholders should be recorded in the shareholders' register. There will be cases where some shareholders cannot be traced and other instances where they will have died. This will always happen in a large company. In such circumstances the credit due should be transferred to a special suspense account and held separately, the credit of which is shown as an accrual in the balance sheet. Dividends which are due to deceased shareholders become payable to their executors. Other dividends not claimed become statute-barred in accordance with the Statutory Limitations Act. Forfeited dividends can be transferred to the revenue reserve.

Taxation

Full provision must be made for taxation due on all profits or capital gains which is normally paid after the balance sheet date. There may also be value added tax due to be paid as well as income tax and National Insurance contributions deducted from employee salaries. On top of this there will be claims for capital allowances (depreciation) for vehicles, plant and equipment.

The auditor should request a schedule of tax computations which reconciles with the estimated tax calculation shown as an accrual in the balance sheet. The auditor may be a trained tax specialist but the reality of the situation means they probably will not be. However, if there are serious errors in the tax computations, it is very likely that Her Majesty's Revenue & Customs (HMRC) will be quick to point them out. The auditor can be reassured that today's software packages can be a great help and most practices which offer themselves for audit always have a tax specialist. Even small practices usually have a consultancy arrangement with a specialist tax practitioner. Tax itself is a minefield for some and the auditor must be aware of this and recognise the boundaries involved.

Audit objectives for balance sheet verification of both assets and liabilities have been well stated previously.

In respect of taxation, the auditor will undertake the following substantive tests:

- Agree the company tax computation itemised between different groups of taxes with the balance sheet.
- Obtain the previous year's estimated tax computation and agree with the level of tax paid. Question why differences have arisen. They may help with the current year's computation.
- Ask for the P11D proforma. This deals with deduction of tax from employees' salaries. Test check by sampling its accuracy. Ensure that tax deducted from staff salaries, including National Insurance, is paid over to HMRC.
- Check calculation and additions of the statement.
- Compare the tax accrual with the previous years.

Overdraft

The overdraft is a current liability because it is money that is owing to the bank at the balance sheet date. It is likely that many companies will have several bank accounts, but the current account may go into overdraft because it is considered to be a convenient means of obtaining cash, particularly if the company has cash flow problems. However, the problems of overdraft are that, if unauthorised, they can be expensive and, secondly, the bank can require them to be paid at close of business the same day, which is basically immediately. Many treasury managers use the overdraft as a convenient form of short-term finance and it must be used in that context. The auditor in order to achieve the audit objectives will want to:

- inspect and verify the bank statement;
- check and test the bank reconciliation;
- call for a bank certificate to confirm the balance, albeit a negative balance.

Analytical review

The purpose of analytical review procedures is fully dealt with in Chapter 14. These procedures are designed to ascertain whether there is a material error in any recorded or posted account. If it is not possible to fully explain the differences in trends or between years then clearly the auditor must carry out a full investigation. Analytical review procedures often identify:

- the reason behind what was probably ignored in the past;
- budgeting errors;
- material posting errors in the financial information system;
- deficient management controls;
- a failure of responsible officers to investigate potential problems;
- deficient and ineffective internal controls.

It is worth stating the purpose of analytical review procedures:

- to make comparisons with the previous accounting period;
- to make comparisons with the industry average;
- to make comparisons with the market leader or a competitor;
- to identify significant variations from the budget either anticipated or not anticipated;
- to provide output data for what the company has achieved and how it compares with previous accounting years.

This chapter focuses on the liabilities part of the balance sheet. Analytical review procedures have a part to play here. Changes and comparisons to the financial structure, the implications of capital investment on gearing policy must be reconciled to the policy of the board. The auditor may be required to provide an independent opinion on financing policy and will expect to see a degree of prudence exercised. Changes in patterns of reserves held and creditors' payment periods as part of the working capital cycle are all areas to be included in the analytical review.

Summary

This chapter concludes the verification audit of the balance sheet. It states the audit objectives and provides a checklist of checks and balances to be carried out. The chapter concentrates on liabilities, both long-term and short-term, and how the auditor should confirm the accuracy as part of the statutory duties.

The chapter concludes by restating the purpose of analytical review procedures and the use that can be made of them before, during and at the end of the audit. It states that this is a technique by which comparable balances and trends are compared between financial years. This technique can be carried out manually, using, for example, accounting ratios, but if a more complex approach is necessary then it is prudent to use computer-assisted auditing techniques.

? PRACTICE QUESTION

Prepare an audit plan to test the reliability and accuracy of the creditors figure in the balance sheet.

Chapter 16

Going concern

Objectives

After studying this chapter you should be able to:

- describe the audit approach to the assessment of 'going concern' reviews;
- describe the relevance of going concern reviews;
- explain the procedures applicable to performing going concern reviews;
- discuss the implications of the findings of going concern reviews.

Introduction

When an investment is made in a company there is an expectation that it will be lucrative, unlike the purchase of a car to travel back and forth to work where it is expected that the investment or capital outlay will diminish in value (unless of course the car is a vintage one). Investors purchase shares in going concern entities where there is an expectation that turnover and profit will continue as it currently stands or, even better, that they will increase in the foreseeable future. Institutional investors, in particular, are looking for a safe return on their investment as they have a duty to their own clients or fund contributors, such as pension funds and insurance companies.

Companies wishing to attract long-term investors need to display that they are a going concern, if they are to maintain credibility in the market. This is where the financial statements are required to be properly prepared in accordance with the Companies Act of 1985 to give a true and fair view. This true and fair view will reflect the management's (executive directors) assumption that the business is going to continue in the foreseeable future.

When auditors undertake the role of forming an opinion on the financial statements, they must plan and perform their audit work by taking into account the management's use of going concern assumptions in the preparation of the financial statements.

The going concern assumption

The going concern assumption is a fundamental principle in the preparation of the financial statements. When planning and performing the audit and in the evaluation process, the auditor needs to consider the appropriateness of management's use of the going concern assumption in the preparation of the financial statements. ISA 570, Going Concern, requires the auditor to consider material uncertainties that may cast doubt on the entity's going concern status.

Under the going concern assumption, a company is ordinarily viewed as a continuing business for the foreseeable future with neither the intention nor the necessity of liquidation, ceasing trading or seeking protection from creditors. Assets and liabilities are recorded on the basis that the company will be able to realise its assets and pay its liabilities in the normal course of its business activity.

Those charged with governance, namely the directors, must, according to the Companies Act 1985 (para. 10, Sch. 4), ensure that 'the company shall be presumed to be carrying on business as a going concern'. The Financial Reporting Standard FRS 18 (Accounting Policies) states that: 'The information provided by financial statements is usually most relevant if prepared on the hypothesis that the entity is able to continue in existence for the foreseeable future. This hypothesis is commonly referred to as the going concern assumption.'

IAS 1 (Presentation of Financial Statements) reiterates this but adds that: 'In assessing whether the going concern assumption is appropriate, management takes into account all available information about the future, which is at least, but not limited to, twelve months from the balance sheet date.'

Management's assessment of the going concern assumption

Undertaking an assessment about future activities, events, conditions and outcomes that are uncertain will involve management, i.e. those charged with governance, in making judgments as to the possible outcomes

A number of factors will influence these assessments:

- When there is a degree of uncertainty (an inherent uncertainty) associated with an outcome, the uncertainty increases significantly the further into the future a judgment is being made, as the element of the unknown has very few supporting factors. For this reason, most financial reporting frameworks that need a definite management assessment will normally identify a specific period that has to be taken into consideration.
- When judgments are undertaken about future events, known factors or previous experiences are used as a basis to guide these assessments of future outcomes. It may be that subsequent events or the actual outcome will contradict management's judgment, but it has to be assumed that the decision at the time it was made was a reasonable one.
- The assessment of the outcome will rest upon the size and complexity of the company, the type of business activity, and the condition and the complexity of the business. The impact of external factors on the company will also have a certain amount of influence on the assessments made by management.

Risk to the going concern of an entity

The risk to the going concern of an entity is defined as a threat individually or collectively that can cast a significant doubt about the going concern assumption. Examples of risks that an entity can face are shown in Exhibit 16.1.

Risks and uncertainties relate to the future. There is likely to be limited information on possible outcomes – leading to the need to consider them from a probabilistic point of view. The situation can often be negative and this relates to unwanted or undesired outcomes, which can threaten objectives. It is inevitable that risks and uncertainties cannot be wholly eliminated – they are part of life.

As with life, certain situations can be mitigated by taking the appropriate action. People avoid being knocked down by a car by looking both ways before crossing the road; in the same way businesses need to be forward-looking in their actions. Appropriate action by management to ensure a constant supply of raw materials will mean not relying solely on one supplier. Thus, when one supplier fails to deliver the goods, the loss can be mitigated by increasing the order from another supplier.

Exhibit 16.1 **Risks faced by an entity**

Business risk

■ Failure to assess changes in the economy, leaving the business dependent on a few product lines where the market is depressed.

■ Failure to develop business activity in line with technological developments.

■ Technical developments which render a key product obsolete.

■ Loss of major markets, franchise, licence or principal supplier to a competitor.

Financial risk

■ The net liability or net current liability position is such that it indicates possible liquidity issues.

■ When the necessary borrowing facilities have not been agreed, there is a likelihood that either debts or investment opportunities will not be fulfilled.

■ When there is a major restructuring of debt, it may indicate that the finance position is not as healthy as originally anticipated.

■ When fixed-term borrowing matures without any realistic prospects of a renewal or repayment, while excessive reliance on short-term borrowings to finance long-term assets will eventually lead to a situation that is not sustainable.

■ When major losses have been encountered, or where there are cash flow problems which have arisen since the balance sheet date, the going concern potential may become questionable.

■ A change from credit to cash on delivery truncations with suppliers may make sound business in terms of cash flow, but if the suppliers are demanding cash on delivery it may indicate that the credit rating is suspect and is not well received by suppliers.

■ The inability to obtain financing for essential new product development or other essential investments undoubtedly indicates that the company is not considered a good investment by the borrowing community.

■ Asset stripping by undertaking a substantial sale of fixed assets that are not intended to be replaced can indicate drastic measures being taken to meet creditor demands.

■ Continued inability to pay creditors on due dates, with excessive charges for late payments, court action and stoppage of vital supplies of basic arterials.

■ An inability to comply with the terms of loan agreements will indicate financial problems that can lead to further actions for foreclosure of the debt.

Compliance risk

■ Non-compliance with company or other statutory requirements.

■ Pending legal or regulatory proceedings against the company that may, if successful, result in claims that are unlikely to be satisfied.

■ Change in legislation or government policy expected to adversely affect the company, where failure to comply can lead to additional costs that the company may not have budgeted for or be able to pay.

Operational risk

■ The loss of key management without replacement because a decision based on cost savings may be short-sighted when there is a need to have appropriate staff with the right skills managing the operation or department.

■ Failure to recruit the appropriate staff due to labour or skills shortages.

■ Loss of key staff without replacement – e.g. IT department staff in a lottery syndicate could, on winning the jackpot, decide not to come back to work, thus leaving the company in a situation where no one is able to manage or operate the IT systems.

■ Labour difficulties where staff may take action against the company due to unfair practices, poor or unsafe working conditions.

■ Local or world shortages of important supplies, which in the short term cannot be resolved without recourse to supply and demand rules, leading to extortionate prices that are not feasible and sustainable in the longer term.

Auditor's responsibility

The auditor's responsibility is to consider the appropriateness of management's use of the going concern assumptions in the preparation of the financial statements, and to consider whether there are material uncertainties about the company's ability to continue as a going concern that need to be disclosed in the financial statements.

In planning the audit, auditors need to ensure that they have an understanding of the company in terms of establishing whether there are any events or conditions and related business risks which may cast doubt on the company as a going concern.

The auditor will look at the period used by the directors in assessing the going concern aspects, i.e. the period used by those charged with governance and the relevant information that they were aware of at the time. They will be looking forward in terms of their assessment, but in reality it is going to be difficult to specify exactly the length of time, as there is no 'cut-off point'. The length of time will depend upon the company's reporting and budgeting systems and the nature, size and complexity of the company. The larger or more complex the company, the more likely it is that the information available to the auditor will need to be more sophisticated in order to support the audit assessment of whether to adopt the going concern basis. If the information relates to future events, there is the question of how far into the future the events lie. There will inevitably be an element of estimation involved.

The audit approach to the assessment of 'going concern' reviews must involve checking:

- whether the period applied in assessing the going concern is reasonable in light of the company's circumstances;
- the systems used for identification of warnings of future risks for the company;
- budgets and forecasting are in place to produce the information and its updating;
- whether the assumptions underlying the budgets and forecasts are appropriate;
- the sensitivity of budgets and forecasts to variable factors within the control of the directors and those outside their control;
- any obligations, undertaking or guarantees arranged with other parties for the giving or receiving of support;
- the existence, adequacy and terms of borrowing facilities, and suppler credit;
- the plans of those charged with governance (the directors) for resolving the issues assessed and giving rise to going concern;
- the practicality of the plans in resolving the issues identified.

Period beyond management's assessment

There is a possibility that there may be known facts, events or conditions that will occur beyond the period of assessment used by the directors and management that may bring into question the appropriateness of the going concern assumption. However, as there is a degree of uncertainty the further into the future an event or condition is likely to take place, the impact on the going concern will have to be significant before the auditor takes any further action, although the auditor may ask the directors and management about the potential significance of the event on the going concern of the company.

Procedures when events are identified

When there are issues identified that may cast doubt on the company's ability to continue as a going concern, the auditor will need to:

- undertake a review of the future action plans outlined by management based on their assessment;
- ensure that sufficient evidence is gathered in order to confirm or dispel whether a material uncertainly exists and undertake further audit tests and audit procedures to substantiate this uncertainty;
- obtain written representations from management in relation to their plans of action for the future of the company.

Management assessments

ISA 570, Going Concern, requires the auditor to consider whether material uncertainties affect an entity's going concern status.

In evaluating management's assessments, the auditor will:

- review the same period as used by management, normally that required for financial reporting frameworks of 12 months;
- consider whether management's assessment includes all relevant information;
- inquire of management its knowledge of any events or conditions beyond the 12 months that may cast doubt on the going concern of the entity.

If the auditors are unable to obtain written confirmation of representations considered necessary then they can decide whether:

- there is limitation of scope of the auditor's work which requires a qualified opinion or disclaimer of opinion;
- the failure of those charged with governance to provide the written confirmation indicates that there is concern about the going concern of the company.

Disclosure requirement relating to going concern issues

Based on the audit evidence obtained, the auditor will determine if, in their judgment, a material uncertainty exists relating to the events or conditions that, individually or when grouped together, cast significant doubt on the company's ability to continue as a going concern. The auditor will need to ensure that this concern is documented in terms of the company's ability to continue as a going concern.

If there is a significant level of concern about the company's ability to continue as a going concern based on a material uncertainty, auditors may have to disclose in the financial statements the nature of this material uncertainty, otherwise they will not be able to give a true and fair opinion on the financial statements. On the other hand, the auditor may be able to issue an unqualified report by adding an emphasis of matter section that the noting of the material uncertainty may indicate that the company may not be able to meet all its liabilities as expected in the normal course of business.

Additional procedures when events or conditions are identified

If doubts are cast on the entity's ability to continue as a going concern the auditor will need to obtain further evidence by performing additional audit procedures:

- If management has yet to undertake its assessment then it will be requested to undertake an assessment.
- In evaluating management's future action plans regarding the going concern assessment the auditor will evaluate whether the plans are likely to improve the situation.
- Where management has undertaken financial analysis the auditor will evaluate the reliability of the data and determine whether there is adequate support for the assumptions made.
- The auditor will request written confirmation from management (those charged with governance) of their plans/actions along with their feasibility.

Subsequent events review

Events or conditions which cast significant doubt on the company as a going concern may be identified during the normal audit process and when performing a risk assessment of procedures within the company. However, the auditor will also need to consider whether additional information has become available since the date on which management undertook its assessment. By undertaking additional audit procedures, the auditor can establish whether management's plans are feasible and whether the outcome of these plans will improve the situation.

Audit procedures that are relevant in this case are as follows:

- analysing and discussing cash flow, profit and other forecasts with management;
- analysing and discussing the company's latest available financial statements;
- reviewing the terms of debentures and loan agreements and determining whether any have been breached;
- reading minutes of board meetings, meetings with shareholders and committees for any reference to financing difficulties;
- enquiring of the entity's lawyer as to the existence of litigation and claims outcomes and the reasonableness of management's assessment of possible outcomes, including any assessment of the financial implications;
- confirming the existence, legality and enforceability of arrangements to provide or maintain financial support with related and third parties and assessing their financial ability to provide any additional finance;
- considering the company's plans to deal with unfilled customer orders;
- reviewing events after the period end to identify those that either mitigate or otherwise affect the company's ability to continue as a going concern.

When the analysis of cash flow is a significant factor in considering the future outcome of events or conditions the auditor will review:

- the reliability of the company's information system for generating such information;
- whether there is adequate support for the assumptions underlying the forecast.

In addition the auditor will compare the prospective financial information for recent prior periods with historical data and the prospective financial information for the current period with results achieved to date.

The overall review

The overall review will provide the readers of the financial statements with information as to whether the company is a going concern. The audit report will confirm whether the financial statements include disclosures relating to the going concern, while the audit opinion expressed will draw attention to an emphasis of matter highlighting any material uncertainty or whether the audit opinion is such that it has to be a qualified or adverse opinion if adequate disclosure is not made in the financial statements.

Auditing Practices Board – Bulletin 2008/1

In January 2008 the Auditing Practices Board issued a Bulletin 2008/1, 'Audit issues when financial market conditions are difficult and credit facilities may be restricted'. The bulletin was issued as a result of the 'credit crunch' of 2007, and was intended to provide guidance to auditors when dealing with matters related to it.
The bulletin addressed two key issues:

■ the implications for companies wishing to renew or obtain finance and the possible consequences for the going concern assumption;
■ the impact on valuation of investments, especially where there has been a severe curtailment or cessation of market trading.

The second issue is more relevant to financial institutions and investment funds, but it could also apply to pension funds or companies with developed treasury activities. The going concern issue is applicable to any company that is about to renew or extend its existing borrowing facilities or is in difficulty itself.
The bulletin focused on aspects applicable to the audit engagement in line with the then ISA 220 (UK and Ireland) issued in 2004. This standard has since been amended in 2009, but the key themes remain just as relevant as outlined in the following three points:

■ involvement in the direction, supervision and performance of the audit;
■ the capabilities and competence of the audit team;
■ consultation with other professionals on difficult and contentious matters;
■ in addition the nature and timing of communications with those charged with governance as outlined in ISA (UK & Ireland) 260.

When the going concern aspect is considered, the key audit planning issues that the auditors need to consider are:

■ Establishing whether the borrowing facilities are coming up for renewal within the next 12 months and considering whether the previous ease with which the borrowing facilities were obtained will continue in the current market;

- identifying whether the company has complied with the existing borrowing covenants (this will require the auditor to re-examine the borrowing agreement to establish which covenants apply);
- bearing in mind the indirect impact of the 'credit crunch' and any related issues such as changes in interest rates and any perceived economic slowdown that might affect the nature of the company's business. Indirect impacts include the way that businesses that deal in household items such as furniture and white goods may be affected by the slowdown in the property market.

Audit evidence issues

The auditor will need to consider what the directors plan to do about dealing with the renewal or extension of finance, what the nature of the plan is and how practical that plan is going to be in dealing with the problem. The auditor will, however, need to consider the danger of becoming too closely identified with the company's plan for raising finance through other services supplied and thereby creating a self-review threat or management threat for the audit. There will be a need for the directors' report to provide a fair and a balanced review of the risks and uncertainties faced by the business.

The Companies Act 2006 and going concern issues

The Companies Act of 2006 highlights the importance of the relationship between responsible business behaviour and business success. Section 172 states that the directors have a responsibility to promote the success of the company, while Section 714(3) requires that within the annual report the directors must provide a statement about the going concern. The Act stipulates that the directors must state that, having made a full inquiry into the affairs and prospects of the company, they have formed the opinion:

(a) as regards its initial situation immediately following the date on which the payment out of capital (distribution of dividend) is proposed to be made, that there will be no grounds on which the company could then be found unable to pay its debts, and

(b) as regards its prospects for the year immediately following that date, that having regard to:
(i) their intentions with respect to the management of the company's business during that year, and
(ii) the amount and character of the financial resources that will in their view be available to the company during that year, the company will be able to continue to carry on business as a going concern (and will accordingly be able to pay its debts as they fall due) throughout that year.

In forming their opinion for the purposes of subsection (3)(a), the directors must take into account all of the company's liabilities (including any contingent or prospective liabilities).

The director's statement must have as an annex a report addressed to them by the company's auditor stating that:

He as auditor is not aware of anything to indicate that the opinion expressed by the directors in their statement as to any of the matters mentioned in section 714 subsection (3) as outlined above is unreasonable in all the circumstances.

Summary

The going concern issue is one that current and potential shareholders and stakeholders alike are likely to be very interested in as neither will want to invest in a company that is not going to yield some form of return. Stakeholders such as employees will want to be reassured that their jobs will continue into the foreseeable future. Uncertainties about future outcomes do cause problems in terms of the assessment of outcomes that affect the continuity of a business. Management has to make certain assumptions based on past experience or precedents set elsewhere when making assessments as to the going concern of a business. Government is aware of this dilemma and the auditor and directors have a duty to report on the going concern assumption as part of the feedback to shareholders.

? PRACTICE QUESTION

The going concern assumption is a fundamental principle in the preparation of the financial statements. Discuss why it is of importance to both senior management and the auditor.

Audit reporting

Objectives

After studying this chapter you should be able to:

- explain the requirements of the reporting standard ISA (UK & Ireland) 700;
- describe the circumstances that lead to a qualified audit report;
- distinguish between different types of audit reports;
- discuss the merits of the standardised report;
- describe the difference between management reports and statutory required reports (true and fair opinion reports);
- illustrate and analyse the format of both qualified and unqualified audit reports.

Introduction

The external audit report is a legal requirement for UK listed companies that is outlined in the Companies Act of 1985. The appointed external auditor has to give an audit opinion as to whether the financial statement gives a true and fair view.

The Companies Act of 1985 Section 235 states that: 'A company's auditor shall make a report to the company's members on all annual accounts of the company of which copies are to be laid before the company in general meeting during their tenure of office.' In terms of the auditor opinion, the Act states that: 'the report must state whether the annual accounts give a true and fair view in accordance with the relevant reporting framework'.

The format of the opinion report has to fall into two categories – 'The auditors' report must be either unqualified or modified (qualified) and must include a reference to any matters to which the auditors wish to draw attention by way of emphasis without qualifying the report' – while confirmation of what the directors include within the annual report for the financial year are confirmed by the auditor: 'The auditors must state in their report whether in their opinion the information given in the directors' report for the financial year for which the annual accounts are prepared is consistent with those accounts.'

ISA (UK & Ireland) 700, The Auditor's Report on Financial Statements, provides the framework for the audit report which is in the form of an opinion on the financial statements of the company:

> The auditor should review and assess the conclusions drawn from the audit evidence obtained as the basis for the expression of an opinion on the financial statement. . . . The auditor's report should contain a clear written expression of opinion on the financial statements taken as a whole.

The audit report

The audit report is an encapsulation of the conclusions drawn from all of the audit evidence collected. To the public, it is the only visible means of communication in terms of the assurance given by the auditor as to the true and fair view on the financial statements.

The Companies' Act 1985, Section 235, said the report must state whether the financial statements:

- have been prepared in accordance with the Act;
- show a true and fair view.

The Companies Act 2006, as well as requiring the audit firm's name to be published at the end of the audit report, also requires the name of the person who signed the report, identified as the senior statutory auditor. The following must also be referred to in the report should the circumstance arise if in the auditor's opinion:

- proper accounting records have not been kept;
- proper returns have not been received from branches not visited by them;
- the individual accounts are not in agreement with the accounting records;

Figure 17.1 **Business activity and audit role**

- there has been a failure to obtain all of the information and explanations necessary for the purpose of the audit;
- there are inconsistencies between the director's report and the financial statements;
- directors' transactions have not been disclosed elsewhere.

The circumstances will cause the auditors to consider whether these are material or fundamental to the financial statements, and whether the audit opinion needs to be qualified. The nature of the qualification will dictate how this is conveyed within the report. The expanded audit report format as outlined in ISA 700 is one means by which the 'communication gap' (an element of the expectation gap), the gap between what is expected of the auditors and what the auditors consider their role to be, can be bridged.

Figure 17.1 illustrates how the audit role of giving an opinion on the financial statements and providing assurance to both management and stakeholders fits in to the overall corporate business activity where the investor releases funds to the directors of the organisation on the basis that there is a relationship between the two. This relationship is often referred to as an 'agency theory' where the directors work for the benefit of the investor who expects to receive a return for the investment in the format of dividends and/or increased share value. The directors, in turn, will also benefit, possibly by their own share value or performance-related return or by director emoluments increasing with the corporate business success, not to mention the kudos of being directors of a successful company. The financial statements will act as one format of accountability in displaying how well the directors have directed and controlled the business, i.e. governed the corporate entity. These statements will be confirmed by the external auditor as displaying a true and fair reflection of what has occurred during the preceding year, the audit opinion of a *true and fair view*, which acts as a level of assurance to those investors who are indirectly owners of the company.

In line with the Companies Act, the audit report conveys the basis of the report and the nature of the report. In order to establish consistency, the format of the report, its wording and the end result have been laid out in the standard ISA (UK & Ireland) 700. The APB has not adopted the ISA 700 as issued by the IAASB but has, instead, issued a clarified version, revised in 2009. ISA 700 became effective in the UK as of December 2004. (A recent APB Bulletin, Auditor's Reports on Financial Statements in the United Kingdom, provides a full range of examples of published reports to illustrate the standardised audit report.)

The aims of a standardised audit report are as follows:

- to set the audit report and therefore the role of the auditor in context, i.e. make the user aware of its limitations;
- to illustrate to the user the precise nature of the work undertaken by the auditor;
- to demonstrate the roles and responsibilities of directors and auditors.

The auditor's job is to form an opinion with regard to:

- the appropriateness of any accounting policies dealing with the matter;
- the reasonableness of the estimates included in the financial statements;
- the adequacy of the disclosure.

The unqualified audit report

ISA 700 states that:

> An unqualified report should be expressed when the auditor concludes that the financial statements give a true and fair view (or are presented fairly, in all material respects) in accordance with the identified financial reporting framework.

The auditor's report includes the following basic elements, ordinarily in the following layout:

(a) Title
(b) Addressee
(c) Introductory paragraph
   (i) Identification of the financial statements audited.
(d) Respective responsibilities of those charged with governance and audits
   (i) A statement of the responsibility of the entity's management and the responsibility of the auditor.
(e) Scope of the Audit of Financial Statements
   (i) A reference to relevant national standards or practices as found on the APB website.
   (ii) A description of the work the auditor performed.
(f) Opinion on the financial statements
   (i) A reference to the financial reporting framework used to prepare the financial statements.
   (ii) An expression of opinion on the financial statements.
(g) Opinion in respect of additional financial reporting framework
(h) Requirement specific to public sector entities where an opinion on regularity is given
(i) Opinion on other matters
(j) Date of report
(k) Location of auditor's office
(l) Auditor's signature.

It is important to have uniformity in the form and content of the auditor's report as it helps to promote the reader's understanding as well as clearly indicating any unusual circumstances when they occur.

Introductory paragraphs

The opening paragraph confirms the company, the records audited, namely the financial statements, whether the company is non-publicly traded or publicly traded, the profit and loss account, income statements, balance sheet, cash flow statements, statement of total recognised gains and losses, and statement of changes in equity. Auditors' reports of entities that do not publish their financial statements on a website or publish them using 'pdf' format may refer to the financial statements by reference to page numbers within the published annual report. There should also be a statement to confirm the accounting convention under which the financial statements have been prepared within the annual report. Depending on the nature of the company, the applicable accounting policies will include reference to International Financial Reporting Standards (IFRSs), Financial Reporting Standards for Smaller Entities, UK Accounting Standards and Generally Accepted Accounting Practices (GAAP).

The respective responsibilities of directors and auditors will set out the directors' responsibilities, and will clarify that the auditors' responsibility in this context is to form an independent opinion based on the audit of the financial statements.

Auditors need to distinguish between their own responsibilities and those of the people charged with governance (the directors) by including in the audit report a reference to a description of the relevant responsibilities of those charged with governance when that description is set out elsewhere in the financial statements or accompanying information. Where the financial statements or accompanying information do not include an adequate description of the relevant responsibilities of those charged with governance, the auditor's report should include a description of these responsibilities.

Scope paragraph

This paragraph within the audit report will state that the audit was conducted in accordance with International Standards on Auditing (UK and Ireland), explain where the audit was undertaken using a test basis, provide evidence relevant to the amounts and disclosures, offer an assessment of significant estimates and judgments, and state whether the accounting polices are appropriate.

The definition of an audit is therefore based on:

- transactions (emphasises a test basis)
- estimates
- accounting policies
- presentation.

All of the above will have been planned and performed to collect evidence to provide reasonable assurance that the financial statements are free from material misstatements.

241

Misstatements may be caused by:

- fraud
- error
- other irregularity.

The report should include a statement by the auditor that the audit provides a reasonable basis for the opinion, as in the following example:

> We conducted our audit in accordance with International Standards on Auditing. Those standards require that we plan and perform the audit to obtain reasonable assurance about whether the financial statements are free of material misstatement. An audit includes examining, on a test basis, evidence supporting the amounts and disclosures on the financial statements. An audit also includes assessing the accounting principles used and significant estimates made by management, as well as evaluating the overall financial statement presentation. We believe that our audit provides a reasonable basis for our opinion.

Opinion paragraph

The auditor must advise the reader of the context of the opinion and the financial framework upon which the financial statements are based and must state whether:

- the financial statements are a true and fair view aligned to IFRSs/GAAP;
- they are prepared in accordance with the Companies Act 2006;
- the information given in the directors' report is consistent with the financial statements.

The terms used to express the auditor's opinion – 'give a true and fair view' and 'present fairly, in all material respects' – are equivalent. Both terms indicate, among other things, that the auditor considers only those matters that are material to the financial statements. The term 'presents fairly' is one that is to be found when reporting on public entities such as local authorities. An example of an opinion paragraph is as follows:

> In our opinion, the financial statements give a true and fair view of the financial position of the company as of December 21 201X, and of the results of its operations and its cash flows for the year ended in accordance with International Accounting Standards.

The 'true and fair' concept has not been defined in legislation. In 2008 the FRC published a legal opinion entitled 'The true and fair requirement revisited' (The Opinion). This confirms the overarching nature of the true and fair requirement that the financial statements in the UK are in accordance with international or national accounting standards.

Date, address and signature

The report should be signed and dated only after the auditors have:

- received the financial statements in the form that has been approved by the directors for release;
- reviewed all of the documents which they should consider in addition to the financial statements.

Auditors should date the report as of the completion date of the audit. This informs the reader that they have considered the effect on the financial statements and on the report of events and transactions of which the auditor became aware and that occurred up to that date. In the UK and Ireland, the date of an auditor's report on a reporting entity's financial statements is the date on which the auditor signed the report expressing an opinion on those statements.

The auditor's responsibility is to form an opinion and report on the financial statements as prepared and presented by management. The auditor should not, therefore, date the report earlier than the date on which the financial statements are signed or approved by those charged with governance.

The audit report is ordinarily signed in the name of the firm, as the firm assumes responsibility for the audit. However, it could also be signed personally by the auditor, or it could have both the auditor and the firm. As regards address, the report should name a specific location, which is ordinarily the city where the auditor maintains the office that has responsibility for the audit.

Sample unqualified statutory auditor's report

As an illustration, the unqualified audit report for JS Sainsbury is shown below.

The standard format of an unqualified report for J. Sainsbury plc

We have audited the financial statements which comprise the Group profit and loss account, the balance sheets, the Group cash flow statement, the Group statement of total recognised gains and losses, the reconciliation of movements in equity shareholders' funds and the related notes, which have been prepared under the historical cost convention (as modified by the revaluation of certain fixed assets) and the accounting policies set out in the notes to the financial statements. We have also audited the disclosures required by Part 3 of Schedule 7A to the Companies Act 1985 contained in the Directors' Remuneration report ('the auditable part').

Respective responsibilities of Directors and Auditors

The Directors' responsibilities for preparing the annual report and the financial statements in accordance with applicable United Kingdom law and accounting standards are set out in the Statement of Directors' responsibilities. The Directors are also responsible for preparing the Directors' Remuneration report.

Our responsibility is to audit the financial statements and the auditable part of the Directors' Remuneration report in accordance with relevant legal and regulatory requirements and United Kingdom Auditing Standards issued by the Auditing Practices Board. This report, including the opinion, has been prepared for and only for the Company's members as a body in accordance with Section 235 of the Companies Act 1985 and for no other purpose. We do not, in giving this opinion, accept or assume responsibility for any other purpose or to any other person to whom this report is shown or into whose hands it may come save where expressly agreed by our prior consent in writing.

We report to you our opinion as to whether the financial statements give a true and fair view and whether the financial statements and the auditable part of the Directors' Remuneration report have been properly prepared in accordance with the Companies Act 1985.

We also report to you if, in our opinion, the Report of the Directors is not consistent with the financial statements, if the Company has not kept proper accounting records, if we have not received all the information and explanations we require for our audit, or if information specified by law regarding Directors' remuneration and transactions is not disclosed.

We read the other information contained in the Annual Report and consider the implications for our report if we become aware of any apparent misstatements or material inconsistencies with the financial statements. The other information comprises only the Operating and financial review, the Report of the Directors, the Statement of corporate governance and the unaudited part of the Remuneration report.

We review whether the Statement of corporate governance reflects the Company's compliance with the nine provisions of the 2003 FRC Combined Code specified for our review by the Listing Rules of the Financial Services Authority, and we report if it does not. We are not required to consider whether the Board's statements on internal control cover all risks and controls, or to form an opinion on the effectiveness of the Group's corporate governance procedures or its risk and control procedures.

Basis of audit opinion

We conducted our audit in accordance with auditing standards issued by the Auditing Practices Board. An audit includes examination, on a test basis, of evidence relevant to the amounts and disclosures in the financial statements and the auditable part of the Directors' Remuneration report. It also includes an assessment of the significant estimates and judgements made by the Directors in the preparation of the financial statements, and of whether the accounting policies are appropriate to the Company's circumstances, consistently applied and adequately disclosed.

We planned and performed our audit so as to obtain all the information and explanations which we considered necessary in order to provide us with sufficient evidence to give reasonable assurance that the financial statements and the auditable part of the Directors' Remuneration report are free from material misstatement, whether caused by fraud or other irregularity or error, in forming our opinion we also evaluated the overall adequacy of the presentation of information in the financial statements.

Opinion

In our opinion:

- the financial statements give a true and fair view of the state of affairs of the Company and the Group at 26 March 2005 and of the profit and cash flows of the Group for the year then ended;
- the financial statements have been properly prepared in accordance with the Companies Act 1985; and
- those parts of the Directors' Remuneration report required by Part 3 of Schedule 7A to the Companies Act 1985 have been properly prepared in accordance with the Companies Act 1985.

PricewaterhouseCoopers LLP
Chartered Accountants and Registered Auditors
London
17 May 2005

(Source: J. Sainsbury's Annual Report, 2004/05)

The modified (qualified) audit report

If the auditor issues a qualified audit report, it will be disadvantagous for the company for the following reasons:

- There may be legal consequences, notably the possible restriction of dividend payments.
- The financial statements may be seen as less reliable by contact groups such as banks and suppliers.
- It reflects badly on the directors.

The content of a qualified report needs to reflect why the auditor has decided to qualify the opinion. The reader of the report should not have any doubt as to the meaning and implications in respect of understanding the financial statements. (Examples of published reports can be found on the Financial Reporting Council's website, www.frc.org.uk.)

An auditor's report is considered to be modified in the following situations:

- Matters that affect the auditor's opinion
  - Qualified opinion
  - Disclaimer of opinion
  - Adverse opinion
- Matters that do not affect the auditor's opinion – emphasis of matter.

Matters that affect the auditor's opinion

An auditor may not be able to express an unqualified opinion when there is a disagreement or a limitation or scope and, in the auditor's judgment, the effect of the matter is or may be material to the financial statements. This is summarised in the qualification matrix in Figure 17.2.

Disagreement

In this case, the auditor disagrees with management regarding the acceptability of the accounting policies selected, the method of their application or the

Figure 17.2 **The qualification matrix**

Nature of circumstance	Form of qualification	
	Material	Pervasive
Limitation of scope	Except for . . .	Disclaimer of opinion
Disagreement	Except for . . .	Adverse opinion

adequacy of financial statement disclosures. Examples are as follows:

- accounting treatment, e.g. overhead apportionment to finished goods
- disclosure, e.g. contingent liabilities
- inappropriate accounting treatment of debtors
- prior period qualification unresolved and results in a modification of the auditor's report regarding the current period.

If the disagreements are material to the financial statements, the auditor should express a qualified or an *adverse opinion*. In the latter case, the disagreement is so pervasive to the financial statements that the auditor concludes that a qualification of the report is not adequate to disclose their misleading or incomplete nature. The situation renders the auditors unable to state that the financial statements give a true and fair view. An example is where no provision has been made for losses expected to arise on certain long-term contracts.

Limitation of scope

A limitation of scope of the auditor's work refers to events or circumstances that prevent the auditor from obtaining sufficient evidence, such as the following examples:

- Outside the scope of the auditors – the directors may not permit a debtors' circularisation or may prevent the auditors from attending a stock-take.
- Outside the scope of the auditors and the directors – e.g. records destroyed by fire or the auditor was on the way to the stock-take but the train was late or the car broke down.
- The auditor was not appointed at the time of the stock-take.

  According to ISA 700:

  if the auditor is aware, before accepting an audit engagement, that those charged with governance of the entity, or those who appoint its auditor, will impose a limitation on the scope of the audit work which the auditor considers likely to result in the need to issue a disclaimer of opinion on the financial statements, the auditor should not accept that engagement, unless required to do so by statute … if the limitation is not removed, the auditor should consider resigning from the audit engagement.

Where the limitation to the scope of the audit is such that the auditor has not been able to obtain sufficient appropriate evidence and accordingly is unable to express an opinion on the financial statements, a disclaimer of opinion is made. Examples are as follows:

- auditor unable to observe all physical stock and confirm trade debtors;
- multiple material/significant uncertainties.

Matters that do not affect the auditor's opinion

Emphasis of matter

An emphasis of matter is where the auditor does not qualify the opinion, in other words the auditor's opinion states that the financial statements give a true and fair view, but there is a possible outcome of a lawsuit, and the auditor is unable to quantify the effect on the financial statements.

In certain circumstances, the auditor's reporting may be modified by adding an emphasis of matter paragraph to highlight a matter affecting the financial statements. This is included in a note to the financial statements that more extensively discusses the matter. The addition of such an emphasis of matter does not affect the auditor's opinion. The paragraph would normally be included after the opinion paragraph and would refer to the fact that the auditor's opinion is not qualified in this respect.

An emphasis of matter of paragraph might be included when there is a significant uncertainly, e.g. a possible lawsuit is pending, the outcome of which cannot be determined and no provision for liability has been made in the financial statements. Hence the outcome depends on future actions or events that are not under the direct control of the entity, but the action or event may affect the financial statements. In determining whether an uncertainty is significant, the auditor considers:

- the risk that the estimate included in the financial statements may be subject to change;
- the range of possible outcomes;
- the consequences of those outcomes on the view shown in the financial statements.

Uncertainties are regarded as being significant when they involve a level of concern about the validity of the going concern basis or have a potential effect on the financial statements that is unusually great. Where the auditor gives an unqualified opinion with an emphasis of matter paragraph, the auditor considers that the appropriate disclosures and estimates have been made within the financial statements to warrant this unqualified report. However, if the auditor concludes that the estimate of outcome of a significant uncertainly is materially misstated or that disclosure is deemed inadequate then a qualified audit report will be issued (see Figure 17.3).

An example of an emphasis of matter paragraph is as follows:

In our opinion the financial statements give a true and fair view of the financial position of the company . . . etc. . . . . Without qualifying our opinion we draw attention to NOTE XXX to the financial statements. The company is the defendant in a lawsuit alleging infringement of certain patent rights and claiming royalties

Figure 17.3 The 'uncertainty' matrix

Emphasis of matter	Audit approach
Uncertainty is adequately accounted for and disclosed	Unqualified opinion and explanatory paragraph
Uncertainty is misstated or inadequately disclosed	Qualified opinion

and punitive damages. The company has filed a counter action, and preliminary hearings and discovery proceedings on both actions are in progress. The ultimate outcome of the matter cannot be determined, and no provision for any liability that may result has been made in the financial statements.

Inherent uncertainty and the auditor's report

There are occasions when the auditor will have to recognise that there are inherent uncertainties due to the nature of the subject matter under audit review. This will have an impact on the opinion that the auditor will give in respect of the financial statements. In addition to the use of an emphasis of matter paragraph, as above, the auditor may also modify the auditor's report by using an emphasis of matter to report on matters other than those affecting the financial statements. For example, if an amendment to other information is linked to a document that contains audited financial statements, but the entity refuses to make the amendment, the auditor is entitled to include in the auditor's report an 'emphasis of matter paragraph' describing the material inconsistency. An emphasis of matter paragraph may also be used when there are additional statutory reporting responsibilities.

In 2009 the APB classified some ISAs including ISA 705 and ISA 706 that outline audit requirements regarding modifications to opinions and emphasis of matter.

Disclaimer of responsibility

A court decision in the Scottish case *Bank of Scotland* v. *Bannerman, Maclay and Others* resulted in an additional paragraph disclaiming responsibility to third parties. The case involved a lender who brought an action against a firm of auditors, claiming that they owed them a duty of care. The court's decision was that the auditors had a case to answer and it allowed the case to proceed to determine whether the auditors had been negligent. If auditors were to owe a duty of care to lenders, it could have substantial consequences for auditors. The Audit and Assurance Faculty of the ICEAW issued a technical release – *The Audit Report and Auditor's Duty of Care to Third Parties* – that recommended the inclusion of an additional paragraph just before the paragraph on the auditor's responsibilities. This inclusion has become common practice for the Big Four audit firms. Whilst this disclaimer paragraph will not prevent third parties from suing auditors, it should reduce the probability of such actions being successful.

Comparison between SAS 600 and ISA 700

The introduction of the International Statements on Auditing in 2004 meant that the national auditing standards that existed within individual countries ceased to operate. The Auditing Practices Board (APB) had endeavoured to expand the audit report under the previous Statements of Auditing Standards (SAS) applicable within the UK by moving away from a one-line opinion stating the accounts showed a true and fair view towards identifying roles of both directors and auditors as well as outlining the framework under which the opinion had been arrived at.

Questions still remain, however, about the current ISA 700 in terms of its user-friendly nature for those readers without any financial background or appreciation:

- Is the audit report still written in 'code', where readers need to decipher the meaning of different statements within the audit report?
- Is audit report language 'tortuous' to non auditors?
- Is it clear from the audit report that the opinion 'true and fair' relates to the overall financial statements and not individual accounts?

Management reports, internal audit and review reports

When the external auditors and consultants who undertake a review of internal activities within a company provide their findings in what are known as management reports, these reports are not normally in the public domain. Internal audit reports are also referred to as management reports or internal audit reports, which, again, are not in the public domain. These reports are important to the company as they provide evidence of audit findings, the conclusions and any resulting recommendations which are normally channelled via the Audit Committee as well as directly to those managers concerned. These reports are completely different to the statutory report found within the annual statements as they provide added value in terms of the issues identified and the assurance that the board, Audit Committee and line managers can glean from them.

Internal audit reports by their nature are going to be different from the statutory auditors' reports produced by external auditors. This is because the external auditors' statutory reports are governed by legislation, the Companies Act, as well as the International Standards on Auditing. Statutory auditors' reports are highly codified, in that they are written in a format that is meant to accommodate all limited companies adhering to the Companies Act, irrespective of their size, nature of trading or structure. The objective is to be a report that 'fits all' that is also able to outline the specific responsibilities of the relevant parties, such as the directors and the auditors. The report itself is fairly brief in that it states the framework within which the opinion has been arrived at and the fact that estimates and tests have been employed. By comparison, internal audit reports can come in different guises, depending on the audit undertaken. There is no standardised format, although there will be an expected remit in terms of outlining the audit objective, describing the audit work and findings thereof, leading to possible recommendations and a conclusion. External audit opinion reports are available for public inspection in that they appear in the public domain as part of the company's annual report. Statutory auditors' reports are produced for the benefit of shareholders and other stakeholders whereas internal audit reports are produced for the benefit of management. They are generally private documents and are not normally available for public inspection. When the external auditors reports back to the Audit Committee and the board they will also provide a report of the findings during the annual audit. This report is not in the public domain and is there to act as a feedback to management on any issues identified during the audit which may not have caused a qualification of the audit opinion but may require management's attention.

Summary   In ISA (UK & Ireland) 700 there are two options for the auditor when forming an opinion for the audit report, namely the unqualified audit report and the modified audit report, commonly referred to as the qualified audit report. Inherent uncertainties are attached to some transactions which can have an impact on the audit opinion, which the auditor may decide to note within the report.

The external audit report is the statutory requirement found within the Companies Act, and must comply with the International Standards on Auditing. The external audit opinion report is in the public domain, while the internal audit report or management report is a document that is written for internal purposes only.

? PRACTICE QUESTION

Provide examples of qualified audit reports which the auditor could use as part of the reporting process.

Chapter 18

Public sector auditing

Objectives

After studying this chapter you should be able to:

- describe the differences between private and public sector organisations and their different objectives;

- distinguish between service-orientated and profit-motivated objectives;

- appreciate the primary objectives and the reporting process in the public interest of the public sector;

- describe the role of the external auditor in the public sector;

- appreciate that internal audit is a statutory requirement for public sector organisations, and that there is a changing face to internal audit;

- appreciate the different aspects of governance that impact on the audit activity as compared with the private corporate entity;

- describe the concept of accountability within not-for-profit organisations;

- discuss how the objectives of not-for-profit organisations do not equate with those of profit-maximising organisations.

Introduction

The following definitions highlight the difference between the public sector and the private sector:

- *Private sector* – commercial activities (production of goods and provision of services) run by organisations in order to make a profit, e.g. plcs such as Marks & Spencer, BT and British Airways.
- *Public sector* – provision of services for the welfare of the general public, e.g. local government services such as leisure centres, crematoria and schools, health care services such as hospitals and GPs and central government services such as national security and executive agencies that operate not on a profit basis but on a rate of return basis.

The private sector has one overriding objective, profit, whereas the public sector has different objectives for each area ranging from provision of education and healthcare to the custody of prisoners. In the private sector, profit can readily be turned into measures of achievement and performance like return on capital employed or earnings per share. Public sector objectives are more qualitative and are related to service delivery. It is very difficult to find suitable measures of achievement and performance in meeting these objectives. It is also difficult to derive measures of accountability in relation to complex services where different stakeholders have varying and sometimes conflicting aspirations and objectives. For example, with regard to NHS patients, clinicians and politicians will have objectives that may not always coincide. Also, the intricacies and complexity of parliamentary accountability render it sometimes less than transparent, especially in the post-devolution UK.

The public sector is expected to manage its affairs in accordance with the public service ethic. This is based on a distinct set of values comprising impartiality, openness, transparency and the highest ethical standards of probity and propriety with oversight from bodies such as the Nolan Committee on Standards in Public Life 1994. In the private sector, senior management are responsible for setting the 'tone at the top' and describing the values and standards for the organisation.

The Nolan Committee established seven guiding principles for public life:

- selflessness – act purely in the public interest and not for personal or for associates' gain;
- integrity – be free from any outside influences or obligations;
- objectivity – make choices and decisions on merit;
- accountability – be mindful of public accountability and stewardship;
- openness – be open about decisions and actions and give reasons;
- honesty – declare any private interests and obey the law;
- leadership – promote these principles by example and leadership.

The report also recommended adequate training, where necessary, establishment of internal systems, external scrutiny of activities and formulation of appropriate codes of conduct.

Exhibit 18.1 **Key characteristics of the UK public sector**

- The public sector is a big spender and a huge employer
- Activities are service- and demand-led
- There is an expectation of the best use of resources
- There are fund contributors as opposed to investors
- Accountability is not an option, it is a must
- Information, choices and progress mean it is a balancing act
- Service provision drives the organisation in terms of performance indicators
- There are limited resources due to the nature of funding

Within the public sector there is a political influence; representatives of the public are elected and can be removed from office. Elected members direct policy and are accountable for the actions of civil servants and local government officials. The level and nature of services provided are determined by those elected into office on a central and local basis, with many central government choices impacting directly on a local level. The process for appointment to senior managerial positions is different. In the public sector there are a variety of options, including internal appointments, whereas in the private sector board members are elected by shareholders.

The main difference lies in the fact that one is profit-driven and the other is service-orientated, activity-driven. In the private sector, the source of funding is deemed 'voluntary' in that investors decide whether to invest, whereas in the public sector the funds are raised by governments, normally via taxation, and are hence 'involuntary' or 'compulsory'. Shareholders do not have to invest unless they wish to, while tax payers (individuals and corporate) have to pay their taxes by law. The key characteristics of the UK public sector are given in Exhibit 18.1.

What are the public sector organisations?

The main public sector organisations in the UK are the central government departments, supply-financed agencies and the devolved governments of Scotland, Northern Ireland and Wales.

On a more local and regional basis, there are local authorities, National Health Service Hospital Trusts, fire services and police authorities. These operate on the basis of 'not for profit' as they exist in order to provide a public service. All have their financial statements audited by external auditors in order to provide external accountability to the electorate. Whilst income may be provided by means of taxation, local and national contributions there are also elements of income from fees and charges.

Accountability in the public sector

Accountability is very important in the public sector as the electorate wants to know where their money has been spent. The concept of requiring public funds to be monitored and appropriately accounted for has become an inevitable aspect of the political arena as the amount of public expenditure seems to be forever increasing. The need to demonstrate money well spent with sound performance and achievement to the public means that performance has to be documented and reported. Accountability by directors and executive managers to shareholders and stakeholders in the private sector is relatively straightforward. The directors are accountable to the shareholders (owners) of the company, under what is referred to as agency theory, and accountability is normally found within the annual report. In contrast, accountability in the public sector is a much more difficult task, and despite the existence of an annual report, the lines of accountability are often obscure or intertwined simply because of the nature of the fund contributor and other interested parties. One of the key ways of displaying accountability in the public sector is via the use of performance targets, measures and indicators.

In the private sector, performance is measured in terms of the achievement of a profit or share value. Using the profit gauge means that resources will have to be utilised to their maximum capacity where increased profits will either drive companies to increase prices or find ways of reducing costs – either way the profit element should shine through. The public sector, however, does not have this same profit maximisation objective. In the absence of such a performance measure, the public sector has to use different performance indicators against other targets. Financial accountability will still be found in terms of the annual financial statements, but in addition the external auditor will publish performance indicators to inform the public and interested parties, including the government, as to the success or failure to meet targets. Managerial accountability is identified in terms of output data that is invariably based on population data, cost per person, cost per activity or cost per location, while budgets and forecasts for service delivery all play an important role in public sector accountability.

Parliamentary accountability

All public sector bodies are ultimately accountable to Parliament as it is Parliament that gives them the authority to undertake their activities. As part of this accountability, Parliament will undertake a review or audit of expenditure in the form of a post-event check to ensure that the money has been spent in accordance with the government policies and planned, approved activities. Every organisation will have a different format to their accountability. Local authorities, for example, are accountable to Parliament as well as to the local electorate. Devolution has added a further layer of accountability in the form of the Scottish Parliament, the Welsh Assembly and the Northern Ireland Assembly, each with their appropriate ministers who expect a raft of feedback based on targets set.

Public pressure has also pushed the boundaries of accountability, as follows:

■ There has been pressure to import private sector managerial practices into the public sector, as they have been deemed to be more effective than those within the public sector, relying on the profit motive to drive better accountability.
■ The introduction of the citizens' charter has led to various charters portraying a service dedicated to providing the best service to the public.

- Increased pressure to enhance the quality of service delivered has come from an awareness by individuals of what takes place elsewhere on both a national and an international platform.
- A policy of prudence in public spending has been used to control economic growth, inflation and ultimately the drive to ensure best value for public funds.

Other forms of accountability

- *Stewardship*, where those charged with governance in the public sector display due diligence in their approach to spending public funds. Members of Parliament and local councillors have a duty to act as stewards for the funds entrusted to them by the electorate.
- *Agency theory* is based on the private sector relationship between shareholders and directors. Directors act as agents on behalf of the owners (the shareholders) in working towards maximising wealth creation.
- *Representative democracy* at a national, local and European level includes elected Members or Parliament, and members or assemblies, European government and local councils.
- *Legal accountability* is the requirement that legislation places restrictions and expectation on those charged with governance to operate within the law and produce specific outputs such as annual reports and financial statements.
- *Managerial accountability* means looking at performance reporting which can either be used internally or placed in the public domain where historical data can be used to forecast, plan, review and question activities.

Key points of accountability in the public sector

- It is vitally important for public sector organisations to respond to the expectations of the public. Higher levels of education, better communication links and the influence of the media mean that the public have become far more vocal in their complaints and better able to compare services, which means that service providers must be prepared to respond to public demands and needs.
- There are different forms of accountability in the public sector, each one requiring different types of activity recording and reporting.
- There are problems linked to the delivery and evidencing of accountability, documenting feedback or outcomes can be difficult when the responses are often subjective and non-quantifiable, as quality is difficult to measure.
- The role of audit in the accountability process is different from that of the audit opinion report that focuses on the financial statements. An emphasis on validating data for indicating performance is an important role for audit.

Accountability feedback

There are two types of feedback: financial and managerial.

Financial accountability

The financial statements paint a picture of the resources entrusted to those who govern. They provide a report on how the resources were utilised during the year, and a statement of the movements of those resources as well as the format in which they are now held. The statements are also a reflection of activity during the period.

Managerial accountability

- This provides a platform to assess and review performance in terms of achieving value for money.
- The means of assessment are enhanced by the ability to indicate activity in terms of utilising and illustrating outcomes through performance measures, targets and indicators.
- This form of accountability is an area where the results are not only indicators of activity, but can also be used as important political tools.

Public sector auditors

Public sector bodies are unable to influence the appointment of the external auditor, as this is determined by legislation. The Audit Commission, the National Audit Office, Audit Scotland, the Wales Audit Office and the Northern Ireland Audit Office have the responsibility of either being the auditor or appointing the public sector auditor. The public sector external auditor has a wider remit than private sector auditors, looking at value for money, performance measurement and public interest issues.

National Audit Office (NAO)

The National Audit Office is auditor to all central government departments and agencies. It contracts out approximately 15% of their audits to private firms. Their objectives centre on ensuring the best use of resources, prevention and detection of fraud. The NAO is responsible for the financial and value-for-money audit of central government expenditure. The NAO reports to Parliament on the economy, efficiency and effectiveness of public money spent, and claims to save the taxpayer millions of pounds every year. It is headed by the Comptroller and Auditor General (C&AG), who is an officer of the House of Commons. The reports of the NAO are presented by the C&AG to government, via the Public Accounts Committee (PAC), a senior select committee of the House of Commons, chaired by a member of the opposing political party in the House of Commons. The NAO's role is summarised in Exhibit 18.2.

Formed in 1983 the NAO scrutinises public spending on behalf of Parliament, and is independent of government. It is responsible for auditing the accounts of all government departments, agencies and a wide range of other public bodies.

Exhibit 18.2 **The role of the National Audit Office (NAO)**

- The role of the Comptroller and Auditor General (C&AG), as head of the NAO, is to report to Parliament on the spending of central government money.
- The NAO conducts financial audits and reports to Parliament on the value for money offered by public bodies in the way they have spent public money.
- The NAO helps public service managers improve performance.
- It works closely with the Public Accounts Committee, and with other public audit bodies who have roles in other areas of public expenditure.
- Around 60 value-for-money audit reports are presented to Parliament each year by the C&AG.

The NAO financial audit

- The Government Resource and Accounts Act 2000 stipulates that the C&AG is responsible for auditing the accounts of all government and agencies and to report the results to Parliament.
- Financial audit of individual accounts can range from the Department for Work and Pensions to the Passport Agency.
- The NAO also audits over half of the 'arm's length' public bodies (known as non-departmental public bodies, NDPBs), such as the Legal Services Commission and the Regional Development Agencies.
- The NAO is also responsible for auditing all National Loans Fund accounts.
- It has several international clients, such as the International Criminal Court, the European Agricultural Guidance and UN World Food Programme.
- As external auditor to the government, the C&AG has to form an opinion on the accounts, as to whether they are free from material misstatements.
- The C&AG has to confirm that the transactions in the accounts have appropriate Parliamentary authority.
- Section 9 of the National Audit Act 1983 states that the C&AG has the power to examine and report on the economy, efficiency and effectiveness of public spending.
- If the NAO identifies material misstatements, the C&AG will issue a qualified opinion.
- Nearly all audits are subject to a report to Parliament for consideration by the PAC.
- Where no report is made, the NAO will write a management letter outlining any recommendations for improvement.

Source: Adapted from www.nao.gov.uk and NAO Annual Report 2010

The accountability cycle

1. Government requests and Parliament grants funds.
2. C&AG audits accounts, examines spending and reports to Parliament.
3. PAC reports on significant issues and government responds.
4. NAO monitoring of government action and follow up.

Relations with Parliament and the cycle of accountability

All the main NAO work is presented to Parliament by order of the House of Commons. Each year the reports – value for money and reports on accounts of public bodies – are investigated by the Public Accounts Committee (PAC). The PAC takes evidence from accounting officers, senior governmental officials who have been specially designated by the Treasury and have a personal responsibility to ensure the prudent stewardship of public funds. The C&AG, or his deputy, and a senior official from the Treasury attend all the Committee's hearings.

The PAC will then issue its own report. By convention, the government must reply to their recommendations within 2 months. The C&AG and/or the PAC can decide to conduct a follow-up investigation. The NAO also responds to over 400 queries from Members of Parliament on issues affecting public spending.

Source: Adapted from NAO Annual Report 2010

Review of audit and accountability for central government

In 2000 a review of audit and accountability for central government was undertaken under the chairmanship of Lord Sharman. The resulting Sharman Report of 2001 recommended that the NAO should be able to 'follow the public money'. This means the NAO can follow public money irrespective of the recipient organisation, which may or may not be a public sector organisation, i.e. that it is now able to trail through a range of public and private sector bodies – including the BBC, rail operating companies, Private Finance Initiative (PFI) and Public Private Partnerships (PPP) contractors – examining how public money is spent.

The Sharman Report equipped the NAO with the tools to audit the changing face of the public sector, adding where civil servants are now expected to take risks, partner the private sector and become involved with commercial activities. The Sharman recommendations were regarded at the time as a major boost to the authority of the NAO. The acceptance by government of the recommendations allowed a range of public and private bodies that receive state funds, such as PFI contractors and NDPBs, to open their books to the NAO. The outcome of the review means that all public spending, by whatever organisation, is now subject to Parliamentary scrutiny by the NAO.

Source: Adapted from www.nao.gov.uk

The Audit Commission

The Audit Commission is responsible for the appointment of auditors (from private firms and its own agency, District Audit, with a 30/70 split in terms of workload) to local government in England. It also carries out value-for-money (VFM) studies of these bodies. The Audit Commission is also responsible for the appointment of auditors to health authorities and NHS trusts and also undertakes VFM studies.

It is an independent body established under the provisions of the Local Government Finance Act 1982, the NHS and Community Care Act 1990, and the Audit Commission Act 1998. Local authorities and the NHS spend approximately 15% of the nation's gross domestic product, and it seems only fair that the public should know that its money is being properly accounted for, is well protected and wisely used. Both the government, as the overseer of these services, and the public, as recipients of these services, need assurances about whether money is spent legally, appropriately, equitably and in line with expectations. Like the NAO, the Audit Commission has a role to play in ensuring that its clients are offering value for money. The Audit Commission is also responsible for the audit of police authorities in England.

According to the Audit Commission it has five main functions:

- to carry out a comprehensive performance assessment of local authority services, formerly referred to as 'best value' inspections;
- to appoint auditors to all local government and NHS bodies in England, either from its arm's-length agency, the District Audit, or from a pool of private firms;
- to set standards for those auditors through the Code of Audit Practice;
- to carry out national studies designed to promote economy, efficiency and effectiveness (VFM) in the provision of local authority and NHS services;
- to define indicators of local authority performance that are published annually to facilitate national comparisons, and to secure a review by auditors of each authority's arrangements for producing performance Indicators.

Auditors who are not from the District Audit pool (i.e. the Audit Commission's own auditors) but appointed by the Audit Commission to undertake the audit of local authorities and NHS bodies must comply with the Audit Commission's Code of Audit Practice 2000.

The Audit Commission is self-financing, deriving its income from fees charged to local authority and NHS bodies for its audit work, and as such is independent of government.

The Audit Commission's code of practice and checklist

The Audit Commission's Code of Audit Practice for local authorities and the NHS in England sets out seven major aspects of management practice to which the auditor should pay particular attention, as follows:

- systems of planning, budgeting and controlling revenue and capital expenditure and income, and for allocating scarce resources;
- personnel management, including arrangements for deciding and reviewing establishment levels and for recruiting, training, rewarding and otherwise motivating employees;
- arrangements concerned with the proper management of all the assets of the authority – land, property (including the adequacy of arrangements for acquisition, maintenance, development and disposal of land and buildings), plant, finance and energy;
- arrangements designed to take advantage of economies of scale or skill, particularly in the procurement of goods or services;
- specific initiatives that have been taken to improve economy, efficiency and effectiveness in the performance of the wide variety of duties which have to be carried out by the authority;
- proper codification of responsibilities, authority and accountability;
- monitoring results against predetermined performance objectives and standards, to ensure that outstanding performance is encouraged and unacceptable performance corrected.

The Audit Commission has a checklist as a framework for use by local authority members and officers as well as their auditors. The Commission's remit is that experienced auditors taking into account local circumstances, personalities and traditions use this checklist. The framework contained in the Commission's checklist is as follows:

- vision
- strategy
- structure
- systems:

(a) *Vision* – statement of significant changes, statement of aims, commitment of top management.
(b) *Strategy* – the strategic planning process covering changes in client, service and management priorities, standards of service and allocation of resources. Capital and revenue budgeting systems and contingency plans.
(c) *Structure* – committee and department structures, to deliver services in accordance with objectives. System for reviewing structures. Assignment and allocation of responsibilities.
(d) *Systems*:
  (i) policy review – relevance of services, comparisons with similar authorities, examination of the utilisation of scarce resources (manpower, land, buildings, equipment and energy), insurance, maximising income and using technology to improve services;
  (ii) planning, budgeting – strategy, action plans, annual budgeting procedures and cost centre structure, use of output/performance measures;
  (iii) performance review – budgetary control and reporting system, variance analysis and performance review;
  (iv) style – style of leader and chief executive, communication and consultation procedures, delegation of responsibility, rewards for excellence and the involvement of the public;
  (v) skills and staffing – performance review and assessment reward systems, training and development, recruitment policies.

The Audit Commission's 3-year strategy, *Delivering Improvement Together*, underpins its mission 'to be a driving force in the improvement of public services'.

The corporate plan sets out in detail how the Audit Commission intends to deliver its objectives, which have four linked themes:

- focusing work on the public and on users' diverse experiences of public services and their outcomes;
- helping to improve public services by designing and deploying services differently and by using knowledge and expertise more effectively;
- safeguarding the public interest by working with other regulators to maximise the benefit and minimise the burden of regulation and accountability;
- leading by example through modernising the Audit Commission and delivering more customer-focused services.

The Audit Commission has more independence than the National Audit Office because it is not hampered by being instructed not to be involved in policy issues.

Devolved audit

The Public Finance and Accountability (Scotland) Act 2000 introduced new arrangements for the audit of public bodies under the Scottish Parliament. On 1 April 2000 the existing public auditors, the Accounts Commission and the National Audit Office (Scotland Office), amalgamated to become the new audit body, Audit Scotland. The Act also created the post of Auditor General for Scotland, supported by Audit Scotland, to have the responsibility for auditing the expenditure of the Scottish Parliament and Executive and reporting to Parliament. Audit Scotland is also responsible for local authority audit in Scotland.

The Audit and Accountability (NI) Order 2003 transferred the responsibility for the audit of local government and health service bodies to the office of the Northern Ireland Comptroller (NI C&AG). The local government auditors audit the Northern Ireland councils and report the results to the Northern Ireland Assembly. The audit of health service bodies is contracted out by the NI C&AG, but it is his responsibility to form an opinion on the accounts based on the findings of the auditors. The audit of central government departments, NDPBs and agencies is undertaken by the Northern Ireland Audit Office established under the Audit (Northern Ireland) Order 1987, of which the NI C&AG is head. The Northern Ireland Act 1998 stipulates that the NI C&AG is totally independent.

The Government of Wales Act 1998 established the Auditor General for Wales post to be supported by the National Audit Office in Cardiff. The Public Audit (Wales) Act 2004 resulted in the amalgamation of the National Audit Office and Audit Commission in Wales into the Wales Audit Office (WAO). The WAO has responsibility for undertaking the audit of the National Assembly of Wales Government, its agencies, sponsored bodies, police authorities, local government and health trusts. It reports to the Audit Committee of the National Assembly of Wales as to whether the funds allocated and received by the devolved government of Wales have been spent on the purposes intended. This includes reporting on value for money audits.

The European Court of Auditors (ECA) is responsible for auditing European Union expenditure in all EU member states, including the United Kingdom. The NAO acts as a liaison point between the ECA and UK departments. It reports regularly to Parliament on issues relating to the expenditure of EU funds in the UK, and, on occasion, on wider issues of financial management within the EU.

The ECA examines whether:

- financial operations have been properly recorded;
- they have been legally and regularly executed;
- they have been managed so as to ensure economy, efficiency and effectiveness.

Source: www.nao.org.uk

External audit in the public sector

The external auditor's duties in relation to the audit of the financial statements produced by a public sector organisation are laid down by statute. For example, in a local authority duties are to give an opinion as to whether an authority's financial statements 'present fairly' the financial position of the authority, to ascertain whether there is an adequate internal control system and an effective internal audit function, and to ensure that the organisation has made proper arrangements for securing economy, efficiency and effectiveness. The external auditor has to ensure that the organisation has collected all income and incurred expenditure in accordance with their statutory authority. ISA 700 has a specific audit report format for public sector bodies.

There are three fundamental principles that underpin public audit:

- The identifiable independence of the public sector auditor from the organisation that is being audited.
- The scope of public audit is far wider than that found in the private sector, incorporating the audit of financial statements, regularity (legality) audit and probity (propriety) audit while also reviewing best use of limited resources, commonly referred to as value for money.
- The public sector auditor has an additional reporting arm as compared with the private sector auditor as it can to make known its concerns and findings in the form of reports in the public interest to the public and to democratically elected representatives.

Internal audit in the public sector

The private sector does not have a compulsory requirement for the establishment of an internal audit function. Internal audit has a passing mention in the corporate governance codes published by Hampel, Turnbull and the FRC Combined Code, but there is no compulsory requirement. The Hampel Report of 1998 stated that all companies that do not have an internal audit function should review whether they need to have one. The Turnbull Report of 1999 stated that companies should take account of internal or external factors that might increase the risks they face. It also focused on the importance of ensuring that appropriate measures were undertaken to review the internal control mechanisms in place. This was an implied role for the presence of an internal audit function. The Combined Code on Corporate Governance published by the Financial Reporting Council (FRC) in 2003 stated that it was the responsibility of the Audit Committee to monitor and review the effectiveness of the activities of the internal audit function.

In the public sector, however, there are specific requirements for the establishment of an internal audit function.

Section 151 of the Local Government Act 1972 states that: 'every local authority shall make arrangements for the proper administration of their financial affairs and shall secure that one of their officers has responsibility for the administration of those affairs'.

Regulation 6 of the Accounts and Audit Regulations 2003 states that there should be a: 'responsible officer to maintain adequate and effective systems of internal audit of its accounting records and of its system of internal control in accordance with the proper internal audit practices'.

The Chartered Institute of Public Finance and Accounting (CIPFA) published a code of practice for internal auditors in local government in 2000. The HM Treasury Government Accounting Manual sets out the requirements for the internal audit function in all central government bodies, and the NHS sets out in its *Internal Audit Manual* a benchmark minimum internal audit standard which is mandatory for health service organisations.

Corporate governance codes of best practice, with their increased emphasis on how organisations are managed and controlled, have had an impact on the role of the internal audit function. These factors have contributed to changing the face of local government, which in turn has influenced the role of, and audit approach employed by, the internal audit function in local government.

The changes that have paved the way for a different internal audit include:

- a higher profile for internal audit based on Audit Committee expectations;
- clearer reporting lines to members via the Audit Committee;
- assurances that internal audit reports and recommendations will be acted upon;
- independent monitoring of audit performance;
- the reliance placed on internal audit in respect of providing assurances on the existence of risk management policies linked to corporate governance.

The changing face of internal audit in local government has created a more diverse internal audit service that incorporates the internal control review and the assurance role on risk management (see Figure 18.1). There has been a progression from the conventional, basic and traditional minimum audit service as required by statute to the more corporate image of advisor, business consultant and assurance provider as part of the control mechanisms and risk management linked to corporate governance.

External and internal audit relationships

In 1996 the Audit Commission published *It Takes Two*, a good practice guide to cooperation between internal and external auditors, promoting the concept of the 'managed audit'. The guide contains a checklist for action, and may be used by management and the Audit Committee to stimulate discussion of co-operation arrangements. It also describes how internal and external auditors can work together. The external auditors will assess the organisation, management, staffing and operation of an internal audit function to determine if they can rely on the work completed by them.

Areas of work where the external auditor will normally consider relying on internal audit include:

- review of internal control
- computer audit work
- final accounts work
- visits to establishments
- value-for-money audits.

Figure 18.1 **The changing face of internal auditing in local government**

Basic Audit Provision ⟶ Corporate Assurance

| Traditional position | Positive | Internal audit service with added value |

- Minimum audit standards
- Poor leadership
- No standardised approach
- Very little group working
- Performance not questioned
- No head of audit review
- Lacks audit methodology
- Tolerated relationship with external audit
- Potential for improvement
- Can capitalise on audit experience
- Can claim a certain amount of successes
- Reputation can be improved

- Team motivation
- Can develop a team approach
- Potential for leadership
- Management commitment
- Embrace a team approach and talk
- Audit rotation on tasks for skills
- Added value and quality
- Introduce performance measurement
- Positive attitude towards problems
- Use modern approaches to audit, systems and risk-based, CAATs

Negative

- Unwilling to move from traditional audit approach
- Management failing to show interest
- Objectives not identified
- No management or accountancy skills
- No integration in the business
- Lack of will to standardise
- Lack of knowledge of best practice methodology
- Not reporting to an Audit Committee
- Failure to 'sell' audit as a service

- Recognised business advisers
- Confirming presence of risk management existence
- Displaying the value of audit to clients
- Applying best practice policies
- Offering solutions-based outcomes
- Promoting and 'focusing' change
- Audit services displaying objectivity
- Able to be regarded as a stand-alone service
- Part of the performance monitoring group
- Use of forensic audit techniques

Developments impacting on current auditing practices in the public sector

Public sector services, especially those concerned with public health, public housing and child welfare, have come a long way since the Poor law Act of 1834. Local government, in particular, has developed considerably. Its structure and nature of service delivery and management have developed such that there is a high degree of expectation in respect of the level and quality of service provision and the calibre of those elected to manage the scarce resources. Restructuring and reorganisation in different areas of the public sector have all been driven by the need to utilise scarce resources to their maximum. The streamlining of the operations and decision-making structure for services provided the opportunity to secure them in the most effective and efficient manner, and to ensure they were utilised in the most economic way.

The following aspects deserve a mention with regard to their role in the creation of public sector services as they exist today.

- *Reorganisations, e.g. boundary changes for local government, the establishment of National Health Service Hospital Trusts and Local Health Boards to administer certain services*. Hospital trusts have been the subject of government initiatives to improve the quality of service provision. The flavour of 2001 was that of the star rating system, where it was decided to publish performance indicator data, in which poor performers would be named and shamed into improvement.
- *Local government reorganisation in terms of the reallocation of county areas from urban district councils, and county boroughs to district and county councils in 1974*. Twenty-two years later there was yet another reorganisation that included boundary changes and the creation of unitary authorities in some regions, whereby the previous district authorities were absorbed within the county authority.
- *The abolition of compulsory competitive tendering and best value inspection in favour of the introduction of the Comprehensive Performance Assessment,* and Programme for Improvement (an initiative specific to Wales) have all involved the use of an assessment process aimed at improving service delivery in the form of performance review. Best value replaced the compulsory competitive tendering in 2000 and was not seen to be achieving its objective. Its replacement, the Comprehensive Performance Assessment programme for local government services, was designed to be more of a self-assessment process for service delivery and improvement.
- *Legislation in terms of establishing the Audit Commission, the National Audit Office, the Wales Audit Office and Audit Scotland*. The creation of public sector audit bodies in the format of the Audit Commission in 1982 and the National Audit Office in 1983 provided a formal structure to the external audit function of central and local government. The Audit Commission plays an important role in promoting the key audit processes and procedures within the public sector as well as developing working partnerships between the internal audit function and the external audit function. An example is the Audit Commission's work towards the managed audit approach for better external and internal audit co-operation, and the embracing of the corporate governance code of best practice on encouraging public bodies to appoint an Audit Committee. The Audit Commission has revolutionised the audit approach from that of merely imposing a probity or voucher-bashing audit to that of a sophisticated audit embracing a management, consultancy and advisory role. The National Audit Office's remit is that of helping the nation spend wisely, and its work aims to put forward constructive ideas and recommendations that will help government departments and executive agencies to achieve better value for money. Both organisations have a remit to undertake VFM audit. Following devolution, further legislation established separate audit bodies for Scotland and Wales.

■ *Greater public awareness and interest in public sector management, with a demand for more private sector style financial reporting and management structures,* has led to the application of corporate governance codes within the public sector, duly amended to reflect the unique nature of the public sector. A greater expectation for more accountability has stemmed from interested parties and the media asking more pertinent questions of those elected to govern. There is also an open invitation to stand election; local government management (councillor elections), for example, is open to individuals from all sectors of the community who may wish to participate in local government.

■ *Greater demands on the provision of public sector services, increased need for social housing and social services and an ageing population requiring a greater level of care.* As greater demands are placed on the service providers, the need arises to ensure that all the resources utilised are providing value for money in terms of efficiency, effectiveness and economy. All the concerns within the public sector relating to scarce resources, lack of funds and lack of skilled staff have led to a need to ensure more VFM initiatives are undertaken.

■ *More public accountability leading to a greater demand for more performance comparison, target-setting and the use of performance indicators.* This resulted in the publication of corporate governance reports by Cadbury, Greenbury, Hampel and Turnbull, Smith, Higgs and the Financial Reporting Council (Combined Code on Corporate Governance). Corporate governance issues that came to the fore in the 1990s in the private sector spilled over into local government with the publication of the various reports and codes of best practice. Along with the Nolan Report on conduct of members and officers in the public sector they all influenced and impacted on the management of public sector organisations.

■ *Decentralisation and low level cost centres taking control of their budget* has created a need for additional management information in order to maintain control and awareness of events, activities, outputs and impacts. The increased use of information technology has revolutionised the way in which services are delivered and changed the approach to record-keeping and the management and audit functions. The existence of management information systems, with their ability to create timely reports, has facilitated more substantive testing and analytical review, while the analysis function has enabled both advisors and decision-makers to identify risk areas to enable risk management and corrective action far quicker than would otherwise have been possible.

■ *The creation of Executive Agencies in 1988 by the UK central government to run its departments and business units where practicable within agreed policy and resource frameworks.* The concept of an agency was to enable an improvement in efficiency and quality of service. This was based on the theory that by relating outputs to the costs involved, managers could monitor and manage services having made better choices. Establishing targets at the outset enabled expected achievement plans to act as goals for the subsequent review and evaluation. This in itself generated a method for displaying accountability.

■ *Increased political pressure for government bodies to be more accountable* has led to changes in central government's attitude towards what 'other public sector organisations' are doing. Local government issues have increasingly become an integral part of party politics on a national level, and vice versa. Manifestos and election promises are often linked to local issues which take the limelight and result in dramatic changes. A classic example of this was the introduction of the 'poll tax' and the negative effect that it had on the popularity of the Thatcher government. The abolition of the 10p tax rate proved to be a negative factor in the local elections of 2008 when the Labour Party lost a substantial number of local government seats. The more people who become aware of the decision process and its outcome, the greater pressure there is for those in government to become more accountable. Government cutbacks on funding to centrally funded government bodies has resulted in greater pressures for service provision at a local level, such as care in the community where certain types of mental health provision have shifted from the health sector to the local sector.

■ *Reports in the public interest published by the external auditor of local government have increased significantly in recent years,* resulting yet again in the demand for greater accountability, openness and reliance on the auditor to provide assurances. Members of the electorate are no longer tolerant of poor management and corrupt activities within the public sector. Far more people are willing to express their views publicly and express their concerns by voting against the offending councillors at the next local election if corrective action is not taken. The guiding principles outlined in the Nolan and Neill reports on conduct of public servants have a greater meaning when representatives are held accountable for their actions and decision-making.

■ *The impact of privatisation, private finance initiatives and private public partnerships* has resulted in a need for greater awareness on how to manage projects, undertake risk management and take account of the resulting impact of the public private merger on projects. The creation of internal markets and market testing have resulted in private sector mirroring to generate a better approach to the sourcing of goods and services.

■ *Central government's use of local government issues on the political platform and the presence of pressure groups on a local and national scale* have meant that issues ranging from local groups campaigning for city centre bypasses to Green peace's fight on environmental issues have been placed at the centre of debate.

■ *Devolution in Wales and Scotland establishing the Scottish and Welsh Assemblies* has provided a forum from which local issues can be debated at a regional level, with the intention of generating a more effective decision-making process. The 1998 Modernising Local Government White Paper initiatives encouraged better voices for local people and the desire to attract younger people to participate in local government.

All these factors have influenced the approach and nature of the audit function, both external and internal, in the public sector. Greater emphasis has been placed on value for money, performance indicators and the reporting methods not only in respect of the audit opinion but also in terms of published statistics and special investigations or reports in the public interest. The true nature of the independent external auditor, with the establishment of a dedicated public sector auditor, has reinforced the assurance provided by the audit. Changes in attitude towards those who are charged with governance, with the establishment of Audit Committees, has led to changes in the role of the internal auditor, having to contribute to risk management initiatives and reviews.

Table 18.1 gives an overview of the differences between the audit of a local government authority and that of a listed company.

Table 18.1 **A comparison between the audit of a local authority and that of a listed company**

English local government	Private sector company
External auditor	
Audit Commission appointed auditor, either District Audit or one of the private sector firms	Private audit firms, e.g. Pricewaterhouse Coopers, Ernst & Young, Grant Thornton
Responsibilities	
The responsibilities of the auditor are contained within the Audit Commission Act 1982 and 1998. The Act states that there shall continue to be an Audit Commission for local authorities in England	The responsibilities are contained within the Companies Act 1985 (amended 1989), and 2006
Year end	
The Act states that the accounts of the bodies subject to audit will have a year end date of 31 March	No such date is imposed or required of a private sector company
Appointment	
The Audit Commission appoints the external auditor, either from the District Audit (the Commission's own audit body) or members of a private firm who are private sector 'approved auditors'	The auditor is appointed by the owners (usually the shareholders) of the company, after consideration by the Audit Committee
Duties	
The auditor must ensure that:	Auditors must carry out investigations which will enable them to form opinions on whether:
■ accounts present fairly the financial position of the authority, and are prepared in accordance with regulations in the Local Government Act ■ accounts comply with the requirements of all statutory provisions applicable to the accounts in terms of generally accepted accounting policies ■ proper practices have been observed in the compilation of the accounts ■ the authority has made proper arrangements for securing economy efficiency and effectiveness in its use of resources ■ the body has made arrangements for collecting and recording the information and for publishing it as required for the performance of its duties under that section ■ audit is concerned with value-for-money and performance indicators, and comprehensive performance assessment ■ they understand their role is to identify why, when, what for and how public money is used by local authorities. The auditor is acting in the public's best interest	■ the financial statements show a true and fair view of the financial position at the balance sheet date and of the results for the year ended on that date ■ the financial statements comply with statutory or other requirements ■ the financial statements have been prepared using appropriate accounting bases and policies, applied consistently from year to year ■ the business has maintained proper accounting records ■ there has been compliance with the Code of Corporate Governance in line with the London Stock Exchange listing requirements, 'comply or explain'

Table 18.1 *Continued*

English local government	Private sector company

Guidelines

As well as the auditing standards, guidelines and pronouncements which apply to the private sector, the Commission prepares and regularly reviews a Code of Audit practice. Auditors appointed by the Commission must comply with the code, which prescribes best practice and embodies best professional practice, compliance with auditing standards and accepted procedures and auditing techniques. The auditors must also apply the International Standards on Auditing in their approach to the audit work undertaken

Although the Companies Act sets out in detail what the duties of the auditor are, and what the form and content of the financial statements should be, it does not detail how the audit should be carried out, or what assurance is needed on any particular aspect of the financial statements. To deal with these issues, the International Standards on Auditing provide the necessary instructions for the completion of the audit

Rights of access

The auditor has a right of access at all reasonable times to every document relating to a body subject to audit. The auditor can require information and explanation from individuals employed by the body

Auditors of local authorities (LAs) also have at their disposal a wide range of additional powers that are specific and unique to LA audit, reflecting the fact that LAs are accountable amongst others to their local electorate

The Companies Act provides the following rights and powers:

- Access at all times to the books, accounts and vouchers of the company
- To obtain from the officers of the company such information and explanation as are deemed necessary
- To receive notice of and to attend meetings and to report on any matter which concerns them
- To make a report to the members on their findings, including failure on the part of the officers of the company to supply all the information and explanations which they consider necessary

- The auditor has to consider whether a matter should be brought to public attention: an 'in the public interest' report can be made into an 'immediate report' and issued before the conclusion of the audit
- A local government elector has the right to inspect accounting statements and documents subject to the audit
- A local government elector for any area to which the accounts relate can question the auditor about the accounts and make copies of all or any parts of the accounts and other documents
- A local government elector, as their representative, has a right to make objections to an item or items in the accounts
- The auditor can apply to the court for a declaration that an item is contrary to law
- A prohibition order can be issued if the auditor has reason to believe that the body or an officer of the body is to make or has made a decision which involves unlawfully incurring expenditure or incurring a deficiency

(Continues)

Table 18.1 *Continued*

English local government	Private sector company
Reporting requirements	
Public sector reports also adhere to the guidelines set out in ISA 700	The APB Statement of Auditing Standards ISA 700, Auditors' Reports on Financial Statements, establishes the standard and provides guidance on the form and content of auditors' reports. Under the heading *Opinion on the financial statements* the report will state that *the financial statements give a true and fair view . . . and have been properly prepared in accordance with the Companies Act 2006*
Under 'Opinion' the report will state that the 'statement of accounts presents fairly the financial position of .... Council for the year ended.....', then under the heading 'Certificate' it will state 'I/we completed the audit of accounts in accordance with the Code of Audit Practice issued by the Audit Commission.'	
The Auditor can publish a report in the public interest	

Local authority accountability issues – reports in the public interest

The external auditor of a local authority can apply another form of feedback to the public in the format of a 'report in the public interest'. This is a qualified audit opinion on the financial statement, which is an opinion that the financial statements 'represent fairly' the activities and transactions undertaken during the financial year, as compared with the true and fair view for a company. In this 'qualified audit opinion' the external auditor brings to the attention of the public issues that are deemed to be in the 'public interest'.

These reports are only applicable to audits of public sector organisations and are made by the external auditors on matters which, in their opinion, should be brought to the attention of the wider public rather than just management letters which are purely internal to the local authority and submitted to the Audit Committee who will report back to the Cabinet. Reports in the public interest are intended to notify the public, as 'fund contributors', about serious problems affecting the financial statements of the organisation.

The sort of thing that would call for a report in the public interest is a failure to comply with statutory requirements in relation to accounting procedures or accounting standards which have a material impact upon expenditure. An area that has become increasingly important has been the failure to provide value for money within a local authority's service provision. This failure to display value for money would need to be important and significant enough to justify the report in the public interest. Issues such as unnecessary expenditure due to wastage or an abuse of a councillor's or other officer's position would warrant a report in the public interest, as occurred in a North Wales local authority when a councillor decided to use the council to purchase his wallpaper, therefore obtaining a substantial discount on the cost. Although he then paid the council for the wallpaper, he had abused his position in order to gain an advantage. This situation justified a report in the public interest and all matters of a conflict of interest or an abuse of position, if significant, would justify a report being prepared.

Clearly issues such as misconduct, fraud and matters requiring any kind of special investigation would justify a report being made. Matters such as a late completion of the accounts could lead to a qualified audit report by the external auditor as it may mean that they are unable to complete the audit. However, it may not be significant enough to justify a report in the public interest. There needs to be an additional element before it becomes necessary to inform the fundholders. Another reason for a report in the public interest may be poor management information systems, which in turn can lead to poor management decision-making and therefore impact upon the financial position of the organisation; this is something which external stakeholders should be made aware of.

The external auditor has a significant role to play in the public sector as a result of the letter in the public interest, which can be included in addition to the qualification of an audit report. This means that there is greater public awareness of the failings and problems within the public sector.

Qualifying an audit opinion does not mean there has to be a report in the public interest, as such a report requires sufficient concerns to be made. Reasons for qualification include:

- delays in preparing the accounts;
- failure to comply with statutory requirements;
- inadequate levels of balances;
- poor VFM displayed;
- unnecessary expenditure due to waste etc.;
- poor management information systems;
- deficiencies in internal control;
- misconduct, fraud or special investigation.

Report in the public interest versus the qualified audit report

The Companies Act 1985 requires companies to file the audit opinion with their annual accounts at Companies House, which can be subject to public scrutiny and is a source that all potential investors will examine. The private sector, unlike the public sector, needs to ensure that shareholders retain confidence in the company in order that share prices retain their value. Therefore a qualified audit opinion in the private sector indicates problems within management and can mean that shareholders become uneasy about their investment and the security of their funds within the company. Should this occur, additional equity funding, or even maintaining the level of the same, can become problematic and it may be extremely difficult to obtain credit, as creditors will usually check with Companies House prior to granting or extending any type of credit.

On the other hand, although a report in the public interest can have a major impact on the top layers of management in the public sector, it will not threaten the overall existence of the organisation in the way that a qualified audit opinion (depending on the severity of the same) has the potential to do in the private sector. A report in the public interest will lead to some action being taken but will not threaten the continuing provision of the service. Regardless of their confidence in their local authority, the public will still have to continue to pay council tax and cannot choose an alternative local authority to collect their refuse unless they move outside their existing authority. The service provider is not optional, unlike the situation in the private sector for customers and investors.

Therefore it could be argued that although reports in the public interest do not enhance the public perception of a local authority and may mean that central government becomes involved to help 'sort out' the organisation, it does not present a threat to the continuing operation of the organisation in some form or another. However, the impact of any negative opinion from the external auditor in the private sector can have far-reaching consequences for those both inside and outside the organisation.

Housing associations and charities

Other organisations that provide a public service include Housing Associations, charities, charitable foundations and Friendly Societies, which also operate on a not-for-profit basis. Housing associations exist to provide social housing and, as such, charge a rent that is capped by government. Their aim is to fund new-build properties to provide additional social housing and repay their loan debt and reinvest any excess income. They are in receipt of social housing grants from central government and have emerged as a replacement to the traditional local authority 'council housing' provision, doing away with the need for local authorities to 'ring fence' their council housing income and expenditure to ensure that those in receipt of a council house were not doubly subsidised by other council taxpayers when a deficit occurred on the housing revenue account.

Housing association financial statements are subject to external audit, and, in line with corporate governance codes of best practice, even the smaller associations are appointing internal auditors (invariably on an outsourced basis) to provide assurances on internal control and risk management aspects of corporate governance. The external auditor is appointed at the annual general meeting by the association's membership, namely tenants and board members, both executive and non-executive. The nomination for the external auditor is from the board via the recommendation of the Audit Committee. The board membership consists of executive and non-executive directors and tenant representatives. Due to the nature of the financial statements in terms of rental income, and especially in terms of arrears due to housing benefit payments from local authorities as well as void weeks when the properties may be subject to refurbishment, a number of audit firms have set up specialist departments to tender for housing association work, in both external and internal audit.

Charities exist on fundraising activities and charitable donations. Their aim is to meet their objectives, which can vary considerably depending on the size of the organisation, be it a small local charity set up specifically to meet a local need or an internationally recognised charity such as Oxfam.

A key audit issue linked to charity funding is the source of its income. There is an inherent risk that there will be an understatement or incompleteness of recording the income, especially due to gifts in kind and, cash donations from fundraising events, and legacies. As a number of charities survive on grant income, which is subject to annual review, there is a possibility that there will be an overstatement of cash grants due to their uncertainty and also an overstatement of expenses. Also, quite often, the people working in the charity offices and outlets are volunteers and are not trained in the relevant area of work, which can lead to an inadvertent misstatement of transactions.

Charities are not all dependent on donations and grant aid. Some will have 'surplus' or 'spare' capital money (which can often be in the millions) that is invested in restricted funds, or invested abroad on the instructions of the donor. Both can, however, be subject to fraudulent activity, whether it is on a local small scale of cash manipulation and theft or on the international front. All of this adds to the uncertainty and aspects of risk that need careful consideration by the auditor prior to commencing the audit work. The audit focus will be on ensuring the completeness of income, appropriate accounting for grant incomes, and appropriate security of assets.

Summary

Public sector auditing takes into account the issues that impact on the delivery of services and the use of resources which are generated via public taxation. Auditing practices for the public sector auditor follow the standards prescribed for auditors, but they also take on board additional aspects linked to value-for-money auditing and review of performance data that are used for displaying whether the bodies have met with goals and targets set.

? PRACTICE QUESTION

Critically analyse how the external audit in the public sector differs from that in the private sector.

Chapter 19

Value-for-money audit and performance indicators in not-for-profit organisations

Objectives

After studying this chapter you should be able to:

- describe the constituent elements of value for money (VFM) and the importance of VFM audit in the public sector;

- appreciate that there are different approaches to VFM investigations;

- discuss performance measurement audits;

- explain how limited resources place a different emphasis on audit of public/ not-for-profit organisations;

- appreciate the framework within which performance measurement operates;

- understand the reasons why performance measurement in the public sector is a difficult concept due to quality issues.

Introduction

Value for money (VFM) has a greater relevance within the public sector and not-for-profit organisations than in the private sector, as expenditure that is sourced from the public purse is viewed as requiring more safeguards and assurances than that funded from the private purse. While private expenditure can be assessed in terms of results via output and profit, the complex nature of public sector activities makes the analysis less clear-cut than simply the consideration of company profitability.

Value for money is described as having three main components and all three must coexist in order for an activity to truly display VFM. These are known as the three Es – economy, efficiency and effectiveness – of a service provision and are defined as follows:

- *Economy* – minimising the cost of resources used or required. Economy refers to the acquisition of resources of an appropriate quality at the minimum cost. Economy is often measured in terms of unit costs, e.g. cost per employee, cost per student. The result of good economy is *spending less.*
- *Efficiency* – the relationship that exists between the output from goods or services and the resources to produce them. Efficiency means getting the maximum outputs from the resources consumed by the organisation, or ensuring that the minimum level of resources is devoted to obtaining a particular level of output. This can be measured by comparing actual results with budget, external targets or benchmarks. A number of comparison measures are appropriate here, e.g. comparisons over time, inter-organisation comparisons and comparisons with similar private sector activities. The result of good efficiency is *spending well.*
- *Effectiveness* – the relationship that exists between the intended and actual results of public sector expenditure on services and activities. Effectiveness measures the outcomes and the extent to which they indicate success in the realisation of objectives, e.g. the correct payment of staff in the month that the payment is due. The result of good effectiveness is *spending wisely.*

The most widely used model for assessing and measuring output and performance identifies these three dimensions of performance.

In addition to the three Es there is a fourth element, *quality*, for assessing service provision. Performance targets and indicators can be utilised to generate a picture of activity results using comparisons. The 'quality' measurement describes the usefulness or value of a service, and is linked to the delivery of the service to the recipient. For example, the efficiency of a hospital provision cannot be measured simply by relating the value of inputs to outputs. Instead it is necessary to consider whether or not the output is what the patient needs and expects. This value-added concept makes it necessary to address the problems associated with assigning relative values to outcomes/outputs.

Because it is difficult to measure the outcome of a health service provision, intermediate outputs generated can be used as proxy measurement. For example, the number of beds available can be counted as a measure of the capacity to treat patients. Intermediate outputs must be chosen carefully or they may distort the decision-making process by emphasising an inappropriate outcome.

As VFM has its origins safely established in the public sector, it must therefore be concerned with obtaining the best possible services for the least amount of resources, thereby achieving the three Es by:

- economy – least cost
- effectiveness – best results
- efficiency – best use of resources.

When it comes to VFM auditing, the Auditing Practices Board (APB) in Practice Note 10 (revised) 'Audit of Financial Statements of Public Sector Entities in the UK' requires that the external auditor not only considers the financial statements but also takes into account the three Es when auditing a public sector entity, adopting:

> . . . an audit methodology in which auditors are either required, or exercise discretionary power, to satisfy themselves by examination of the accounts and otherwise, that the audited body has made proper arrangements for securing economy, efficiency and effectiveness in the use of resources.

The role of audit

External audit, internal audit and management's responsibilities for VFM

External auditors have always been concerned with more than just financial and regulatory audit. The unique position they occupy in relation to both organisations and stakeholders means that they become aware of standards of performance and are in a position to suggest or recommend ways of improving performance. Traditionally, the auditor of a public sector entity has had to consider not only the regularity and lawfulness of the financial statements, but also the possibility that loss has occurred due to a lack of economy, efficiency and effectiveness in the use of its resources, in other words, the achievement of VFM. This superimposed duty to perform a VFM audit means that the auditor has an important role to play both in achieving accountability and also in the independent review of the evidence put forward to demonstrate public accountability. It is the responsibility of management to undertake activities that will aid an organisation in achieving its objectives. Part of this responsibility is to ensure that activities are undertaken with regard to economy, efficiency and effectiveness.

Private sector organisations aim to achieve VFM based on operational performance, where cost analysis, projections, business models and review of actual against budgeted expectations (both financial and non-financial) are compared for decision-making. Internal audit may undertake this activity as part of its assurance provision role and even its risk management review. External auditors may include an element of VFM in terms of the three Es as part of their overall review and include their findings and recommendations in their management letter to the board. Invariably, external auditors will undertake the VFM audit as a consultancy exercise, e.g. a review of the human resources department to assess and confirm whether the right employees are appointed to the right job at the right time. This exercise will come wrapped up in a consultancy package rather than being called a VFM audit. The decision to undertake such an operational review will come from management; there is no statutory requirement to undertake a value for money audit in the private sector.

Statutory requirement for a VFM audit

The Audit Commission in England under the Audit Commission Act 1998 requires it to undertake, or at the very least promote, comparative VFM studies for local authorities. In Scotland, Wales and Northern Ireland similar powers and responsibilities were granted under legislation establishing the relevant audit bodies, Audit Scotland, the Wales Audit Office and the Northern Ireland National Audit Office.

The Commission for Healthcare Audit and Inspection (CHAI) carries out VFM studies in the NHS, this became effective in April 2004.

Central government VFM studies are the responsibility of the National Audit Office, as per the National Audit Office Act of 1983.

Often management will identify certain VFM studies that have not been earmarked by the external auditor. In these instances, the internal auditor will undertake the VFM studies and report the findings to the Audit Committee and the relevant departmental officer or cost centre manager. These studies will come under special investigations outside the normal routine audits undertaken by internal audit.

VFM focus

Value for money is deemed a public sector audit activity that focuses on the three Es. These are measured with reference to:

- inputs – obtaining the best possible inputs at the best price or least cost;
- outputs – where the maximum output is gained from utilising the inputs efficiently;
- impacts – achieving the most effective impact in order to fulfil the desired objectives.

The Chartered Institute of Public Finance & Accountancy (CIPFA) takes the view that a structured approach to VFM auditing is to undertake and complete input-based, systems-based and output-based reviews.

Example:
University campus restaurant

In relation to a university campus restaurant, the approach would be as follows.

Input-based review

- Ascertain the organisation structure, approved staffing and budget.
- Review quality statements and objectives.
- Obtain the annual financial statements/accounts/returns for the restaurant and review the cost profile.

- Obtain comparable costs with similar facilitates within the university, if applicable, and where possible utilise published data.
- Ascertain and review the performance measures used.
- Compare costs and performance measures with the private sector or other public sector establishments.

Systems-based review

- Review the structure of staffing and equipment and ascertain if a cost-effective service is provided to the students and other users.
- What information relating to usage, utilisation and costs is provided to management?
- Is there analysis of staff idle time and food wastage?
- Is the latest in terms of electrical equipment, catering facilities and technology used?
- Are meals and function catering completed within target times, rates and presentation, with minimum wastage. If not, what action is taken by management?
- Is the cost of purchasing raw produce, pre-prepared food/supplies etc. regularly reviewed?
- Is there an analysis of overhead costs?
- Does management review the pricing policy and pricing structure regularly?
- Is there a review of the menu? Are customers' views taken on board?
- Is there a review of the eating area in terms of peak time utilisation?
- Can costs be reduced or can the preparation of meals/snacks be carried out more cheaply outside without impairing the quality and standard of meals/services?
- What would be the effect of changing service levels, from current restaurant-style to fast food, takeaway, café-style self-service?

This review will be completed by examining staff shift schedules, budgets, supplier and purchase contracts, menus, catering costing sheets and other records. Questionnaires to customers could also be used where applicable. Interviews will be conducted with management, staff and customers, and there would be direct observation of the restaurant's operating procedures.

Output-based review

- Are clear objectives set for the restaurant? If it is to be subsidised, there is a need to establish whether there is an expected rate of return on activities.
- Are performance indicators used to measure activities? What happens if the objectives are met?
- Is there an effective reporting system on the outcomes and activities to senior management?
- Is there a process in place where policy objectives are regularly reviewed?

Undertaking a VFM audit

Prior to undertaking a VFM study the auditor does a fact-finding review on the client in terms of what exactly is the area that is going to be audited, establishing the client or departmental objectives and routine activities in respect of what exactly goes on and why. The auditor will also assess the adequacy of management information and consider the source of evidence that will facilitate the VFM audit.

Value-for-money studies will invariably look for waste, extravagance, and poor management and planning of activities (examples of VFM studies are given in

Exhibit 19.1 Examples of value-for-money activities and studies

- Financial and management accounting issues of budgeting, controlling, reconciling and income and expenditure
- Strategic and business planning, reviewing past decisions and assessing impact on forecasting
- Contracting arrangements, where the tendering arrangements for larger capital projects are considered, and the repeat contract arrangements of revenue contracts with regular contractors for service delivery
- Human resource management that includes reviewing performance
- Asset management, replacement and renewal policies, including maintenance agreements
- Arrangements for economies of scale, public sector procurement policy where discounted supplies are encouraged to take advantage of bulk orders
- Review of management information for the decision-making process, its reliability, timeliness and accuracy
- Understanding of responsibilities, roles and authority that impact on the requirement for accountability
- Policy objectives that are communicated to everyone in the organisation, including how well these policy objectives are understood throughout the organisation
- Ensuring that performance is monitored and compared to original data, expectations and budgets
- Application of benchmarks and comparative data to enable a realistic review of performance
- Mechanisms for collating the views of customers and service users and what the response and feedback is to these views
- Testing of service costs against comparative costs.

Exhibit 19.1). Changes in the nature of delivery of a service, changes in management and changed policies will mean that some comparative data may be subject to cleansing or adjustment. The tools available to the auditor include performance measures, normally in the form of indicators, and results of analytical review, e.g. data that can be compared with similar providers of the service (either public or private), data that can be used internally where there are a number of identical services sourced from the same organisation. In addition, there are the normal audit sources of information such as enquiries of management, minutes of meetings, observations, third party evidence and the reliability of information provided. The amount, degree and depth of the VFM studies will also be dictated by the risk ranking (high, medium or low) afforded to the service under review.

Categories of VFM studies

Some categories of VFM studies are highlighted below:

- *National projects*, undertaken normally by the Audit Commission (or regional audit bodies), where findings from one study are used as benchmarks levels for comparison to produce a national survey outcome, leading to recommendations on improvement based on best practice from tried-and-tested activities. These are intended to provide a framework of best practice where one service can learn from others leading to a good value for money service.
- *Local projects or projects within 'family groupings'*, the term applied by the Audit Commission to similar local authorities of similar size, demographic nature

and financial standing. Local projects may also mean one-off studies due to the specialist nature of activities but can be relevant to a particular region.

■ *Published performance indicators* – an exercise undertaken by the Audit Commission where all local authorities are identified and their level of service provision compared with others based on various criteria, such as population, number of children, number of establishments, or per pound spent.

■ *Management reviews of services* in terms of VFM provision and internal audit VFM studies will vary according to different pressures, such as these from risk management assessments, public pressure, and departmental manger concerns over identified poor services with high costs.

Performance targets, measures and indicators

Performance measurement has over the past 20 years become an important aspect of service delivery and assessment in the UK public sector. Performance targets are set as goals that those delivering a service must reach, normally by a specified time or within a time period. Performance measures, as their name implies, are precise, quantified outcomes. In the public sector, precise measurement is not as easy as it may initially appear and therefore performance indicators are used to cover the more usual circumstance where it is not possible to be precise in terms of quantifiable measures. An example of a performance indicator is cost of service delivery per head of population.

The objectives of performance indicators are:

■ to develop and improve accountability;
■ to ensure that VFM is being obtained;
■ to monitor the quality of the service provided.

Performance is generally measured against specific targets linked to output or outcome, e.g. financial targets and activity levels that must be met during a set period, normally the financial year. Inputs, outputs and impacts are subject to different forms of measurement in order to indicate levels of performance. The introduction of performance indicators by government is a means of assessing comparative data to establish how well a service is provided. Year-on-year comparison leads to the creation of benchmarks for service providers that should, by setting goals for improvement, lead to better service provision. Local government saw the introduction of performance measurement as a legal requirement in 1990. This resulted in the Audit Commission drawing up a list of indicators for measuring local authority service provision. The first list was published by the Audit Commission in 1992.

The 1990 Local Government Act charged the Audit Commission with three tasks:

■ to specify a set of national performance indicators for local authorities (councils, police and fire services, waste disposal and parks authorities);
■ to arrange for the information to be audited by local auditors;
■ to make appropriate comparisons of performance between authorities and over time.

The audit of performance measurement by the National Audit Office and the Audit Commission relied on the expertise of the external auditor in the realms of VFM audit. The skill of the auditor focused on the three Es, economy, efficiency and effectiveness, but the bias of a results-orientated government towards a focus on outcomes saw the rise of 'effectiveness' as the most prominent 'E'.

The value of performance measurement

To quote the Audit Commission (1995) on performance:

> If you don't measure results, you can't tell success from failure.
> If you can't see success, you can't reward it.
> If you can't reward success, you're probably rewarding failure.
> If you can't see success, you can't learn from it.
> If you can't recognise failure, you can't correct it.
> If you can demonstrate results, you can win public support.
> What gets measured gets done.

The Audit Commission's changing role in the audit of performance indicators led to three initiatives:

- a Library of Local Performance Indicators, jointly with the Improvement and Development Agency (IDeA), to provide off-the-shelf voluntary local indicators with approved definitions and a database of authorities using them to enable benchmarking;
- a national pilot exercise with over 80 local authorities to test a range of quality of life indicators, for use by local authorities and their partners in monitoring their community strategies;
- a Centre for Performance Measurement as a resource for managers across government and the public sector to work with experts at the Commission in resolving their problems with performance measurement and indicators.

Internal and external performance measures that are used to enhance accountability

CIPFA, the public sector accounting body, identified how performance measures can be used both internally and externally to enhance accountability. Internal performance measures promote accountability in the following areas:

- policy – to assist in its formation and execution;
- planning and budgeting – to assist in the planning and budgeting of service provision and monitoring changes to service levels;
- quality – to improve the standards of service delivery;
- economy – to monitor the effective use of resources;
- equity – to ensure fair distribution and access for users.

Performance measures are used by management of the organisation in terms of the planning, development and policy-making process that also enables and facilitates managerial accountability. Indicators enable activities and services to be monitored on a regular basis and at various levels, from lower-level centres and offices up through departments to policy-makers. Internal measures of performance are a means by which senior managers can assess whether they have achieved a satisfactory level of performance and put the organisation in a position to demonstrate accountability to those with a vested interest in the service, both recipients and providers of the funding. Other stakeholders can include politicians, environmentalists, employees and suppliers.

Internal performance measures include costs per unit, per hour, per case load, per individual, per pupil and per patient, budgetary control, monitoring processes, and internal control and comparison of results with pre-set targets. In addition, quality can be assessed via customer satisfaction surveys.

A quality indicator is perhaps the most difficult and contentious area of performance measurement, and is likely to be subject to criticism, because quality is a subjective matter.

Externally, performance measures promote accountability in the following areas:

■ for comparison of performance against targets or previous years or similar organisations;
■ for highlighting areas of public interest or relevance, often used on the political platform both locally and nationally;
■ for identifying trends over time;
■ for enabling the development of benchmarks, norms or targets that can be used by similar public sector bodies.

External performance measures are mainly used more directly as a means to evidence accountability.

In order to obtain an overall view of performance, it can be necessary to use a number of indicators, as very often one indicator may not provide a true picture of output or activity levels. Often a number of indicators taken together will provide a more reliable quality measure. Thus, when evaluating a school, a prospective parent would evaluate not only the examination results and pupil per teacher ratio, but would also take into account all the other resources available within the school and the impression given by current parents and pupils.

External performance measures are normally a result of initiatives from central government, which usually include the use of predetermined targets. The use of indicators can often lead to a system of rewards or punishment, such as naming and shaming, or the withholding of additional funding or resources.

The purpose of performance measurement is to:

■ improve service delivery
■ demonstrate efficiency
■ identify goals within departments
■ help motivate personnel to achieve their objectives
■ aid management in assessing staff performance
■ give an indication to outsiders that money is not wasted in the public sector

- provide a standard by which to gauge the change in level of activity from one year to the another
- give a basis for comparison with other organisations
- provide a base from which to assess activities when preparing tenders for work
- provide objective quantifiable measures on which to judge performance and VFM

Evaluation of performance indicators

An important question to ask when evaluating performance indicators is: what exactly does an indicator or meeting a pre-set target tell the reader about the service? It must be remembered that meeting a goal or target in itself cannot be regarded as adequate proof of the provision of a worthwhile service. Performance indicators therefore have to carry a health warning, as the end output may not always provide the complete picture in terms of a service provision.

Role of auditor

When it comes to discussing the role of the auditor in performance measurement, there are three areas that merit mention:

- the auditor as assurance provider
- the auditor's monitoring function
- the auditor as producer of comparable results that act as indicators.

Once indicators become part of an organisation's measure of activity, the source data used needs to be carefully chosen in order that it does not become misinterpreted. Consistency and accuracy are important to ensure that the indicators are not subject to manipulation and incorrect interpretation by the providers and recipients. Audit can provide the review process here and give a level of assurance regarding the data. The behavioural implications of indicators can be both positive and negative: the failure to meet targets can be demotivating for staff and managers, while the demands placed on individuals to meet the targets can be stressful if they prove to be unrealistic. Some targets can be manipulated and thereby make the indicator unrealistic or useless in terms of its overall objective of providing information about the service. Audit can provide assurance that targets have not been manipulated.

Measures of effectiveness

Measures of effectiveness may be divided into two broad areas:

- *Measures of output*, i.e. the service that an organisation provides. Examples include the number of surgical procedures performed by a clinical speciality, or the examination results for a school or college. Problems arise when trying to measure productivity. Audit and review bodies will need appropriate skills here to assess the output.
- *Measures of outcomes*, which are linked to the longer-term objective. Examples would be mortality rates, homelessness levels and unemployment levels. The

problem with using these types of measures as performance indicators is that they may be influenced by a number of factors. For example, the mortality rate of the population may improve as a result of improved health care provision, or it may be because of improved housing, reducing pollution levels, better employment prospects and/or improved dietary standards.

Setting of targets and measures

There are important factors that need to be taken into account when targets are set and when the performance measure is identified as a mechanism to confirm target achievement:

- How were the targets and indicators set?
- When were they set?
- Who was responsible for setting them?
- What is the timescale for achieving the target?
- Is there provision for reviewing and monitoring the process of setting indicators?
- What will be the behavioural impact upon the managers and personnel involved in meeting these targets?
- What will be the short- and long-term implications on performance, if activity merely revolves around achieving targets?
- Are there any influencing factors that need to be taken into account when interpreting indicators?
- How will the targets be communicated to the service managers and officers delivering the service?
- Are there any compensating factors to consider where failure to meet one target may be compensated by the achievement of another target?
- Are the indicators prioritised and set accordingly in terms of key indicators, primary or secondary indicators?

Performance indicators interpreted in isolation need to be viewed carefully, as external factors may have a bearing on the results provided by the indicators. The measurement of units of production and activity has progressed from the measurement of outputs to the measurement of outcomes, which has become an important focus for public services. It has changed from the conventional measurement of cost of resources and cost of teaching staff per pupil, to the amount of time spent in exam preparation, the number of GCSE A–C grade passes and the number of pupils going to higher education establishments. Measuring outcomes that relate to the well-being of society or the quality of life is far more difficult as it relies on perceptions and expectations and subjective feedback from participants.

Public pressure on accountability from elected representatives has resulted in governments seeking ways of demonstrating that public money has been put to good use, and as the demands on public money and public services increase, so the emphasis on performance measures, targets and indicators continues to increase in order to display improved service provision. Examples of measures that yield evidence about activity levels are given in Exhibit 19.2.

Exhibit 19.2 Examples of measures that yield evidence about activity levels

- Inputs – e.g. staff numbers per establishment, level of expenditure
- Outputs – e.g. quantity of service provided in terms of hours of home care
- Quality – e.g. % of household waste collections missed
- Speed – e.g. % of emergency housing repairs completed within 24 hours
- Efficiency – e.g. cost per person in residential care
- Outcomes – direct measures of the achievement of service objectives (e.g. to educate children)
- Consumer satisfaction – e.g. the % of users satisfied with a service
- Equity – e.g. % number of public buildings that provide access for the disabled
- Targets – e.g. achieve a 6% annual rate of return
- Comparative indicators – inter-authority, per school or hospital.

For performance indicators to fulfil their role in yielding positive information, they need to possess the following characteristics:

- They must be of an appropriate consistency in terms of indicator information – there should be recognition of changes that will affect the comparison level that may render the results meaningless. Care has to be taken when data is adjusted to take account of changes as the resulting data could be subject to mistrust and manipulation.
- They must establish a system for measurement – target measurement must be understood so that there is no misinterpretation, while targets should not be set at a level that make their achievement regarded as 'easy' to reach irrespective of actual activity.
- They must maintain a strong focus – key indicators should not be swamped by an endless list of lower-level indicators that can cloud the objective of the process of measuring the service. Key areas need to be in identified so that the resulting data will prove informative and worthwhile.
- They must be challenging – an annual review of targets should be undertaken to ensure that they remain challenging but achievable.
- They must be capable of audit and verification – ensuring that the targets and indicators can be audited and verified means that the data has the credibility of having undergone an independent review.

Limitations of performance indicators

In spite of the usefulness of performance indicators, they do have limitations. The measurement of performance through inappropriate indicators may be a waste of resources. The following caveats should be borne in mind:

- The whole picture needs to be considered, not just selected or individual aspects that may not give the full picture.
- The reason for using the published indicators is to influence, inform or undermine other information; interpretation is therefore vital within the correct context.
- The collection and analysis of the data will often dictate the reporting format, as will the remit of the report writers. The access to data and the source of the data may themselves be subject to interpretation.

■ Meeting targets does not automatically indicate good performance – target setting may be subject to constraints or external influences that led to them being set at an inappropriate level; for example, a standardised rate of return on capital employed for an array of bodies may mean that some are already meeting this arbitrary target.

■ Meeting targets year on year may not be a true indicator unless the targets used are consistent or take into account changes in activity levels.

■ Performance-related pay schemes may encourage false reporting of achievements.

■ The reliability of some indicators may be suspect when they are not subject to independent audit.

■ People can react adversely to targets set when they perceive that there is very little chance of meeting them; this can lead to undue stress on the workforce and management involved.

Pressure to 'perform' in terms of achieving targets can have behavioural and psychological implications for staff. There may be a shifting of blame, by concentrating on an individual's effort and not on a holistic view of the overall activity and performance, and the increased pressure on individuals can be counterproductive in terms of output. Budget holders may adopt a 'watchdog' attitude, where they work in direct conflict with other departments. There can be a culture of 'picking holes' in order to ensure they are not looked upon in an unfavourable light. Ill-feeling in an organisation as a direct result of target-setting can leave that organisation facing service delivery problems and even staff welfare issues.

Behavioural issues related to target setting are summarised in Exhibit 19.3.

Exhibit 19.3 Behavioural issues related to performance targets

Staff

Failure to meet targets and goals could result in:

■ a loss of interest at work; staff can become demotivated
■ a lowering of the standard of achievement
■ a loss of confidence
■ a tendency to give up quickly
■ a fear of change and a reluctance to accept new working methods or jobs
■ an expectation of failure
■ a loss of concentration – escaping from this 'expectancy of failure'
■ difficulties in working relationships – 'out of their depth'
■ a tendency to blame others.

People will be motivated to achieve targets if there is a reward or an incentive.

Management

■ Unnecessary pressure from targets can lead organisational or divisional managers into uncharacteristic behaviour.
■ These pressures can push them into making poor decisions.
■ Pressures may skew the main priorities towards meeting artificial targets and away from solving real problems or delivering complex or expensive services.
■ Where performance-related pay (PRP) is in existence, managers may have a greater incentive to meet pre-set targets, but for the wrong reasons.
■ the situation may lead managers to manipulate data, results and accounting figures, distorting the information simply for self-preservation.

Table 19.1 **CIPFA performance indicators for inner London boroughs**

London boroughs	Average time taken to re-let dwellings (weeks)	% of tenants over 13 weeks in arrears
Inner London		
City of London	3.0	5.9
Camden	10.0	22.8
Greenwich	9.7	20.4
Hackney	37.4	19.8
Hammersmith & Fulham	13.4	29.0
Islington	12.8	15.2
Kensington & Chelsea	6.0	13.8
Lambeth	15.0	34.4
Lewisham	8.6	16.0
Southwark	3.4	32.8
Tower Hamlets	13.8	7.1
Wandsworth	8.4	10.5
Westminster	6.3	10.0

Source: CIPFA Statistical Information Service, The Chartered Institute of Public Finance and Accountancy (CIPFA)

Performance indicators may need to be read with caution. To avoid misunderstanding and misinterpretation, data must be carefully selected. There needs to be an awareness of non-financial issues affecting the service, while other information not immediately identified may impact on the data. Target completion times for activities can vary between providers, which will render comparison difficult.

Performance indicators come with some health warnings. They may not be comparing like with like, and auditees will no doubt be quick to point this out. Indicators can, however, be used together and are at their best when benchmarked or put in a league table. An example of this is shown in Table 19.1.

The auditor may be examining local government housing statistics for two areas: re-letting times after tenants vacate, and tenants' rent arrears. Using the table the auditor will want to benchmark with an average and will be concerned if the authority in question is one or two standard deviations above or below the mean, as follows:

	Vacancy period	Rent arrears
Average	11.4 weeks	18.3%
Lows	Southwark and Westminster	Tower Hamlets and Westminster
Highs	Hackney	Southwark and Hammersmith

Clearly the areas identified as high are well out of line with the average. Something may well be going wrong in these boroughs.

Example:
BDM Hospital Trust

Value for money covers the three concepts of economy, efficiency and effectiveness (the three Es) in the use of resources. A sound, reliable and accurate accounting information system (AIS) can provide source data that yields useful information in the assessment of whether BDM is achieving VFM in its provision of health care.

Performance targets and indicators can aid in the evaluation of whether VFM is being achieved within the organisation. A target is a quantifiable objective set by management to be attained at a specified future date. For example, an output target for BDM Hospital could refer to the objective of increasing patient vision by performing a target number of 12 cataract operations per week.

A performance indicator provides a measure by which the level of activity can be assessed in terms of performance in meeting the three Es. Both financial and non-financial data are utilised in this exercise to produce information that provides results for comparison, action or decision-making:

- *Performance measure – economy.* As a result of changing suppliers of disposable surgical gloves, the cost per operation was reduced by 5% compared with the previous year.
- *Performance indicator – economy.* Vacancies for unskilled workers indicate that pay scales are comparable to those for similar jobs in the locality.
- *Performance measure – efficiency.* The unit cost of cataract operation is £xx.
- *Performance indicator – efficiency.* The operating theatre is only used 80% of the time due to excessive overtime costs associated with payments to professional staff.
- *Performance measure – effectiveness.* The success rate of all the cataract operations is 97%.
- *Performance indicator – effectiveness.* More referrals are made to this hospital, indicating that it is highly regarded by general practitioners and patients, and is therefore producing better results.
- *Performance measure – quality.* The average waiting time after referral is 2 weeks.
- *Performance indicator – quality.* The number of complaints received from patients and their relatives is only 1 in 600 patients.

Quality issues are often based on factors affecting the recipient, e.g. length of waiting time at hospital emergency department prior to being seen by a doctor.

Other performance indicators can relate to activities that are not directly medical, such as the provision of meals to patients, e.g. patient food costs per week, compared with pre-set allowances or rates, or comparative unit costs of patient meals on a per-patient-day basis.

Comparative data

To determine the standard to set for a given performance measure or indicator, it is useful to make comparisons against a like activity or organisation. There are four main performance comparators:

- against targets
- over time
- against comparable organisational units
- against benchmarks.

Comparisons against benchmarks assess the performance that should be expected by adoption of best practice standards built on rational argument and professional judgment. Benchmarking substitutes measures with absolute standards.

A basic comparison between organisations is expenditure levels. This includes data that is capable of being measured in financial terms such as unit costs. Unit costings have several uses as performance measures for evaluating services:

- to aid in the setting of prices for other providers;
- to compare prices/costs for purchases;
- to establish realistic criteria on which to invite tenders for goods and services.

Examples of indicators include:

- cost per in-patient day
- cost per in-patient episode
- cost per outpatient attendance.

All of these can be speciality-related, e.g. medical, surgical, obstetric, or geriatric.

The information relating to the BDM Hospital could be used to undertake a VFM audit, and a series of audit tests would need to be undertaken to establish the validity of the information available, with analytical review procedures used to analyse the data.

Summary

Value-for-money and performance indicator reviews by the auditor are important features in public sector auditing. This is because the different objectives of public sector organisations and the use of public money demand accountability. Auditor skills must therefore be expanded to meet this level of auditing, where reviews assess not only the validity and verification of data but also aspects of achieving effective and efficient service with the economical use of resources.

? PRACTICE QUESTION

What are the advantages and limitations of performance indicators to be used in a National Health Service hospital trust? Provide examples of areas where they can be used.

Chapter 20

Emerging issues in auditing

Objectives

After studying this chapter you should be able to:

- appreciate the issues surrounding forensic auditing;
- recognise that reports other than financial statement reports require audit assurance;
- understand the changing role of the auditor in terms of risk management;
- discuss the concept of added value audit.

Introduction

Forensic auditing, the application of auditing skills to situations where there is a legal consequence, is a new discipline under the auditing umbrella which has become a necessity in today's demanding and complex world. The 20th century brought an array of technological developments that allowed enormous leaps to be made – the laptop, mobile phone and credit card are just the tip of the iceberg. Information and communication are key words used to describe the activities affecting everyday life as well as the business environment. While the new technology has been beneficial in providing high-speed transactions, storage facilities for data capture and analysis, it has also provided an opportunity for fraudsters to benefit from the overload of information, the accessibility and often the ease of manipulation of data.

During 2007 and 2008 there were high-profile losses and theft of information of data in the UK. For example, a staff member from the Ministry of Defence lost a laptop and other government officials left laptops containing sensitive information on the train. HSBC bank lost customer data while Her Majesty's Revenue & Customs lost a CD containing the personal details of millions of taxpayers by forwarding it in the post to the National Audit Office without first encrypting the data. While these examples display poor security controls or lack of awareness of procedures, financial crime involving intentional theft or manipulation of data is on the increase. Fraudsters use stolen data to commit crimes, especially identity theft, which has seen a huge increase since the introduction of electronic transfer of information. Accidental loss may be unavoidable, but data security risk assessment should be a high priority that is reviewed by management and subject to audit. As criminal activity becomes more prevalent and more sophisticated, it is important that internal audit, in particular, plays a role in giving added value to management by highlighting the need to apply effective controls over the risk of data loss, data manipulation and data theft.

When data is manipulated and used whether for identity theft or corporate fraud, the aftermath in terms of identifying and quantifying the loss often falls to the accountant or auditor in the initial stages. The terms forensic accounting and forensic auditing conjure up the image of a far more exciting job than the traditional auditing roles of number-crunching, checklist-orientated activities and following the trustworthy audit trail. The new image is far more judgment-driven, with an ability to apply investigative techniques and evaluation processes along with displaying an appreciation of social considerations. Forensic auditing and accounting bring the professional accountant and auditor into a world of criminal investigations, interviewing techniques beyond those of systems confirmation, and appearing as an expert witness in the courts.

Fraud is not normally discovered during the normal audit. Something usually triggers the discovery. Whether it is discovered accidentally or by the actions of a whistleblower, it is the task of determining that the fraud actually took place that places a great deal of work on the shoulders of the auditor. The mindset of the auditor has to change when dealing with fraud, as financial auditing is about taking things apart and is more procedural than forensic audit. The premise of financial audit is that it is not designed to detect fraud but rather material misstatements which, although they can be one and the same, are also different. Forensic auditing and accounting is more about putting things together while being intrusive rather than deductive. This is why fraud detection should be considered an art and not a science, and one that requires innovative and creative thinking; the auditor has to be determined, persistent and a problem solver. Data mining, data analysis and data interpretation are all weapons in the forensic auditor's armoury when carrying out fraud investigations.

Forensic audit

The forensic auditor will be concerned with identifying the weakest link in the system which can create the 'opportunity' so often capitalised upon by the fraudster. Recognising the best way to compromise the system can help the auditor to evaluate the risk. There will also be opportunities to deviate from generally accepted accounting practices, and this is something the auditor needs to be aware of. In an environment where transactions are automated, the auditor will need to ensure that any offline transactions are appropriately documented and authorised, as this may be the weak link. The 'bypassing' of standardised controls by higher authorities may, in itself, lend a hand in enabling fraud; this is a common source of management fraud.

The forensic auditor will need, in addition to the skills commonly attributed to the auditor, the following:

- to be a detective – an ability to think like a fraudster
- objectivity without any personal bias
- to be a problem solver
- the ability to read body language
- the ability to act on hunches and intuition

While the financial auditor may take the information apart in terms of what happened, the forensic auditor will have to put things together in terms of why it happened. Auditors see their main goal more in preventing fraud and corruption than in the area of detecting fraud. There is an expectation that auditors are alert to situations that can lead to fraud and will aim to rectify the situation prior to the fraud taking place. This type of forensic auditing is known as 'proactive', as opposed to 'reactive', where an investigation take place after the fraud has occurred.

Proactive forensic auditing

Proactive forensic auditing enables a better understanding of areas of possible risk and threats to the company, which in turn can identify the audit focus that eventually determines the audit report. System review and assessment on a regular basis can act as a deterrent to fraud and corruption; this is where the auditor takes on the role of a policeman in the company in terms of an audit presence and is therefore proactive.

Reactive forensic auditing

Reactive forensic auditing takes place when fraud is suspected and there is a need to prove or disprove these suspicions. The discovery of supporting evidence and identification of the fraudster are important in terms of further action, whether this involves criminal or disciplinary proceedings, and also in terms of information for any insurance claims for losses incurred. When evidence is gathered that is relevant to criminal proceedings, it is important that it is appropriately documented, safeguarded and that it can ensure that the case against the fraudster is sustainable. There is an emphasis here on ensuring that the audit is appropriately planned and executed to enable the reporting to be in a manner that meets with legal requirements as well as company requirements.

Working with others

Other investigative agencies, (police, serious fraud office) will become involved at some stage and the working relationship between forensic auditors and these agencies has to be one of co-operation and respect. When the fraud falls into the category of a criminal investigation, there has to be set procedures in place especially when the auditors themselves may be subject to questioning, and be part of the investigations team.

Forensic auditing and IT

Information technology plays an important role in forensic auditing as the ability to process at speed large volumes of data that may be dispersed in its original format helps in the search for the fraudster. This aspect of forensic auditing expects the auditor to have a higher level of IT understanding than may be required for routine financial auditing procedures. The complex nature of some of the frauds encountered in the last decade (Enron being a prime example) means that the forensic auditor must possess the skills necessary to collect proper evidence to ensure conviction of the perpetrators.

The expert witness

Increasingly the role of the forensic accountant and forensic auditor has gone down the path of the expert witness: the professional with the ability to explain technical issues in lay terms. In a court case this will mean the auditor (who will now be an 'expert witness') may be subject to direct cross-examination which could involve courtroom techniques such as:

- using physical presence to intimidate;
- maintaining non-stop eye contact;
- challenging the space of the witness;
- posing fast-paced questions to confuse the witness;
- not allowing the expert to explain or deviate from the exact question.

The auditor will therefore be faced with a new dimension in terms of how to report on the evidence collected. Thus during a forensic audit this evidence will have to:

■ be reliable and supportive of the case assessment;
■ possess all documents required for the case;
■ be detailed to support the assumptions, opinions and conclusions;
■ be able to be reconstructed if necessary.

In order to survive the expert witness stand, the auditor will have to maintain composure, answer clearly, be free from bias (objective), not become argumentative and recognise any limitations in terms of knowledge. Material will have to be prepared completely, in line with the standard on working papers but with added detail for the court. A number of these issues are recognised qualities expected of the auditor and hence being an expert witness in a fraud case may not be as difficult as it sounds.

The development of the 'added value' audit

There may be a case for 'reinventing' the audit as a result of both technological developments in business and management's requirement for added audit assurance in the assessment of risk. This leads to an audit that:

■ has a wider scope
■ considers business risks
■ makes recommendations for improving business performance.

Many company directors have in the past looked upon the external audit function as a necessary evil, seeing them as extracting funds merely to state that the financial statements show a 'true and fair view'. The internal auditor has traditionally been viewed as part of internal check within the organisation to confirm the existence of internal controls. However, as both types of auditor have invaluable insights into the company and its business activities, they should be utilised to their maximum to provide assurances and advice.

Changes in the nature of auditing

Apart from the emerging role of the forensic auditor, other changes have influenced the audit profession and its approach to auditing, as follows:

■ Major international audit firms have been steadily introducing innovative audit methodologies which have been implemented throughout the profession.
■ Professional accountancy and auditing institutes have also provided the profession with new applications to aid the completion of auditing. An example is the Canadian Institute's development of Interactive Data Extraction and Analysis (IDEA) as a computer-assisted audit tool.

- Business processes have been subject to their own technological developments, which in turn have impacted on the audit.
- The posting of audited financial information on the internet has brought with it the need to ensure data integrity.
- Assurance services have grown beyond the traditional financial statement audit.

Globalisation

- The globalisation of corporate activities has required audit firms to become more global in their approach.
- The fast pace of change due in many respects to globalisation has resulted in a bigger focus on audit involvement in business risk.
- Audit practice is often ahead of audit theory, as practical auditing at grassroots means that auditors have been forced to adapt to the challenges and demands of the emerging global business environment.

Wider use of technology

The wider availability and use of technology by businesses means that:

- Sampling data that is computerised has become virtually redundant as computerised accounting systems can be subject to a 100% check.
- The development of the internet means virtual audits can take place remotely, although asset verification may still need to be undertaken on site.
- Audit reports and management letters are now generated via integrated audit software, which means they can be produced from the audit working papers, enabling the auditor to focus resources on higher-level tasks.
- With the growth of e-commerce and e-business, it seems traditional audit methods may become something of the past.
- Interim reports, annual reports and other financial information are increasingly being posted on the internet; the integrity of the information is important, which in turn has implications for the future role of audit.

The growth of audit assurance services

Management of risk

Risk-based auditing is the 'modern' approach to auditing, and emphasis on areas of concern and risk drive the external audit activity. Internal audit has increasingly become involved with the control risk self-assessment employed by management to embed risk management within an organisation. Auditors are therefore providing more assurances than before in a display that provides added value to the conventional audit of the past.

External auditors are in a position to contribute to internal audit's work in respect of assurance provision as well as relying on the work undertaken by internal audit. This is especially important if the scope of the external audit may expand further in terms of corporate governance assurance. This then becomes a means of meeting both a statutory requirement and a service to management. These audit activities require good co-operation between internal and external auditors if the reports are to be worthwhile. The management of risk covers not only financial risks but all aspects of the business, including environmental and social risks.

Risk management and audit

- Achieving the right working relationship and chemistry between management and auditor is fundamental.
- While auditors generally have the same level of competence, there still needs to be a good 'fit' between the client and the auditor; personalities often play an important role in effective working relationships.
- Achieving the correct balance often means practice, experience, judgment and knowing where to draw the line.

Environmental audit

A key risk faced by organisations today is that of risk associated with the environment impacting on the business. Audit will be drawn into these issues by the very nature of compliance with regulations, which can have an impact, both in terms of reputation and financially, on the business. These include:

- breaking laws that are aimed at limiting pollution of earth, water and air;
- not meeting recycling targets set by government;
- loss of reputation and public image as result of failure to comply, in terms of publicity, fines or closure of certain business activities.

Auditor skills

It is unlikely that a traditional auditor will have the appropriate skills and competencies to meet the requirements of an environmental audit. Audit teams will inevitably become multidisciplinary in order to meet these new challenges, while also closely working with those who have the appropriate knowledge and skills. This will require a reliance on the work of other professionals.

Environmental issues that auditors may encounter

Environmental factors that impact on a company can have an impact on the audit work required to arrive at an opinion on the financial statements, as follows:

- Environmental factors affect the values recorded on assets, as they may need to be replaced or altered in order to meet new legislative requirements.
- Environmental factors may have created liabilities in terms of fines or clean-up work.
- Environmental factors may have an implication for the future cash flows of the business, which may affect the organisation's future viability.
- Environmental factors may create fundamental uncertainties due to pending court cases and resulting corrective actions and court costs.

- Environmental factors and related risk assessment of the impact on the organisation may identify that the insurance cover is inadequate.
- As a preliminary task, the auditors will in future need to ask for a statement of the review of the environmental matters affecting the company, which will include any potential liabilities.

Social audit

Pressure from government and campaigners in general has led to the realisation by companies that they must act ethically and responsibly when it comes to their business activities. The Primark retail group was found to be purchasing clothing from Asia where children as young as 10 were employed to sew sequins onto garments destined for the high street. This was brought to the attention of the public by a television special report on child labour exploitation. In response, Primark promised to review their purchasing policies. This example illustrates the importance of companies acting in a socially responsible way and the influence of both the media and pressure groups. Companies are realising that there are risks associated with social responsibility, e.g. non-compliance with employment laws such as the minimum wage and the use of child labour.

The Co-operative Bank in the UK follows ethical investment policy, encourages sustainable development and has capitalised on its ethical reputation as a caring bank. It is an example of the growth in ethical investment not only by the bank but by investors generally, and shows that there are benefits to be gained by trading ethically.

Annual reports are not just about accountability in the financial sense; social accountability is becoming very fashionable, with firms producing separate annual reports on their 'social' performance, which include verification statements.

Summary   The views on auditing are changing due to e-business, environmental concerns and awareness of social responsibility. The statutory audit may no longer fulfil the needs of stakeholders; there is increasing pressure for audit to move from its stewardship context to one of social responsibility that meets stakeholder as well as shareholder expectations. Globalisation and the growth of large multinationals, which have turnovers greater than some countries, require an audit that provides more than just the audit opinion. Internal audit functions are also changing in line with risk management processes within organisations.

In line with developments in e-business, the audit role has been expanding, with more growth appearing on the horizon to take account of a greater need for audit assurance linked to social and environmental issues.

? PRACTICE QUESTION

Write an audit programme to carry out an environmental audit in a university. The organisation has never in its history been through an environmental audit.